ALPS 4000

75 peaks in 52 days

MARTIN MORAN

DAVID & CHARLES

KEY

▲	PEAKS OVER 4000m
△	OTHER PEAKS
●	TOWNS/VILLAGES
➜	ROUTE TAKEN
┼┼┼	RAILWAYS
═	ROADS
───	CABLE CARS
▨	LAKES
⌂	MOUNTAIN HUTS
⮏	CYCLE
ξ))	GLACIERS
～	RIVERS
Λ	CAMP/BIVOUAC
⋯⋯	FOOTPATHS/TRACKS

A DAVID & CHARLES BOOK

A catalogue record for this book is available from the British Library.

ISBN 0 7153 0690 1

Printed in Great Britain
by Butler & Tanner Limited, Frome
for David & Charles
Brunel House   Newton Abbot   Devon

Many climbers dedicate a lifetime to the conquest of the '4000ers' – the peaks over 4000m in the Alps. Not so Martin Moran and Simon Jenkins who, to the disbelief of their colleagues, set out to make the first ever traverse of all 75 peaks in one continuous journey. To add spice to the challenge they shunned motorised transport, using bicycles to travel from one starting point to the next. Encountering the worst summer weather for many years, facing blizzards, white-outs and sudden thunderstorms and fighting hunger, exhaustion and near despair, the two men succeeded in their attempt, covering over 1000km (620 miles), including over 70,000m (229,000ft) of ascent, in just 52 days. This is the account of their remarkable journey.

———————

Martin Moran is one of Britain's most able and experienced winter mountaineers. In 1984 he became the first climber to make the complete ascent of all 277 Scottish Munros (peaks over 3000ft) in one winter season. His highly acclaimed book *The Munros in Winter*, also available in paperback, records the feat, which took him just 83 days. He is a British Mountain Guide and runs a climbing school in the north-west highlands of Scotland with his wife Joy and their children, Alex and Hazel.

Cover photographs: (*front*) Simon on the upper East Ridge of the Weisshorn looking across the Mattertal to the Mischabel range; (*back*) On the summit ridge of the Aiguille Verte (4122m); (*inset*) Simon (l) and Martin on the Barre des Ecrins, 13 August 1993 (*Martin Welch*)

TO JOY
for taking the strain
and still loving

CONTENTS

SUNDRY INFORMATION

Conversions

All heights, distances and other measures are given in metric scale in the book. Sample conversions to the Imperial scale are as follows:

1 metre	=	3.2808ft
1000m	=	0.6214 miles
1 kilometre	=	0.6214 miles
100 km	=	62.14 miles
1.6093km	=	1 mile
1 kilogram	=	2.2lb

Placenames

All general placenames are given in the form that they are regularly used in the English language. For example, the equivalent terms *glacier, ghiaccio, vadret, gletscher* are not recognised. All such features are called glaciers, as they would be spoken in English. Therefore we have Aletsch Glacier rather than Aletschgletscher. Likewise, the book speaks of the Margherita Hut rather than the Capanna Margherita.

Where a mountain has two alternative names, the form most regularly used in English is given. Therefore we speak of the French Mont Blanc rather than the Italian Monte Bianco.

The Glossary in Appendix I translates all the foreign-language terms for topographical features which are used in the book.

THE FOUR-THOUSANDERS CHALLENGE

Although surpassed in height by many ranges in the world, the Alps have inspired more homage and endeavour than any other mountain massif. Stretching in an arc of nearly 1,000km from the green hills of Provence to the limestone turrets of Slovenia, they form the backbone of Western Europe and contain no less than 439 peaks over 3500 metres and 50 major mountains which exceed 4000 metres in height.

Through the ages, clerics, poets, painters and, more recently, mountaineers have fallen prey to their beauty. Until quite recently the Alps occupied the centre stage in the development of mountaineering and, as a result, the finest peaks, particularly the Matterhorn, Eiger and Mont Blanc, have acquired a renown which brings thousands flocking to their slopes every year. Due to their accessibility and relatively modest elevation, the Alps remain the most popular climbing playground in the world. They are a paradise where the dream of standing between heaven and earth on an ice-bound peak can be the most easily realised by those who want to escape the pressures and strains of modern life.

Nearly a century has passed since the last great summits of the Alps were scaled for the first time. The period between 1850 and 1914 was rightly dubbed the Golden Age of alpinism. Not only were the summits attained but their every ridge and some of their faces were also explored. The mountaineering achievements of this era were all the more remarkable in that, with very few exceptions, ascents were accomplished with the most rudimentary equipment and in rapid time.

We now look back on this period fondly and with some envy. It saw the flowering of classical mountaineering, in which the style of an ascent came to be as important as its completion. How wonderful it must have been to stride across uncharted passes and feast one's eyes on summits as yet untrodden by man, as Edward Whymper and his contemporaries were able to do.

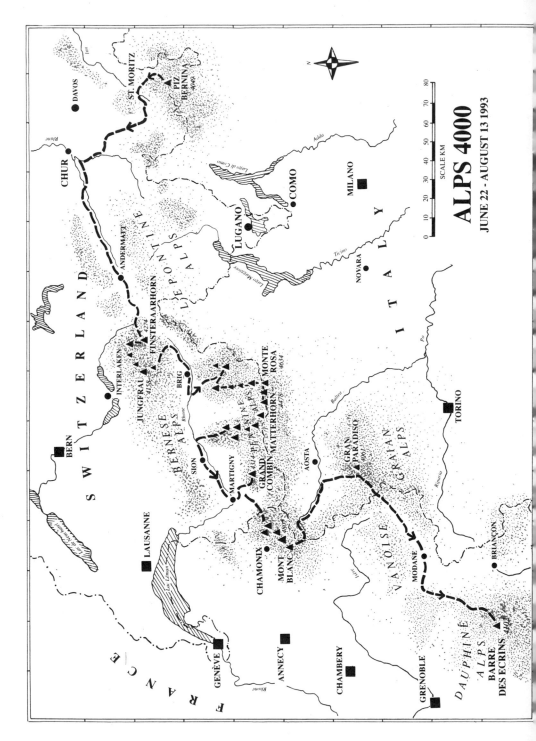

However, the 1930s saw the dawning of a new epoch of extreme alpinism in which the steepest faces and buttresses were tackled with the necessary employment of technical hardware. Although the boldness and purism of many early extremists is without compare, the concept of style became increasingly blurred as the relentless search for the steepest or most direct line on a mountain progressed. By the late 1960s extremism had reached a depressing stalemate in the realisation that, with siege tactics, fixed ropes and the use of drilled bolts, any face in the Alps could be climbed in any season.

The time was ripe for a reversion to the classical approach. With the remarkable solo climbs of the likes of Reinhold Messner, speed and style regained their rightful place in the sport during the 1970s. Routes which had taken several days to pioneer were now climbed in a few hours. Personal skill and fitness once more became the pre-eminent requirements of the mountaineer.

Far from being exhausted, the Alps have become the focus for new styles of adventure in the last twenty years. Sensing the dwindling potential for making worthwhile new routes on the mountains, the younger generation of alpinists sought fresh challenges and began linking groups of summits or faces in single expeditions, which the French have aptly termed *enchainements*. Such exploits may be more contrived and their rules more artificial than on the climbs of old, but they have certainly recaptured the adventurous spirit of mountaineering as it was practised by the early pioneers.

One objective that appeared on this new horizon was a non-stop traverse of all the 4000m peaks of the Alps. If executed without detours or delays, this expedition would commit the challenger to follow some of the finest and most difficult ridge routes of the classical era. In duration it would surpass any continuous mountaineering journey previously attempted.

Peak-bagging is an irresistible and incurable disease among mountaineers. The aim of completing the ascents of a published list of peaks, however arbitrarily defined, adds a discipline and direction to one's climbing career once the initial thrill of discovery has waned and particularly when one has reached a plateau of technical achievement.

The alpine '4000ers' form an obvious goal for the collector of mountains. They include a host of magnificent peaks of every imaginable form, from rock spires to towering pyramids and lofty ice caps. They are grouped in three main ranges – the Bernese Oberland, the Pennine

Alps and the Mont Blanc massif – with only three outlying mountains. This neat geographical arrangement adds to their appeal.

The man responsible for spreading the '4000ers' affliction among alpinists was Dr Karl Blodig, a practising optician born in Vienna in 1859. He developed an exceptional physique through wrestling and gymnastics and became a formidable mountaineer. He could impress his companions equally by performing acrobatics on the wire stanchions of a mountain hut or surviving the most arduous ascent on a diet of neat alcohol and butter.

Blodig made the ascent of all the '4000ers' his lifetime quest. In 1906 he completed all sixty-five, with ascents of Mont Brouillard and the Aiguille Blanche de Peuterey. Unfortunately for Blodig, this was the era when minor summits were still in the process of being identified and he was forced into renewed activity in 1911 with the acknowledgement of two new points as '4000ers', the Pointe Marguerite on the Grandes Jorasses and Pic Luigi Amedeo on Mont Blanc's Brouillard Ridge. He beat his main rival, Dr Puhn, to the latter peak by just seven days, and thus secured the first completion by the slimmest of margins.

Given the difficulties of travel in those days and the absence of cableways on the mountains, it was a magnificent achievement; one of his companions on the Pic Luigi Amedeo, Humphrey Jones commented: 'Blodig was so happy that, if the rest of the party had had no other reason for feeling the same, the fact of having contributed in some measure to his happiness would have been enough.' Such is the contentment which the ascent of an obscure pile of crumbling gneiss can give when it is the last on a hallowed list.

Then 52 years of age, Blodig settled to a happy retirement from serious climbing, and his book, *Die Viertausender der Alpen,* was published in 1923. However, twenty years after his apparent success came the devastating news that six more tops had been added to the list, the Aiguilles du Diable of Mont Blanc du Tacul and the two subsidiaries of the Aiguille Verte, the Grande Rocheuse and Aiguille du Jardin.

Incredibly, Blodig returned to the high mountains at the age of 73 to settle this new score. On 27 July 1932 he made a solo ascent of the Jardin and Rocheuse by a couloir that is today graded *très difficile* (TD–) and which had only received its first ascent a few days previously. This was the act of an obsessive but exceptional character and one of the most remarkable in alpine climbing history. It is small wonder that Blodig lived to the age of 97.

Many others followed in his steps, and most early completions of the '4000ers' are documented. Eustace Thomas became the first British mountaineer to succeed in 1932 after a whirlwind eight-year campaign, largely in the company of the guide, Josef Knubel. Thomas himself was no stripling, being 62 years old when he added the Aiguilles du Diable as his final tops. Unfortunately, no official list of completers of the '4000ers' has been made in the way that the Scottish Mountaineering Club has a maintained a record of Munroists (completers of Scotland's 277 3000ft mountains). As a result, we do not know how many people have succeeded in climbing the '4000ers' since the days of Blodig and Thomas, although the numbers must surely run into many hundreds.

One particular problem in documenting the feat is that there has never been a definitive list of the '4000ers'. There is fairly general agreement on the 50 major mountains, but it is the classification of the subsidiary summits which gives the trouble. The subsidiary tops undoubtedly add spice to the challenge of the '4000ers', committing the climber to visit many remote and difficult places, which must be included in the itinerary. Most mountaineers have followed Blodig's list, which totals 76 summits, including subsidiaries. However, Robin Collomb, Britain's leading alpine archivist, has published a table naming 79 tops. To further add to the confusion, the German climber Richard Goedeke listed 150 points over the magic mark in his climbing guidebook to the '4000ers' published in 1990.

In 1993 the UIAA (Union Internationale des Associations Alpinistes) went to the extent of appointing a committee of experts to decide the issue. They produced a list of 82 summits which unfortunately is no more consistent than its predecessors. Three of the 82 tops are little more than the shoulders of bigger peaks, whereas individual towers of far greater prominence in height are excluded from the list.

Ideally, some objective criterion is required which will define all significant tops, while ignoring the dozens of other minor eminences. In planning a traverse of the '4000ers', I applied a minimum height separation of 35m from the nearest higher neighbouring peak and obtained a list of around 75. Even this is open to residual doubt since a few of the lesser tops have not had their height separation accurately confirmed. The debate on classification will doubtless continue, but as long as everything of importance is included, it is the climbing of the '4000ers' that really matters. This is exactly what Simon Jenkins and I set out to do in the summer of 1993.

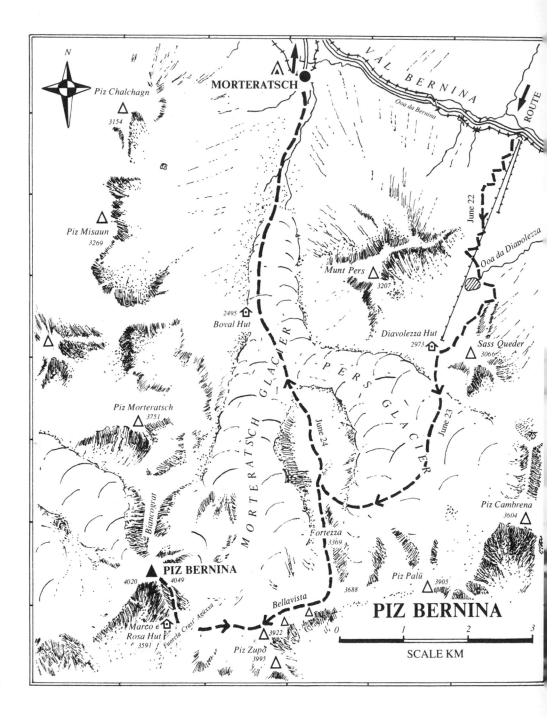

N

Piz Chalchagn
3154

Piz Misaun
3269

MORTERATSCH

VAL BERNINA

Ooa da Bernina

ROUTE

June 22

Ooa da Diavolezza

Munt Pers
3207

2495
Boval Hut

Diavolezza Hut
2973

Sass Queder
3066

PERS GLACIER

MORTERATSCH GLACIER

June 23

June 24

Piz Morteratsch
3751

Biancograt

Piz Cambrena
3604

Fortezza
3369

PIZ BERNINA
4020   4049

Bellavista

Piz Palü
3688   3905

PIZ BERNINA

Marco e
Rosa Hut
3591

Fuorcla Crast' Agüzza

3922

Piz Zupò
3995

0   1   2   3

SCALE KM

1

BATTLE ON THE BERNINA

The Piz Bernina

Rain drummed on the roof of the Diavolezza Hut in the final hour of darkness on the morning of 23 June. The moment of truth had arrived. We had to get out of bed and face up to the prospect of climbing the 75 4000m peaks within the next 60 days. All the plans and projections which we had made over the last six months now seemed mere bravado.

We were at the base of the Piz Bernina, one of the three isolated '4000ers' and most easterly of the 4000m peaks. The Bernina is the crowning point of the massifs of the Upper Engadin Valley in Eastern Switzerland. Neither Simon nor I had set foot on the mountain before. When planning our adventure, this seemed of little importance since the climb to its 4049m summit is technically simple and is given the lowly grade of *peu difficile* (PD).

Indeed, the Piz Bernina was seen as a gentle start to the summer, but no alpine mountain is easy in a blizzard and our first route made up in complexity what it lacked in difficulty. Over the coming hours we had to find our way across the Pers Glacier, climb the Fortezza Ridge and then make a traverse of 2km at an altitude of 3700m across the glacial shelves of the Bellavista Terraces in order to reach the Bernina's South Ridge.

The previous afternoon we had bade our wives farewell and walked 880m up to the hut from the Bernina Pass, following bulldozed ski-ing pistes up under the pylons of the cablecar lift which services the hut. At the moment of leaving the road at the pass, we had taken the vow that we would forsake all motorised forms of transport until the day we descended from our final '4000er', the Barre des Ecrins in the French Dauphine Alps. Between the Bernina and the Barre we had estimated that we would walk, ski and cycle 1040km overland and climb some 63,000m in ascent. However it was achieved, our journey was to be entirely self-propelled. Our minimum schedule for the traverse from peak to peak was 48 days, but this allowed for no delays for bad weather and a time of between 50 and 55 days was our most reasonable hope.

We were supposedly standing at the threshold of a great adventure, but in that dark hour I could find no reason as to why we had imposed this enormous task on ourselves and our families, why we had spent our savings and given up a whole summer of our work as mountain guides, and why we had committed a respectable charity to a venture that was fraught with risk. We folded our blankets and trooped downstairs to a lonely breakfast of lemon tea with the usual stale bread and jam. Hard though I searched, there was no inspiration either in the rain-swept gloom outside nor in the soulless hut in which we had slept.

I looked at Simon and tried to gauge his thoughts. My climbing partner of ten years was busying himself fitting contact lenses and tying boot laces while supping at the weak and lukewarm brews of tea he so much loves. He looked just as he does preparing for any other day on the mountains – quiet and relaxed but with the serious demeanour that suggests there is a job of work to be done.

I felt reassured by his presence, for there was no other companion I would have chosen for this trip. Through long years of apprenticeship we had developed an effective teamwork that had borne us safely through some harrowing moments on climbs in both Scotland and the Alps. While our friendship was never especially demonstrative, we each had the ability to ignore the other's irritations. Simon's strength and stamina had carried me through some difficult days on the mountains. Yet I wondered if he, too, was feeling some doubts.

The morning's weather dampens our spirits, but is something we just have to accept. Much of the challenge of this summer will come from riding the inevitable storms. Neither Martin nor I have ever climbed continuously for ten days, let alone sixty, but the uncertainty of our undertaking is very much part of its appeal. Ever since first climbing in the Alps I've looked for climbs to test my ability and strength of mind against the wild and savage beauty of the mountains. This traverse will give a myriad of new experience and our first day looks as though it will give a suitably testing start.

Although sited on the fringe of the glaciers, the Diavolezza Hut is really a skiers' hotel, grossly in excess of the needs and pockets of most mountaineers. Its empty corridors had been sealed recently with a noxious mastic and ducted central heating ensured that no guest would ever be exposed to any chill or damp from outside. Last night we had been the only customers for dinner, and a staff of some ten cooks, waitresses and chambermaids floated around trying to look useful. Evening entertainment was provided by satellite television while the kitchen staff caught up on their knitting. The place exemplified all that we were trying to escape over the next two months, but just at that moment the world we sought was hidden somewhere high in the clouds.

We left at 3.50am and strapped on skis down on the glacier. On the Fortezza Ridge a driving sleet assailed us and even the narrow ridge crest was banked high with fresh snow. To our right, steep slopes plunged to the Morteratsch Glacier, which is the longest ice stream on the Bernina's flanks. Our circuitous route to the peak would keep us above the steep and crevassed upper slopes of this glacier.

The first ascent of the Piz Bernina was made on 13 September 1850 by the Engadin surveyor Johann Coaz and his guides Jon and Lorenz Tscharner, and they climbed direct through the most chaotic section of the glacier, now known as the Labyrinth, in order to gain the mountain's East Ridge. Glacial shrinkage and the discovery of the safer Bellavista route, which we were following, have led to the abandonment of the Labyrinth passage. Even climbers who approach the Bernina from the Boval Hut on the lower Morteratsch Glacier now steer well to the left of the Labyrinth and join the Bellavista route.

We were forced to remove our skis at a rocky section and ploughed up the crest in a rising blizzard. As we gained height, the wetting sleet transformed into thick snowflakes and then to fine dry powder, which swirled in the wind to create a virtual white-out on the plateau above the Fortezza. Now that the ridge had lost its definition, we had to embark on a critical piece of navigation, changing our direction in order to hit the 100m wide entrance to the terraces.

If we missed the line we could find ourselves veering up steep avalanche-prone slopes above the shelf or else stumbling into the bands of seracs below. We might have kept our skis off and counted paces in order to measure off the map distance involved, but had we done so we would have wallowed up to our thighs in every fold and hollow of the traverse. Even with skis we sunk knee-deep in the bigger drifts and found it increasingly difficult to extricate our feet in order to execute kick turns. Simon's altimeter proved to be our saviour as we tackled the traverse. With sure knowledge of our height we could follow the exact contour line of the terrace as shown on the map.

In a spell of fine weather there would doubtless be a track the width of a motor-road over these slopes and each day a hundred climbers or more would wander across at their ease. They might have laughed to see our laboured progress in the storm. Had the forecast suggested weather this bad, we might have postponed our departure by a day, but we had been given to expect a mixture of sunshine and showers. Now, having made a start, we had to keep faith with whatever the elements threw at us.

At 10.15am we were only half-way over the traverse and our first radio call to the valley was due. We had bought four lightweight transceivers in order to maintain essential communication with our support teams throughout the expedition. I opened our set with my gloved hands and adjusted the wavelength to our pre-arranged channel. Although we were 9km from the campsite at Morteratsch, Joy's encouraging voice came over loud and clear and I could even hear a background babble of shouts from my children, Alex and Hazel. It was wonderful to know that the radios worked so well after we had invested £1200 in their purchase, but rather less cheering to receive the news that the weather forecasters had awoken to the reality of the storm and were promising no significant improvement in the next twenty-four hours.

From the end of the terrace we had to descend 150m before resuming horizontal progress to the broad saddle of the Fuorcla Crast'Aguzza. For the long climb and traverse we had used adhesive brushed nylon skins on the base of our skis to provide grip, but in the thick cloud we were equally glad of our skins to slow our rate of descent. Roped together 10m apart, we slid slowly downhill with our legs wide apart in a beginner's snowplough stance. Simon went hesitantly ahead.

The visibility, though nearer to 30m, feels like five as fresh snow blankets all features with a uniform whiteness. Caution reduces my pace as I search for signs of crevasses or steepening slopes. I feel a constant unspoken pressure from Martin who can judge the surrounding terrain better against my position out in front on the slope. A controlled side-slip and gentle snow-plough are the best we can dare.

One of the greatest fears of climbers is that of losing more height than is necessary during a temporary descent, with the result that they invariably keep too high, and so it was with us. Soon after resuming our traverse, I sensed darkening shadows to both my left and right. We were ski-ing into a steeply inclined crevasse field, but not until my ski-tips were hanging over a considerable vertical drop was I convinced that our way was barred. We tried going higher but hit a minor maze of ice towers connected by bridges of soft snow. Despite our delicate position, we decided to consult the map and spent the next few minutes passing it back and forth to one another while hypothesising on our likely position.

It is testimony to the superb accuracy of the Swiss 1:25000 maps that we were eventually able to pinpoint the exact band of crevasses in which we were stuck and realised that we needed to be 50m lower down. If any humble cartographer of the Swiss national survey has ever questioned the worth of spending his days sketching the countless lines of crevasses on to its maps, then please let me convince him otherwise.

A strong wind rose on the open plateau of the Fuorcla, driving the snow into our chests. Until then I had thought we might have kept going all the way to the summit, which was only 440m above us, but now the penetrating damp and chill lowered our horizon to the shelter of the Marco e Rosa Hut which lay 500m beyond the saddle. It was not a target that one would want to miss, as it is perched right on the brink of the Bernina's southern cliffs.

The gentle undulation of the pass was highly confusing. By following in exact line and constantly checking the back-bearing down our ski tracks, we held our course. At the same time we tried to interpret the fall-line of the slope which would tell us on which side of the pass we lay. There was a rising sense of excitement as we neared the presumed hut location. We had taken every possible precaution to keep our line, but the thrill of mountain navigation is that you are never absolutely sure of your position until the moment of arrival.

We passed just above a rock outcrop and suddenly met the cliff-edge. With forward progress no longer possible, we first explored up the slope, but without success. Then we searched below our point of arrival. The fear that, despite our careful navigation, we might be lost was just beginning to form when we discovered that the rock outcrop was, in fact, the hut roof. However, we were dismayed to find its windows shuttered and the doors all bolted. We hadn't exactly expected to be greeted by a friendly guardian with a cup of hot tea, but it is normal practice that at least one room of a hut is left open throughout the winter for the use of climbers and skiers.

Then Simon spotted a second rock island a few metres lower and, with a bit of digging, this transformed itself into a second and older refuge, and indeed its door was unlocked. It is some indication of the foul weather outside that we were more than thankful to enter what was no more than a glorified refrigerator. The idea of a hot cup of tea was plaguing our thoughts. We had brought no stove with us, thinking that we would be up and down the mountain comfortably within a day. Now it looked likely that we would be stuck here all night and we could only hope that there was a wood or gas stove in the hut.

We searched the shelves and equipment boxes, procuring frozen Mars Bars and cake left by previous visitors, but could find no cooker. With some despondency, we stuck our water bottles outside so that they could catch the drips which fell from the roof whenever the clouds thinned and transmitted a little of the sun's warmth. The Italian mountaineers Marco and Rosa de Marchi founded the hut in 1913 and this was the original building. Judging from their flea-bitten and dog-eared state, its blankets were of equal vintage. Wrapped up in five of them we achieved a semblance of warmth and settled down to an afternoon of dozing and waiting. Yet for all its privations, the Marco e Rosa Hut was infinitely preferable to the Diavolezza. At least we were on the hill and fighting.

Our rest was punctuated only by the buffeting of the wind on the hut walls and the whistling vibrations of its wire supports. Occasionally, Simon would pass up a square of Highland toffee – some two hundred slabs of the stuff had been donated by a sweet manufacturer to sustain our summer's effort. With the first bite we realised that, at sub-zero temperatures, Highland toffee is as tough as glacier ice and that we were lucky to survive without breaking any teeth.

By 5pm we were becoming restless. Already a day of our schedule had slipped from our grasp. We should have been ski-ing the last slopes back towards the valley at that moment with our first summit under our belts. Now we were wondering if we would get down by tomorrow night. With increasing regularity we poked our noses out of the door only to meet the same blast of snow and wind. The final climb to the Bernina's summit would take three hours at most, but we needed a lull.

Our scheduled radio check at 6pm forced us to climb 20m up to the crest of the ridge where we had a line of sight to Morteratsch. Joy reported more bad weather for tomorrow. As I closed our radio set I sensed that the snowfall was abating and the wind dropping. If we waited until the morning, a new storm would likely be upon us, and in truth I could barely face another 12 hours cooped up in an ice-box with nothing to drink. My thought was sudden and decisive.

'I think we should go for the top.'

Simon was a little taken aback.

'Do you think we've got time? It might be clearer in the morning and the snow could be dangerous now.'

I stamped around on the snow trying to demonstrate its consistency in an attempt to win his agreement. Simon is less a creature of impulse than I am. He was finally converted to the plan with the logic that if we failed tonight, it wouldn't stop us going back up again tomorrow morning.

There were $3^1/_2$ hours of daylight left when we set out. We left our skis and all spare gear at the hut. A long plod up 25° slopes took us to a steeper face at the foot of the final ridge, the Spallagrat, which crosses the forepeak of La Spalla in order to gain the summit. I was enervated by the altitude and started to feel that strange detachment of mind and matter which is a sure sign of oxygen starvation. No amount of general fitness training can compensate for proper acclimatisation and it was nine months since either of us had climbed above 3000m. Had we been able to nip up and down the mountain in a few hours as planned, our bodies might not have noticed the deprivation, but after 12 hours at 3500m, there was no chance that we could play such a trick on ourselves.

The wind had blown the steeper ground bare of fresh snow, so we put on our crampons and made more satisfying progress towards misted pinnacles under La Spalla. The windward south-west side of our ridge was caked with great cascades of rime ice while the lee slopes were banked with deep drifts. In the gloom of evening we felt anywhere but on a *voie normale*. The guidebook promised a rock step of grade II to gain La Spalla.

In dry conditions grade II denotes what is no more than a glorified scramble and involves only the briefest pause in upward progress, but now we were confronted by sloping frosted rocks with no pitons or visible scratches to indicate the line. We briefly examined the problem and decided that somehow the step had to be avoided if we were to escape benightment during the descent. A ledge banked steeply with snow traversed under the rocks on to the east face. Putting in occasional running belays on the rope between us lest the snow should give way, I led across this and up a steep runnel to regain the crest.

In normal summer conditions our little detour is probably a shattered slope of dangerously loose rocks which should be avoided at all costs. Under snow it gave a simple solution. Heavy snowfall often renders rocky ridge routes all but impossible, but alternative lines are opened on the faces on either side, and these invariably give a quicker passage. Nevertheless, the risk of avalanches must be borne in mind when taking to the flanking snow-slopes.

At La Spalla the Italian border turns to the south-west and heads down the linking ridge to the Piz Roseg, leaving the Bernina itself to be claimed as a Swiss peak. Such discrimination is a slight affront to Italian sensitivities, but it is one repeated around the frontier peaks of the Pennine Alps. We now descended the airy arête northwards and made a short but wearying climb to the Bernina's summit.

At 8.38pm our '4000ers' traverse began, the two protagonists slumped on the topmost rocks trying to summon the energy to take the necessary photographs. We had even lugged up a borrowed video camera in order to record the moment, only to discover that the batteries were flat. The only fresh member of the summit party was 'Tartan Ted', a miniature teddy with a tartan scarf given as a good-luck mascot by my three-year-old daughter, Hazel. I had every intention that he should still be with me on the Barre des Ecrins in two months' time.

Remarkably, there was a flat calm on the top, and briefly the mists parted to give us a glimpse of the Piz Zupò over on the far side of the Crast'Aguzza, which at 3995m comes as close as any top to joining the Bernina on the '4000ers' rollcall. There is much else in the area to commend a return visit. Besides the Piz Zupò, both the Piz Roseg and Piz Palü exceed 3900m in height. The North Face of the Palü is a magnificent snow climb, first opened by the great Engadin guide, Christian Klucker.

However, the most compelling route of the Bernina Alps fell away under our feet to the north: the Biancograt, which is one of the most beautiful snow ridges in the Alps. Its renown as a classic route was enhanced when the great Austrian climber, Hermann Buhl, soloed it up and down from the Boval Hut in six hours in 1950 in order to win a 200 franc wager. Buhl's feat funded his assault on the Grandes Jorasses North Face later that summer, but the thought of it made our own protracted ascent by the easy way look rather ridiculous. I vowed that on a fine day I would return to climb the Biancograt and see the Bernina at its best.

The descent brought an immense physical relief and with it the satisfaction that our gamble had paid off. We regained the hut just after nightfall at 10.10pm and after taking a few sips of water fell to the sleep of the just.

We were far from finished with the Bernina, but the sight of a few bright patches of sky at dawn encouraged the thought that we might yet be able to ski off the mountain in recompense for the previous day's toil. Therefore, we left with some enthusiasm at 6am, but before we had skied a kilometre, we met a new mass of cloud boiling up from the Morteratsch Valley. Almost immediately we hit a second obstacle, the 150m reascent to regain the Bellavista Terraces, so easily forgotten yet a real trial to two parched climbers.

The night's sleep had produced only a feeble recovery and my body felt shackled by the altitude. Simon could hardly have been feeling much better, judging by the regularity with which we were swopping the lead on the return journey. For the second day running, the Bellavista failed miserably to live up to its name, but on the plateau above the Fortezza we removed the skins from our skis and chanced a little downhill running. The mist coupled with gentle snowfall continued to impair visibility however, and the sudden appearance of a cornice edge a few metres to our right persuaded us to discontinue the experiment. With some disgust we removed the skis altogether, strapped them to our packs and resigned ourselves to hiking back to the valley.

At least our skis were wonderfully light and eminently portable since they were only 130cm in length compared to a normal touring ski of 180 or 190cm. We had foreseen the likelihood of carrying our skis considerable distances and had obtained two pairs of the extra-short Kastle Firn Extrem model, which are not normally available for sale in Britain. With the addition of the Silvretta 404 binding, we not only had a light ski, but also one which could perform excellently when wearing ordinary plastic climbing boots. Although the ski-ing experience of the

Bernina was anything but enthralling, we already appreciated the wisdom of our choice.

Instead of returning via the Diavolezza we sought a more scenic end to the trip and headed directly north towards the Morteratsch Glacier, emerging below the clouds at 3000m and blinking in the shock of unaccustomed light. At the first meltwater stream we drank long and deep, and reflected that a couple of litres of hot tea some time in the last 36 hours would have made the Bernina a rather easier proposition. We reached the main iceflow just at its junction with the Pers Glacier and there met a large guided party which was enjoying a day trek down from the Diavolezza to Morteratsch. I swallowed hard when one of their guides, a grizzled chap in his fifties who looked much in the Christian Klucker mould, bemoaned the lack of snow that spring.

The Morteratsch Glacier is a kilometre wide with a huge lateral moraine stranded high above its western bank, upon which stands the Boval Hut. At the junction the glacier's surface is a sea of ice waves, but lower down the ice is obscured by the masses of debris so typical of the shrinking Alpine ice sheets. It is the sort of terrain where one can easily waste time and energy in fruitless routefinding, so we were glad of the guide's directions, particularly in hitting the best route off the glacier snout.

Below the snout a flat and stony meltwater plain stretched down to the encroaching forests of the Val Bernina. A series of signposts charted the retreat of the glacier in each decade since 1900, the total diminution being a remarkable 1318m. Already a young forest is regenerating on the land so recently abandoned by the ice. At these rates of retreat one wonders just how many of the alpine glaciers will be left in another century. Perhaps we were tackling the '4000ers' traverse not a decade too soon!

A good track leads from the glacier down to Morteratsch station and 2km further lay our campsite where Joy and Carole were waiting. They had just had a first taste of their routine over the coming two months, a game of patient waiting and time-filling. Never being sure just when they would be needed, they were unable to pursue life with the singularity of purpose that we enjoyed.

Having been unsuccessful in attempts to get some commercial sponsorship for the expedition, Joy and I had ploughed our savings into the purchase of a motor-home for the summer. Our only security lay in the caravan dealer's offer to buy the vehicle back at the end of the journey.

Had we not obtained that guarantee we might have faced insolvency on our return. However, without its comfort and convenience Joy would have faced an impossible task in caring for the family. On getting back at 2pm, I stretched out on its settees and waited for the kettle to brew while a pair of excited children climbed all over me.

By contrast, Simon and Carole's accommodation was rather more cramped, consisting of a Land Rover loaned by our designated charity, Blythswood Care, and a nylon dome tent. Blythswood had converted the vehicle into a field ambulance for use in Eastern Europe and it was now packed to the gunnels with their food and equipment. As newly-weds of just two months, they would have no justification were they to complain about living at such close quarters, but Carole was already developing a love-hate relationship with their new home.

> *Never in my wildest dreams had I expected my first three months of married life to involve driving a temperamental Land Rover around the Alps. Simon and I had been very grateful when Blythswood offered us the vehicle as we would never have been able to have got all the equipment into our car. Not only did we have our personal gear but also all the hill food needed to supply Martin, Simon and support teams for the whole trip. Imagine living with 40 cans of tuna, 10kg of trail mix, 100 packets of oatcakes, 150 chocolate bars and a host of other items. There had already been times when it was necessary to sleep in the van, among all these provisions and on stretchers that were only 2ft wide!*

We kept our camps proximate but never intimate. Coming off the mountain we looked forward to immersing ourselves in our respective family lives more than anything else, and certainly Simon and I needed time apart if our relationship was to survive intact. We had scheduled the expedition so carefully that it was rare for us to need more than a few minutes of chat to plan the next day. On our return to Morteratsch our plans focused on one thing only, and that was a good lie-in in the morning.

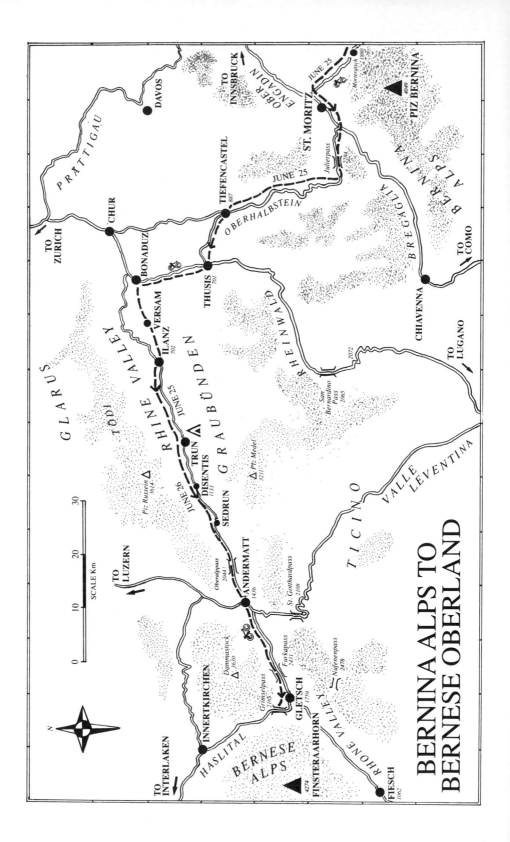

BERNINA ALPS TO BERNESE OBERLAND

2

ACROSS THE DIVIDES

The Bernina Alps to Bernese Oberland

The morning of 25 June dawned crisp and clear. Just as the sun's first rays were brushing the frost off the grass, two very different characters emerged from the Alps 4000 support vehicles. From the pair of tousled climbers who had descended the Bernina, Simon and I had been transformed overnight into lightweight racing cyclists, complete with sleek chamois-leather shorts, purple lycra vests and matching helmets. The only detail we had forgotten was the shaving of the legs that seems obligatory to all top bikers!

We felt more than a trifle embarrassed parading in this gear like a pair of strutting peacocks, since neither of us could be described as cycling enthusiasts. However, when we had planned our traverse it quickly became obvious that we could save many days of overland walking if we biked between the main massifs. This would also provide a welcome change of exercise and perhaps would save our knees from the progressive wear and tear that might cause injury later in the journey.

We had been royally kitted out by my local bike dealer, Dryburghs of Dingwall, and had been loaned a pair of fine Dawes touring bikes. Strictly, our bikes were termed hybrid models since they had straight handlebars and a tyre tread of sufficient thickness to allow a little off-road running. For our purposes they were light enough for road touring and amply geared for the switchback gradients we were going to tackle over the coming weeks.

The Bernina group is separated from the main massifs of the Western Alps by a complex series of ridges and passes that form the core of Central Switzerland. These are mainly aligned on a north-south axis which is most unhelpful if, like us, your intention is to travel from east to west. In the next two days we had to cycle 215km over four major passes in order to reach Grimsel, the eastern portal to the Bernese Oberland. In doing so we would span the headwaters of Western Europe's greatest rivers – the Danube, the Rhine and the Rhône. Whatever the effort involved, the journey promised to be a geographical education.

The first fine day after a storm is always a revelation. The air is at its freshest, coolest and clearest. The mountain world seems reborn, especially when the peaks are thickly draped in virgin snow, as they were today. As we prepared for departure, the Piz Bernina and her satellites were arrayed in brilliant splendour at the head of the Morteratsch cirque and every detail of our tortuous route of the last two days could be picked out even at our distance of 10km. The frustration we felt at our mistiming of the Bernina climb was mitigated by the prospect of perfect cycling weather. The only outstanding question was whether our fitness was sufficient for the task. As Simon put it: 'The bikes will become either our friends or enemies over these next two days.'

Mountaineers tend to consider that their particular brand of fitness is sufficient to cope with the rigours of other outdoor sports. The reality can be rather different. Mountaineering is essentially a low intensity but highly prolonged activity. Simon and I had built up great stamina and endurance through our years of climbing and in our daily work as mountain guides. Cycling, on the other hand, is a much more intensive and specific exercise. It burns up energy reserves at a faster rate and relies on the efficiency of a limited group of leg muscles. If one doesn't keep topped up with food and liquid and if the quadriceps and calf muscles are insufficiently trained, one can be overtaken by a sudden and alarming depletion which athletes call 'the bonk'.

Our cycling training could hardly be regarded as exhaustive. I had done a couple of runs up my local road pass at home, the 600m Bealach na Ba, and one long hilly run in the Lake District over Wrynose and Hard Knott Passes and Birker Fell, and hoped that this might be sufficient insurance against undue suffering. By contrast, if Simon had been pursuing a secret training programme, then he was keeping the details closely guarded. I rather imagined that he intended to rely on his inner strength over the next two days.

We set off at 9.30am, spinning smoothly down the Val Bernina, past the village of Pontresina, to meet the main valley of the Engadin, which carries the waters of the River Inn towards the Danube. A climb of

550m would take us past the famous resorts of St Moritz and Silvaplana and up to the 2284m Julierpass. The upper Engadin looked groomed ready for a garden show. Its waters rushed in icy torrents down through green meadows to glistening lakes and its villages grouped in enchanting clusters of sloping eaves and church spires. Even the vehicle fumes on the hairpins of the Julier could not dispel the image that we were pedalling through a giant wonderland.

On gaining the pass we enjoyed a final retrospect of the Bernina group, now burning with a silvery glare in the midday sun. We could already sense the pleasures of travelling cross-country, fond regret at leaving a familiar horizon behind, mixed with anticipation of the new scenes to come. We now embarked on 35km of continuous descent with a height drop of 1400m to Tiefencastel in the Oberhalbstein Valley, and Simon made most of the pace.

> The almost effortless ride down the zigzags is exhilarating and opens into long straights where just an occasional turn of the pedal keeps my speed. We stop briefly at Savognin to allow Carole to catch up so we can take on more liquid and a little food. Although the exertion is not great, it is easy to forget that we must maintain our fluid balance through the day. With little pedalling to do we can absorb the scenery. The surrounding peaks rise to 3000m, their tops still covered with the remains of winter snow. Grazing pastures sweep downwards to the valley between swathes of pines, interrupted only by the wires and pylons of small ski installations. Above us a few paragliders drift with the light morning breeze and add small splashes of vivid colour to the expanse of blue sky.

I found myself working increasingly hard to match Simon's pedalling power throughout the run. He may have lacked training, but he seemed as strong as an ox. Nevertheless, he was setting a pace which got us places quickly without blinding our senses to the beauty around us. These are the Alps you never see if your horizons are limited to the fleshpots of Chamonix or Zermatt, and on this early summer day they were exquisitely lovely.

After Tiefencastel Carole shadowed us through a series of tunnels down to Thusis. Neither of us had lights on our bikes, so we appreciated having the Land Rover right on our tail. The string of cars behind thought otherwise and we were accompanied through the tunnels by a cacophony of blaring horns. We concluded that maybe the Swiss are not the most patient of motorists.

Going into the first tunnel at a speed of 40km per hour, I made the

mistake of forgetting to remove my sunglasses, and was suddenly
plunged into near darkness. With one hand desperately trying to hold
my handlebars straight, I shoved the glasses on to my forehead but the
brim of my helmet quickly knocked them back down on to the bridge
of my nose. Eventually I had to pull them down to my neck where their
retaining cord held them safely in place. Later in the journey, with
increasing confidence, I gained a thrill from riding the short tunnels
with the glasses on.

   Just past Thusis we enjoyed hot tea and flapjacks and Alex joined
me on his bike for the gentle run down to Bonaduz, where we met the
main Rhine Valley. At Bonaduz we were at the lowly elevation of 600m
and in the next 70km would make a steady overall ascent towards the
2044m Oberalppass. Initially, we had a choice of two routes: the main
road on the north side of the river, which was longer in distance, or
else a very hilly short-cut to the south.

   By choosing the adventurous option we were rewarded with a most
scenic and peaceful ride. The road commenced with a long straight
section through young forest, then rose through a series of hairpins to
emerge on a lofty balcony high above the Rhine. The river flowed sinu-
ously through a gorge of glacial conglomerate and a range of attractive
peaks lined the opposite skyline. We sped round a series of curves satis-
fyingly close to the retaining parapet, dipped sharply to cross the trib-
utary valley of the Rabiusa, then dropped into lowest gear for a tight
sequence of turns up to the pastures of Versam and Valendas. Thanks
to their secluded position, these villages were untainted by the whirl
of commercialism which has infected so many alpine valleys. With
quiet industry and an appreciation of traditional values, the people
here seemed to have preserved a rural idyll while still enjoying the
material comforts of modern life. Few nations have better achieved a
marrying of an agrarian society with a wealthy and sophisticated
economy. Usually, the one destroys the other, but the Swiss show no
intention of abandoning their agricultural heritage.

   We rejoined the main road at Ilanz and again I struggled to keep
abreast of Simon's relentless pace on the long level sections or gentle
climbs. I noted with dismay that he was always pedalling two gears
higher than me, while my feet spun crazily in the effort to keep up.
Perhaps I should have asked him to slow down a little, but my personal
pride was at stake and I also realised that if either of us started
complaining on this trip, our mood could easily degenerate into one of

mutual recrimination. My best tactic was to get into the lead and then dictate a slightly slower pace. I would pant up alongside and gasp: 'I'll take it for a bit now if you like,' then try to get my wheels in front before Simon could notice my pained grimace.

Joy and Carole had driven on ahead, promising to stop at the first good camp-ground. There were sites marked at Trun after 18km and Disentis, a further 12km upvalley, and I was now praying hard that Joy had chosen the first. We turned into the site at Trun and to my relief she was there. We had covered 125km with 1150m of climbing in the day. As I laid down my bike and staggered over to our van, there was cold comfort in the thought that tomorrow's ride was considerably shorter. Although only 86km in distance, it promised a total of 2550m of ascent over the Oberalp, Furka and Grimsel passes. With a leg massage, hot shower and an enormous meal, I might hope to recover most of the strength I'd lost during this first day, but tomorrow's climbs went far beyond what we had so far achieved. I tried to relax that evening playing with the children on the swings and in the camp sandpit, but could not escape the sense of pending torment.

By doing two hard days on our bikes we were saving five days on the quickest walking route between the Bernina and the Bernese Alps. In 1988 two British climbers, Paul Mackrill and John Rowlands, had, like us, set out to make a non-stop traverse of the '4000ers'. Like us, they had the support of their families and had started on the Piz Bernina. However, they had elected to walk the whole distance and had started in early May when the lower mountains are still well covered in snow.

After two abortive attempts, they climbed the Bernina on 13 May and then commenced a complex trek westwards. Their route stayed well to the south of ours, traversing a series of passes into the canton of Ticino in continuously wet and depressing weather. They then headed north-westwards and crossed the Nufenenpass on the 21st to gain the southern flanks of the Bernese Oberland. Already Rowlands had twisted his knee on a tree root hidden under the snow and his injury forced a three-day rest at Fiesch before they could tackle the Oberland peaks.

From such a tough initiation their expedition developed into an epic struggle as time and again they were rebuffed in the Oberland by bad weather. Alpine weather in May and June is often very unsettled. Just at the time when anti-cyclones tend to dominate the weather of

Northern Europe and the Scottish Highlands enjoy their finest and driest spell of the year, the Alps lie along the deflected track of a series of depressions. So the conditions faced by Mackrill and Rowlands in 1988 were not exceptional. In 1992, for instance, it had rained with monotonous regularity in Chamonix from the middle of May until late June. On those spring days when it isn't raining, the Fohn wind has a tendency to blow up from the Mediterranean, bringing hot and dangerous conditions to mountains loaded with fresh snow.

By starting on the first days of the summer season, we hoped to avoid the worst of the spring weather. We anticipated unsettled conditions for the first couple of weeks, but the dominant feature of the summer weather over the last decade has been a large and stable anti-cyclone, the Azores High, which settles over the Alps in early July and guarantees largely fine conditions through to late August. The timing of the anti-cyclone is variable. In 1991 it was firmly installed by 10 July, in 1992 the onset was delayed until the 13th, but its occurrence was sufficiently regular that we relied on its presence to speed us across the great ranges of the Pennine Alps in three or four weeks' time.

When Mackrill and Rowlands hit the equivalent period in 1988, they were already far behind schedule, but were unable to make up time because of a lack of high-level support which forced them to return to the valley every two or three days. Rowlands' leave from work expired on 18 August, but Mackrill battled on with two other partners until 19 September when he completed the 50 Swiss '4000ers' alone on the Grand Combin, fully 130 days after his journey began.

This was the only known continuous attempt on the '4000ers' until the summer of 1993 and for sheer determination it was a remarkable effort. However, Simon and I intended to complete all 75 in less than half that time and had chosen our tactics accordingly. We also knew that our many years of mountain guiding in the Alps had given us a level of experience sufficient to keep moving even in doubtful weather, and the Bernina had been the first proof of this theory. Between us we had previously climbed 57 of the summits, a degree of familiarity which would speed our progress without eliminating the sense of adventure from our enterprise.

Our chosen schedule demanded the utmost of our endurance and allowed us very little breathing space, as was self-evident during our overnight stay at Trun. We continued the ride at 7.45am on a second fine morning, hoping to get the bulk of the work over before the heat of midday. The early start gave us an hour on quiet roads, gaining height steadily through the towns of Disentis and then Sedrun. We were now only 12km from the Oberalppass, yet still had 700m to climb, and my stomach tensed with anticipation of the effort to come. I scanned every gap in the hills ahead trying to guess where the pass lay, but it was only on rounding the long bend by Tavetsch that at last we could see the road snaking up to a definite conclusion in a right slanting defile.

For me, the thought of the final climb proved far worse than its reality. My morale was boosted to see that we both dropped into the second-to-bottom of our 21 gears when the gradient increased to 10 per cent, and no longer was Simon dragging me at an untoward pace.

Near the top of the pass I am struggling. I have not found a rhythm as I did yesterday, and as a result am expending too much effort to hold my own with Martin. It is with some relief that the top of the pass is reached.

The truth was dawning that although I couldn't match Simon's strength on the flat, his extra weight was counting against him on the stiffest climbs. He had started the summer weighing some 82kg compared to my own 72kg. Although Simon is prone to bemoan his extra bodyweight when hanging by his fingers on a rockclimb, it was no bad thing to embark on this prolonged endurance test with a surplus. Indeed, we had both happily allowed our weight to creep up in the weeks before leaving for the Alps, knowing that in the early days of the trip our bodies would convert any surplus fat into extra muscle. There would also be many times in the next two months when we would be glad of those extra energy reserves. It would have been quite the wrong tactic to have embarked on the trip in a peak of condition from which one could only decline. As far as Simon was concerned, Alps 4000 was an ideal way to lose weight while still enjoying 5,000 calories a day, a technique that confounds most dietary advice, but one which works effectively on the high mountains.

Rounding one of the final hairpins, we were greeted by two familiar faces. Our first support team, Ian and Sandra Dring, had been due to meet us on the Grimselpass the previous evening. As we were running a day behind schedule, they had driven their caravanette back along our cycling route in the hope of meeting us. I'd first met them rock-climbing on Froggatt Edge in the Peak District back in 1983 when they were students at Sheffield and, despite my moving up to Scotland, we had never lost touch. In sharp contrast to their days of student poverty, they were now pursuing extremely remunerative careers, Sandra as a dentist and Ian as a research scientist with ICI. Indeed, Sandra was currently regretting their indulgence in a week's heliski-ing in the Canadian Rockies which had depleted the funds she had earmarked for a new house. Impecunious friends such as hard-grafting mountain guides viewed their extravagances with benign amusement but no jealousy, for affluence had not dimmed their dedication in all mountain sports from biking to alpinism, and they retained a refreshing modesty and youthful enthusiasm in all they did. In 1991 Ian and I had spent seven days making a new route up the prow of Bhrigu Pathar in the Garhwal Himalaya and throughout that week of exiguous living not a word of anger had passed between us. He and Sandra were going to provide support during our traverse of the Bernese Oberland and they would be joined by Ian's brother, Craig, later that day.

A half-hour break was called on the top of the Oberalppass. While Ian showed Alex the intricacies of his latest computer 'Game Boy', Joy cooked me a large plateful of fried eggs and tomatoes with hunks of buttered bread. Diluted with several mugs of hot tea, this would hopefully be ingested by the bloodstream during the descent to Andermatt and be readily available to sustain the 1100m climb to the Furkapass which followed. Several other groups of cyclists were congregating on the pass when we set off into a stiff west wind at 11.30am. Ian was pacing us on his mountain bike on this section and led us down 600m of wild hairpins which ended abruptly on the cobbled streets of Andermatt.

We then had a 6km respite on level roads to Realp where the Furka motor-rail tunnel commences its 14km journey through the mountains to Oberwald in the Rhône Valley. At 2431m, the Furkapass is exceeded only by the Grand St Bernard (2469m) and the Nufenenpass (2478m) as the highest road pass in Switzerland and is closed by snow for six months of the year. The tunnel diverts much of the summer traffic and leaves the road pass itself for the pleasure of tourists, cyclists and motorbikers.

The pass commenced in a series of loops so tight that Ian decided that at one point it might be quicker to get off his bike and carry it up the steep hillside to the next hairpin. His sudden disappearance puzzled us for several minutes, and it was only a good deal higher up that he finally rejoined us, his experiment having proved a decided failure. We maintained the same steady pace that had got us up the Oberalppass, but Simon was now labouring under what he discovered to be a cruel misconception.

> *We are now under the full glare of the sun and the heat in the valley stifles any breeze as we gain height on the precisely engineered road. I count the remaining hairpins to the summit where a building stood on the skyline. There are six, maybe seven, and I focus on them as a goal. Each bend gives a slight easing in angle and I look forward to the extra momentum they give to the following straight. The only other relief comes from jets of water shot from the pistols which Alex and Hazel aim at us as we pass the Morans' van.*
>
> *Turning what I had perceived as the final bend by the building, which is a café-pension, I see the road snaking up into the distance for another 6km. We have gained the perfect false summit and I realise I've only 'psyched' myself up for half the distance. Forgetting Martin, I get my head down and make my own pace. My back has tightened with cramp and, seeing no easing in the slope, I search within myself for more strength, barely aware of my surroundings.*

For me, it was some relief to be able to ride on gently ahead without feeling the edge of unspoken competition that was inevitable when our wheels were together, and I was pleased that my own stamina had held out. Perhaps those hilly training rides had made a difference. Ian took on the job of shielding Simon from the wind, and we reached the cluster of hotels and cafes on the true summit as a threesome at 1.30pm.

The sky had progressively clouded over from the west through the morning and a cool breeze blew across the pass, making us glad of the shelter of our vehicles. We were high enough that extensive fields of spring snow fringed the road and fanned out among the cliffs of the high mountains. The Furkapass is an excellent base for middle altitude climbing on the Winterberg massif. The beautiful snow-cap of the 3583m Galenstock rises directly above the pass and behind it lies the Dammastock, at 3630m the highest peak of the group.

This is the sort of area which British climbers should consider visiting during their first season in the Alps, being highly accessible and offering a variety of climbing without the intimidating atmosphere of the Mont Blanc or Zermatt massifs. Too often novice alpinists are deterred by the scale and reputation of the biggest mountains and spend their first holiday either failing on the longer routes or pecking round the edges on lower level training climbs. Places like Arolla or these ranges of Central Switzerland offer a far more thorough and friendly grounding in the skills of alpinism, but lacking charisma they are ignored by the majority who rush to the famous resorts like bees to the honeypot.

Only the Grimsel now stood between us and successful completion of our trilogy of passes, but this is a much shorter climb, being merely 400m above Gletsch at the head of the Rhône valley. Sandra now took over from Ian as our pacer and we rode off over the brow of the pass with some anticipation of the westward view. The Furkapass was our gateway to the Western Alps and we were not disappointed by the panorama that opened before us. Just 20km away the Finsteraarhorn, monarch of the Bernese Oberland, rose in a giant pyramid above a sea of cloud. To its left, the Rhône valley cut a 40km trench down to Brig and 20km further rose the noble form of the Weisshorn together with other '4000ers' of the Pennine Alps. It was a great moment of arrival. At last we were in the heartland of the high Alps.

The descent to Gletsch was, if anything, more hair-raising than that to Andermatt. The terminal icefall of the Rhône Glacier tumbles down by the side of the road, giving birth to the river that feeds the great cities of Lausanne, Geneva and Lyon and drains into the Mediterranean close to Marseilles. There are few other places in the Alps where the car-bound tourist can get as close to an impressive glacier and inevitably there were hordes of vehicles at the car park which gives access to a grotto under the ice.

A low stone wall alone protects road traffic from the precipitous slopes of the valleyside below the glacier snout. Swooping down the bends in a line of cars I realised that our polystyrene cycling helmets offered little more than psychological protection had one of us missed a turn. As a result, I elected to stay some way behind Simon and Sandra and maintained an unvarying grip on my rear brake lever until the worst was over.

Looking back during the ascent to the 2165m Grimselpass, the maze of hairpins made the valley look like a giant Formula 1 racing circuit, an impression which was reinforced by the constant roar of motorbikes as the youth of urban Switzerland enjoyed a weekend spin. All this was a far cry from the flowered verges and pretty villages of yesterday. No number of souvenir shops could hide the grimness of the Grimsel on a clouded afternoon, a barren landscape of bare granite and barrage dams raked by a cold wind. We stopped only a minute on the summit to regain breath before descending to the Hospice.

This former monastery is now a hotel and is besieged on all sides by the concrete bastions of hydro-electric power development. A paved road led across the access dam and then twisted 50m up an agonising 25 per cent gradient to the hotel entrance and car park, proving a nasty sting in the day's tail. The Hospice was our point of embarkation for the Bernese Alps. Behind it lay the long reservoir of the Grimselsee, and tomorrow we would walk its 6km length to gain perhaps the wildest and most expansive mountain area of the Alps.

As an overnight stopping place, the Hospice left much to be desired. Although our traverse was intended as a continuous route, I could not allow this rule to impose a night of chill misery on Joy and the children. We quickly hoisted the bikes on our vehicles and drove off down the Haslital to an official campsite at Innertkirchen. We would return to the Hospice in the morning.

This motorised deviation off-route mattered little while we were on the road network, but was not a tactic we could contemplate on the mountains whenever we passed a handy cableway. However tempting a quick ride down to the valley for a change of clothes and infusion of extra oxygen might be, such manoeuvres would be tantamount to cheating and would negate the whole concept of a high-level traverse. All the famous mountain railways and cableways of the Alps like the Jungfraujoch, Klein Matterhorn and Aiguille du Midi were therefore out of bounds to us for the duration of the trip.

Less than an hour after leaving Grimsel, we had spread ourselves out on a green and sheltered campsite and Simon and I were washing off the salt and stains from the day's effort. Although relieved to have survived the day, my buttocks and knees were tender and my legs as stiff as boards, but more significantly my brain circuits were slowed with fatigue. I could only imagine that Simon was feeling considerably worse after his buffeting on the Furka. We now faced the necessity not just of making a physical recovery by the morning but of immediately switching all our mental energy into planning and psychologically preparing for eight days away in the mountains. Yet all I longed to do that evening was to stretch out, reflect on a couple of magnificent days' cycling and then let my thoughts drift far away.

3

OBERLAND
ODYSSEY

The Bernese Oberland

For a distance of some 40km from Kandersteg across to Meiringen in the Haslital, the Bernese Oberland presents to its north a near-continuous series of ice faces and limestone precipices. This great wall links a string of summits hovering around the 4000m mark and plunges into valley trenches less than 1000m in altitude. Viewed from the foothills to the north, no mountain chain in the Alps has a more hostile appearance, and the conquest of these faces in the 1920s and 30s forms one of the great passages in mountaineering history.

Pride of place goes to the Eiger, whose 1800m north wall towers above the resort of Grindelwald and remains a touchstone of high-standard alpinism; but other faces like the Gspaltenhorn, Gletscherhorn or Fiescherwand yield little in scale or fearsome grandeur. However, the Eiger fails by just 30m to pierce the 4000m barrier, and several other summits on the skyline fall short by a similar margin. Of all the peaks along the crest of the wall, the only '4000ers' are the Fiescherhorn, Mönch and Jungfrau.

Behind this savage facade lies an extensive plateau of ice sheets and lonely peaks which give birth to tremendous glacier streams flowing south- and eastwards, including the 20km Aletsch Glacier which is the longest in the Alps. A further five mountains and one top over 4000m lie in this remote outback. Strictly, the name Bernese Oberland applies only to the hinterland of Bern on the north side of the range, and the mountains of the interior should more properly be called the Bernese Alps. However, the term Oberland has commonly been used for the whole massif and conjures up contrasting visions, the one of steely-eyed Germanic youth battling on some merciless *nordwand* in the pre-war years and the other of ski tourers skinning across vast glaciers from one lonely hut to another.

Undoubtedly, the area is the premier high mountain wilderness of the Alps and the thought of a continuous traverse across its 4000m summits was particularly daunting to Simon.

I am less familiar with the Oberland than any other range. Having only the Bernina as acclimatisation, it is not certain whether we can hold to our schedule. Climbing early in the season, we are likely to encounter large amounts of fresh snow with the added possibility of early summer storms. Coupled with the unknown terrain, we are assured of a few surprises here. I have spent many hours over the last months of preparation working through the Oberland traverse in my mind and it is still the section that presents me with the most uncertainties.

Indeed, our route plan required a good deal of forethought. Once we went into an area like the Oberland, we had to complete all of its summits before we returned to the valley, or else we would fall far behind our schedule. The commitment was considerable and a single mistake in our choice of route could cost us dearly.

Any approaches from the north would involve us in technical difficulties and enormous height differentials. We had therefore ruled out visiting Grindelwald or Lauterbrunnen, deciding instead to use the high-level eastern access from Grimsel to climb first the Finsteraarhorn and then the area's most difficult summits, the Schreckhorn and Lauteraarhorn. A tenuous link over the Fiescherhorn would take us over the watershed of the Aletsch basin, from where the remaining peaks could be tackled in more leisurely fashion. Finally, we would exit southwards to the Rhône Valley, ready to move across to the Pennine Alps. With regular support at huts, our schedule was eight days for the whole traverse.

We also anticipated that our skis would provide a crucial help during the coming week. Our overall plan to traverse the '4000ers' from east to west was based upon this assumption. To take advantage of its skiing potential we needed to be in the Oberland early in the season when an extensive snow cover still remains on the glaciers which would enable fast running between the mountains. Conversely, the more technical peaks and pinnacles of the Mont Blanc massif would be better left until much later in the summer when their ridges are usually clear of snow. The east-to-west route choice thus dovetailed in a logical fashion.

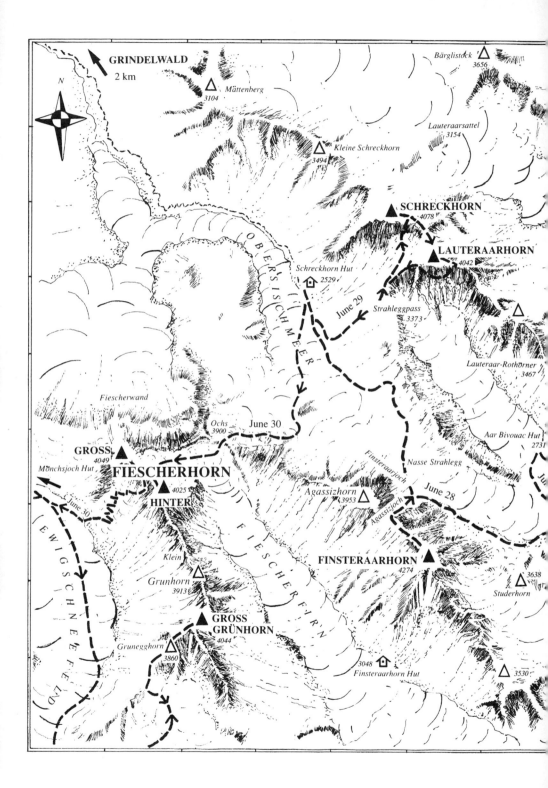

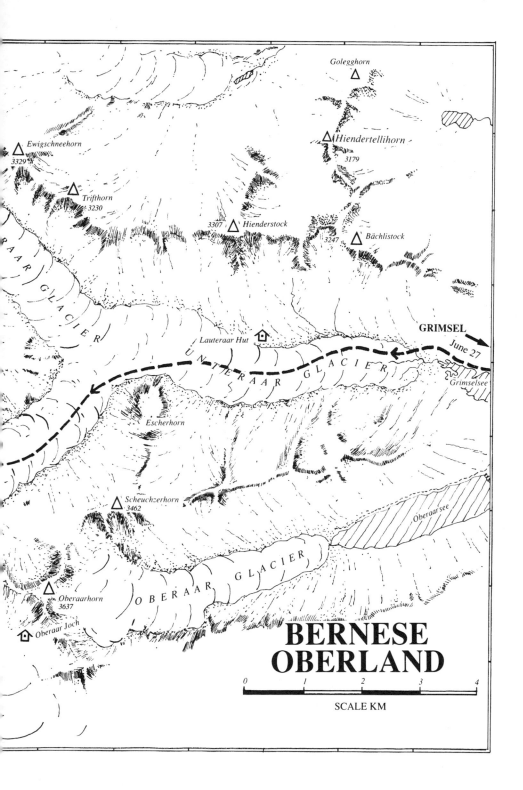

Golegghorn
△

Hiendertellihorn
△
3179

Ewigschneehorn
△
3329

Trifthorn
△
3230

3307 Hienderstock
△

Bächlistock
3247 △

AAR GLACIER

GRIMSEL
June 27

Lauteraar Hut
⌂

UNTERAAR GLACIER

Grimselsee

Escherhorn

Oberaarsee

Scheuchzerhorn
△
3462

OBERAAR GLACIER

Oberaarhorn
△
3637

⌂ Oberaar Joch

BERNESE
OBERLAND

0   1   2   3   4

SCALE KM

Carole drove us back up to Grimsel late on the morning of 27 June. The Land Rover's gears crashed and the engine roared on the long climb, while Carole battled for control of the steering wheel at every hairpin bend. The vehicle was certainly not designed for light-hearted road touring. Its power was wholly geared for the churning mud and unmetalled roads of Albania, where it was destined after the summer.

On both sides of the Haslital, magnificent granite cliffs soared above the road. The Handegg walls are renowned for providing some of the most accessible and finest slab climbing in Europe, most of it protected by expansion bolts. This being a Sunday, there were many parties already engaged on the slabs, but judging from the blackening sky they were going to get a drenching before they reached the tops of their climbs.

The threatening weather made it imperative to get a weather forecast for the next two days, so I popped into the hotel at the Hospice to enquire. The news was heartening. The rain and clouds would gradually clear today, tomorrow would see a continuing improvement and Tuesday was to be fine. Since we had scheduled the crucial Schreckhorn-Lauteraarhorn traverse for that second day, we were most relieved. Had we to face poor weather or fresh snow, we would find ourselves hard-pressed to climb those two peaks individually over two days, never mind compressing them both into a single outing. The Drings had now driven round to Grindelwald, from where they would walk up to the Schreckhorn Hut to meet us with our first re-supply of food on Monday night.

As we set out on the 18km trek to the Aar Bivouac Hut our mood was optimistic, despite the prevailing drizzle. The pain of saying goodbye to my family for a week was eased by the excitement that again we were treading new paths into hitherto unknown country, and the concrete jungle around the Hospice was soon forgotten as we hiked along a stone-flagged path high above the Grimselsee. The verges of the trail were vivid with the flowers of orchid, gentian and even the shy butterwort, a plant more typical of boggy Scottish moors than high alpine pastures.

The clouds were clearing when we stopped for lunch a kilometre before the head of the lake beneath the Eldorado cliff. This great dome of burnished granite looked much the finest of the crags in the area and all the more attractive for its secluded location. A number of parties were strung out across its slabs and dièdres.

Mountaineers who pass this way might hope that the high peaks of the Oberland are composed of material of similar quality, but they are likely to be disappointed. A rough red gneiss is the best that can be anticipated up at 4000m. Only in the Mont Blanc and Bregaglia massifs are the intrusions of granite so pronounced that they form the bones of the high mountains. Elsewhere in the Alps the granite is largely confined to altitudes of 2500m or less and it is the overlying sediments which outcrop at the summits.

Climbing at Eldorado is currently threatened by a scheme to raise the level of the Grimselsee in order to increase its potential for power production. It is difficult to decry hydro-electric projects when they produce cheap, clean and virtually unlimited supplies of energy. Nevertheless, in many parts of Switzerland one cannot help feeling that the scenic destruction caused by such projects has gone far enough. Perhaps the time has come when schemes for energy conservation should take priority over those for its increased production.

Just beyond the head of the lake we climbed up to the dirty snout of the Unteraar Glacier and followed widely spaced cairns over to its left medial moraine. The going can be indescribably bad on the lower sections of receding glaciers. The shattered rock debris which covers the ice is continuously on the move so that permanent tracks cannot develop, while the dying ice tends to shrink into great mounds clothed in loose boulders. These drumlins give an endlessly undulating terrain where each kilometre of progress can take close on half-an-hour.

We were lucky on the Unteraar Glacier. By keeping to the long moraine crest we avoided the worst of the hollows, and within an hour were marching up under the Lauteraar Hut towards the confluence of the Lauteraar and Finsteraar ice flows. The dividing ridge between the two glaciers was crowned by an attractive rhomboidal peak which eventually we realised was the Lauteraarhorn. Under the playful projection of afternoon clouds and shadows, the surrounding cirques acquired the austere majesty of an Arctic mountain wilderness and for a while I felt lost in the vastness of the place. Occasionally we caught a sobering glimpse of tomorrow's objective, the mighty Finsteraarhorn whose North-East Face towered 1000m through the gathering cumulus.

The tiny Aar refuge was the sole shelter in these barren wastes, but remained hidden in the side valley of the Strahlegg Glacier throughout our approach. At 2400m the stony glacier surface ended quite abruptly and thereafter was covered by wide fields of spring snow, which had melted and refrozen into a sea of bumps and ripples. Immediately we took the opportunity of putting on our skis and fought against a rising headwind to cover the last 2km to the Strahlegg Glacier junction. Hut approaches in the Oberland are notoriously long and arduous, and this one was no exception. At 6pm we rounded the last corner and gave silent thanks when finally we spotted the hut situated just 50m above the glacier.

The refuge proved not just to be a welcome shelter but also a haven of wood-panelled luxury. It has no resident guardian and was deserted, but judging from its immaculate condition had recently undergone an annual spring clean. No need was left unattended with the provision of everything from solar-powered lighting to minutiae like toothpaste and brushes. Would that we had comparable facilities in Scottish bothies. Visitors to these unguarded huts are honour-bound to sign the hut logbook and pay the appropriate charges either in the money-box provided or by post. The cosy atmosphere of small huts is far removed from the credit-card alpinism practised from establishments like the Diavolezza.

We had recovered well from the rigours of the cycling and the walk had proved that we could marry the two forms of exercise without the one adversely affecting the other. Indeed, we could see a walk as a rest from cycling and vice versa. However, such reflections were of little import up in the Finsteraar basin. Our minds were much too busy adjusting to the high mountain setting and preparing for tomorrow's task. Our route to the Finsteraarhorn ascended complex glacial terrain to the Finsteraarjoch, followed by a 500m snow couloir to gain the summit ridge at the 3749m Agassizjoch. The overall grade of the climb was *assez difficile* (AD) and guidebook times to the summit added up to nine hours. This would have required us to have left at 2am in order to be on top much before midday. Unwilling to advance our reveille any earlier than 3 o'clock, we went to bed banking on our ability to undercut the guidebook estimates.

At a little after 4am we clattered down the frozen sun-bumps of the glacier towards a slim corridor rising under the Studerhorn. This is the sole passage through the icefall which bars access to the upper Finsteraar Glacier. At the ramp we removed our skis, roped up and began what was to be a climb of 1670m to the summit. To face such a daunting height gain requires keen motivation and an ability to split the climb into sections and concentrate on one stage at a time.

The corridor formed our first section and was not a place to linger, for it passed close under the seracs of the Studerhorn's North Face. The sun touched the top of the Finsteraarhorn when we gained the upper glacier and within an hour we, too, were bathed in its amber glow. A fine day was promised and the night had been suitably cold, but the snow deteriorated the higher we climbed. From marching on a supportive frozen crust we increasingly found ourselves breaking through into soft dry powder which the sun of recent days had failed to melt, and it took a further hour and a half of hard slogging to gain the base of our couloir at 3300m.

Throughout the approach, the Finster's North-East Face riveted my attention. The scale, severity and looseness of its ribs and gullies could not be doubted from such close quarters and I marvelled at the feat of Fritz Amatter and Gustav Hasler in climbing it as long ago as 1904. The route is challenged only by the South-West Face of the Täschhorn as the hardest in the Alps before 1914. Still graded *très difficile* (TD+), the face is ignored by all except connoisseurs of serious alpinism and is best tackled in winter when its rocks are cemented by ice.

Although clearly the dominant peak of the region, the Finsteraarhorn was not named with certainty until publication of Coxe's *Travels in Switzerland* in 1789. Its first ascent is still clouded by a controversy which will probably never be resolved. Dr Rudolf Meyer took a party to it in 1812 in the era of initial mountain exploration long before the growth of climbing as a sport. Dr Meyer himself did not reach the top, but the ascent was claimed by his three guides, Arnold Abbuhl, Alois Volker and Josef Bortes. Their route by the South-East Ridge is today classed as AD, a grade which was not established in mountaineering until nearly half a century later. Detractors have suggested that the party actually climbed, in mist, Altmann, a completely different peak which is 800m lower than the Finsteraarhorn. The climbing ability of the early chamois and crystal hunters should not be underestimated, but it is thought more likely that they reached a forepeak on the South-East Ridge, not the summit.

In 1829 the mountain received an undisputed ascent by the North-West Ridge from the Fiescher Glacier by the guides Jakob Leuthold and Johannes Wahren, and this remains the normal way to the top. Our own route would join it for the last 200m. First we had to climb the big 45° couloir to the Agassizjoch, which yielded only to a determined burst of step-kicking on crusted snow that was already thawing under the power of the rising sun. At the top the angle steepened to 50° and we began to fear the risk of snowslides during our return journey three or four hours hence.

The Agassizjoch is named after the glaciologist Louis Agassiz who spent a series of summers in the nineteenth century camped on the Unteraar Glacier recording ice movements. Its guardian peak, the 3953m Agassizhorn, is a beautiful horn of snow rising direct from the saddle and would make a worthy consolation for parties unable to climb its bigger neighbour. We were met on the saddle by a fierce north-west wind and stopped only to add a layer of clothing. The ridge above rises to the Finsteraarhorn in three pronounced steps. There were a few delicate moves on loose snow-covered rocks on the first riser, but the second was an easy snow ridge leading to the Hugisattel where the normal route from the Finsteraarhorn Hut is joined. Then the last 200m gave a fine rocky scramble. We reached the summit cross at 11.30am, well pleased with our time of seven and a half hours from the hut.

Throughout the descent of the ridge we were harassed by the rising gale which blasted needles of ice across our faces and cut through our clothing. Such conditions gave us a sporting fight on the Finsteraarhorn, but would not be welcome tomorrow on the Lauteraargrat when we would be traversing a knife-edge for several hours. The contrast in temperature on dropping back into the couloir was hard to tolerate. From a windchill temperature of −10°C on the crest, we were at once plunged into a furnace exceeding +30° in absorbed heat as the sun reached its zenith.

Reeling in this oven we ploughed down the disintegrating steps of our ascent and at 1.15pm regained our skis at the base of the couloir in a state of total enervation. I hung my head, stuffing handfuls of melting snow into my parched mouth to dilute our remaining snacks. The only redeeming thought was of a long simple ski-run down to the Obers Ischmeer basin and the Schreckhorn Hut. The watershed lay just 500m away at the Finsteraarjoch. This is the most difficult of the three crossings from Grindelwald to Grimsel, the others being the Strahleggpass and Lauteraarsattel which lie to the north.

As we packed up we saw, to our dismay, a mass of boiling cloud rise out of the basin and envelop the pass, and, sure enough, we skied into white-out conditions. As if the day had not already brought enough trials, we spent the next hour navigating by altimeter on a long north-wards traverse to avoid the crevasse fields of the Obers Ischmeer.

> *With visibility now cut to 20m, we decide to rope up for safety, and then continue traversing the slope. Suddenly we find ourselves amidst large crevasses. Martin is in the lead and slides with care over a snow bridge, then side-steps up the slope beyond, while I tentatively move on to the bridge wondering at its solidity. We are now at the point where we must descend 500m to the lower glacier. With visibility opening a little we take the rope off and try a few tentative turns.*

My hopes of pleasurable swings down the slopes were dashed at the first turn. Just as I prepared to plant my pole, my skis disappeared under a layer of slush and I was projected head over the tips. Although far superior in ski-ing skills, Simon was not faring much better. The slush was so heavy that we could only glide close to the fall-line in a controlled slow motion. This alternated with blocky avalanche debris which gave a bone-jarring rollercoaster. We bumped and waded in long zigzags until a better run of compact, firm snow enabled us to achieve a semblance of style and speed.

Down on the main glacier at 2700m the atmosphere was steamy. We were surrounded by great bands of tottering ice cliffs and the layer of cloud above us trapped the day's sunlight to create a sweltering heat. Indeed, I felt we had entered a snare, for in two days' time we would have to climb up through those seracs to escape from the basin. If we failed to find a route, there would be no alternative save for a retreat to Grindelwald. Despite all that we had achieved today, I was gripped by depression. All our efforts so far suddenly seemed futile.

As we scrambled down one last icy steepening in the glacier we spotted the figures of Ian, Sandra and Craig ski-ing towards us. They had hiked up to the Schreckhorn Hut, a brutal 1200m climb from Grindelwald, the previous day. Their loads had been so heavy that they had had to help each other to their feet after every rest stop. To see them then, just at a low point in morale, gave me a tremendous fillip.

'We'll take your gear,' said Ian, and with lightened loads we followed them across the glacier and up the 100m climb to the hut. After a few brews, a beer and a huge plate of spaghetti, my fears lifted. The clouds cleared and we sat on the balcony admiring a retrospect of the Finsteraarhorn framed at the head of the cirque while a herd of ibex grazed beneath the hut. A new moon rose in the south-east and as the shadows lengthened the temperature plunged.

We were thus to be granted ideal conditions for the first crucial test of the summer, the Schreckhorn-Lauteraarhorn traverse, graded *difficile* (D+) and given a cumulative guidebook time of eighteen hours. It is a route rarely completed and was known to us only by its reputation. Even given the fine weather, we were frightened that there could be excessive snow on the linking ridge which has many sections of grades III and IV rock climbing. The hut guardian, Hans Balmer, already disenchanted by Ian's lack of attention to hut housekeeping, was sternly pessimistic. 'I think there is too much snow,' he warned. We replied humbly to the effect that we could only try.

Whatever our fatigue, there could be no lie-in tomorrow and we bedded down at 8.30pm with our alarms set to ring just five hours later.

The Schreckhorn (4078m) ranks as one of the toughest half-dozen of the fifty major '4000er' mountains. If its name 'the peak of terror' is not sufficient deterrent, then the foreshortened view of its towering gneiss buttresses that we enjoyed from the hut might well persuade cautious parties to try something easier. The mountain was first ascended by Leslie Stephen with guides Peter and Christian Michel and Ulrich Kaufmann in 1861. Stephen was attracted to the peak with the thought: 'Was there not some infinitesimal niche in history to be occupied by its successful assailant?'

Sadly, posterity has not looked kindly on Stephen's Schreckhorn climb. The achievement, though considerable, was overshadowed by the dramatic events on the Matterhorn four years later, and his route of ascent via the Schreck Couloir and East-South-East Ridge has been largely superseded due to avalanche and stonefall risk.

Nevertheless, we judged that early in the season the Schreck Couloir would be well banked with snow and on a cold night would be safe and reliable. All five of us left together at 2.35am. The Drings were to climb the Lauteraarhorn and would wait for us on the summit so that they could assist our final descent. We reversed yesterday's route for a kilometre, then climbed off the glacier, passing the site of the old Strahlegg Hut which was destroyed by an avalanche, and entered the narrow valley that would take us to the Strahleggpass.

The snow was frozen so hard that we needed to wear crampons from the outset. It was hard to credit that the abominable slush of yesterday afternoon had been formed of the same material. I felt in tremendous form and led all the way to the pass, round to the Schreckfirn glacier bay and up into the couloir. In the interests of speed we climbed unroped. Every minute saved could be vital later in the day. The couloir was a beautifully simple climb, just like an extended grade I Scottish gully, and we were on the Schrecksattel at 3915m soon after dawn.

We now traversed an icy convex slope on the east side of the ridge, no longer buoyed by the surety of step that we had felt in the couloir. The slope merged into a horizontal ridge of awkward icy rocks where a series of iron stanchions were cemented in place. This was the notorious Elliotswengli where the Reverend Julius Elliot had slipped to his death in 1869 when climbing unroped like ourselves. The place remains just as treacherous 125 years later, and we got our rope out at the first available ledge.

The ridge then steepened into an arête of solid rock and the climb terminated in a level snow crest 150m in length. We reached the top at 7.50am, nearly two hours inside the guidebook time. Despite climbing regularly for many years, I have found few routes where conditions, fitness and personal temperament combine in perfection, but this was one of them. But our day was only a third done and we were concerned to see high clouds spreading rapidly from the west. As we reversed the route back to the saddle, a light snowfall commenced. We kept too high on the Elliotswengli and ended up on a rock pulpit high above the ice slope. We were carrying only a 40m length of 8.2mm rope of some vintage, which did not give us scope for lengthy abseils, and it took two rappels of 20m to regain our ascent route.

The consequent loss of time, plus the deteriorating weather, brought a sudden tension to the day. I rushed on in front, pausing only at the first major step on the Lauteraargrat. Ahead of us lay some four hours of ridge climbing with no possible escape. If we continued and were then forced into a protracted retreat in a storm, we would not only fail today but might lack the strength to attempt the Lauteraarhorn again tomorrow, so this was not a decision to be taken lightly.

Simon joined me and we scanned the skies. The westward prospect remained gloomy, but the reappearance of the sun gave us sufficient impetus to continue. We knew from experience that weather in the Alps often threatens but doesn't actually clamp down. A residual doubt remained, but it was a risk we had to accept.

Simon led off strongly along an exhilarating arête. Wherever possible, he arranged running belays on the rope on each tricky section, but we kept moving continuously without taking fixed belays until the first of two prominent towers on the ridge. The rock left much to be desired in solidity and roughness, and its slanting bedding planes produced an alternation of smooth slabs with steep incut walls. Snow patches still choked all the gaps, but we were able to climb without crampons. Had a blizzard blown up, this sort of terrain would have become well-nigh impossible, but our trust in the weather increased as the day settled to one of haze and sultry sunshine.

The traverse of the two towers, Points 4011m and 4015m, was quite sensational. In places we could barely credit how the overhanging fins of rock remained attached to the mountain. The towers are ignored in all the lists of 4000m tops and yet they come close to attaining our own requirement of a 35m height separation. Those who include them on their '4000er' itinerary will be guaranteed some of the most exciting ridge climbing in the Alps.

In July 1902, somewhere on these rotting gendarmes, one of the more infamous meetings in Alpine climbing history took place. Quite independently, two eminent female alpinists, Miss Gertrude Bell and Fräulein Kuntze, hired guides with the intention of making the first traverse of the ridge, Bell starting at the Lauteraarhorn and Kuntze at the Schrecksattel. The scent of competition was undoubtedly in the air and Bell recorded in her diary before the climb: 'I shall laugh if we meet half-way across the arête but shall not be at all surprised.' In the event, the two parties did cross somewhere near the half-way point and their guides noted that the meeting of the two ladies was greeted with no enthusiasm.

A week later, Bell spent fifty-seven hours on the North-East Face of the Finsteraarhorn attempting its first ascent. Remembering their epic climb and storm-lashed retreat, her guide Ulrich Führer commented that he had seen no climber, man or woman, to match her in coolness, bravery and judgement.

Difficult climbing is all-absorbing and the four hours it took us to traverse the arête from the Schrecksattel to the 4042m summit of the Lauteraarhorn passed in a trice. From the top we made radio contact with the Drings who had retreated from 3700m when the weather threatened. Therefore we had the job of finding the way down ourselves and no descent could be more tricky in its routefinding. To get back to the Strahleggpass, we had first to descend 120m down the South-East Ridge back towards the Strahlegg basin. This is the route by which the mountain was first climbed by a party of glaciologists and geologists in 1842. Then we descended a couloir on the west flank until a traverse line led round under the terminal buttress of the peak to gain the South-West Ridge at a prominent shoulder.

Below this shoulder lay one of the most lethal pieces of ground I have ever trodden. Totally shattered rocks were banked at 70° in angle and covered with a thick layer of slush. There was no protection, only a 400m drop to the Schreckfirn if either of us slipped.

> *Martin leads us down. With crampons on I find this mixture of loose rock, snow, and hidden patches of ice tortuous in the extreme, and I have to exercise the greatest care not to knock any stones down on to Martin. Descending these steep crumbling steps, depending on questionable footing and imaginary handholds, I find myself holding my breath as if it alone might be able to support my weight. On finally reaching easier ground, I find it hard to credit how this ridge can be classed as an ordinary route up the mountain.*

That 100m of zigzagging descent took us an hour. Now we unroped and scrambled along the interminable lower ridge to the pass. This is a route that I would scarce recommend to my worst enemy and it blemished what was otherwise a great day's climbing. Parties are far better advised to climb the Lauteraarhorn from the Strahlegg Glacier, even though this involves a much longer approach.

We got back to the hut at 6.35am, exhausted but elated at the first big breakthrough of the expedition. Our sixteen-hour traverse had saved a day on our itinerary and we were now back on our base schedule of forty-eight days. Even our taciturn host, Herr Balmer, showed a flicker of admiration for our day and he visibly warmed to us after Ian bought a couple of rounds of drinks at dinner and then wiped all the tables clean. Maybe these British were not quite so bad after all!

Having been warned of poor weather, we held no real hopes of getting out of the Obers Ischmeer and over the Fiescherhorn on the morrow, and in truth we were too tired to much care. A thick fog outside deterred any movement at 4am, nor when I woke again at 5.30am, and it was 7.30 before we stirred from our blankets. The morning's weather was as lazy as we, warm and drizzling with the cloudbase shifting slowly around the 3000m mark.

As we lingered over breakfast the realisation dawned that our little honeymoon of pleasure was over. The weather forecast was increasingly confused. Herr Balmer reckoned that if today was mediocre then tomorrow would be, in his words, 'not better'. We could happily spend a day here resting, given the certainty of a fine night to come, but if conditions did deteriorate, then we would be really trapped. Reluctantly, we decided we should move despite the criminally late hour and the thawing conditions. Just as the return of the sun had confirmed our decision to continue on the Lauteraargrat, so the raising of the cloudbase to reveal our route through the serac bands persuaded us to go that very morning.

We would have liked at least one of the Drings to have joined us, but they were seriously encumbered, first by full-length touring skis and clumsy ski boots, and second by a duplication in their provisioning which had caused them to bring nearly twice as much food as was required for the two nights. They could barely lift their sacks to their shoulders, even for the return journey. I felt a little guilty that they hadn't achieved a summit for themselves in reward for all that effort. Had we not despatched them towards the Lauteraarhorn yesterday to serve our own interests, I was sure they would have succeeded in doing the Schreckhorn. Their next task was to bring three days of food up the Jungfraujoch railway and meet us the following afternoon at the Mönchsjoch Hut. Maybe then they would make a summit and get some decent ski-ing.

We left at 10am, fully aware that we were in for a long day and a very late finish. Due to glacial retreat, only one feasible line remains through the bands of seracs which guard the west side of the basin. This climbs into a glacier bay beneath an active ice cliff and traverses out left to the crest of a rock buttress and safe ground. With the illogicality that sometimes possesses mountaineers, I suggested to Simon that we dispense with the rope in order to move more quickly through the danger zone. However, the most apparent dangers we encountered were those where the rope would have provided vital security – namely, hidden crevasses and saturated snow-slopes which threatened to avalanche under our feet.

Above the ice band we donned our skis and commenced a long diagonal ascent on a broad terrace leading towards the Ochs summit of the

Fiescherhorn. The clouds now enveloped us and the sound of big wet snowslides on the faces both above and below us emphasised our isolation. We removed our skis and waded laboriously up a steeper rib from which a short traverse took us to the 3694m Fiescherjoch. This is the only simple exit gap on the west side of the Obers Ischmeer basin and took us over to the upper plateau of the Fiescher Glacier.

Our day's two peaks, the Gross Fiescherhorn (4049m) and its neighbouring top, the Hinter Fiescherhorn (4025m), lay a kilometre distant at the head of the plateau. Having quitted the steeper slopes we could rest easier in our minds regarding avalanche risk, but now a thickening of the mist and a blizzard of heavy wet snowflakes brought new concerns. Would we succeed in hitting the saddle between the two summits, and how would we get down its far side once we had climbed the tops? The fresh snow was so wet that it built up in great clods on the base of my ski-skins so that after a couple of hundred metres I was walking on 12cm platforms.

At the point when we were beginning to question our arrival at the saddle, the snow stopped and the skies quickly began to clear, giving us tantalising glimpses of the twin peaks poking through the clouds. Although the approaches are long, both summits of the Fiescherhorn give excellent short summit scrambles. They took us an hour apiece, but I felt devoid of energy, even without my rucksack which I had left on the saddle. Perhaps we should have eaten more of that surplus food before leaving the Schreckhorn Hut, but there is a limit to what you can force down when as tired as we were last night. Nor were our sacks well provisioned, for we carried just the minimum necessary to get us through to tomorrow afternoon.

By 7.15pm we had descended to the long glacier slope above the Ewigschneefeld, one of the three main feeders to the Aletsch Glacier. From now on, the Oberland we would be in was the great Aletsch basin. We had made our escape and, given the clear weather, could now anticipate an effortless 500m downhill run to the main glacier stream. The warm evening lighting provided an exquisite backcloth for the descent – but much to our ire the snow was just as rotten as it had been two days previously. So again I was thrust unceremoniously head-first into the slush on every second or third turn.

On the final 150m the slope steepened above 25° and we edged more cautiously forwards, peering over the convexity of the ice for a feasible route down. Once convinced that we had a line, I set off ahead on a

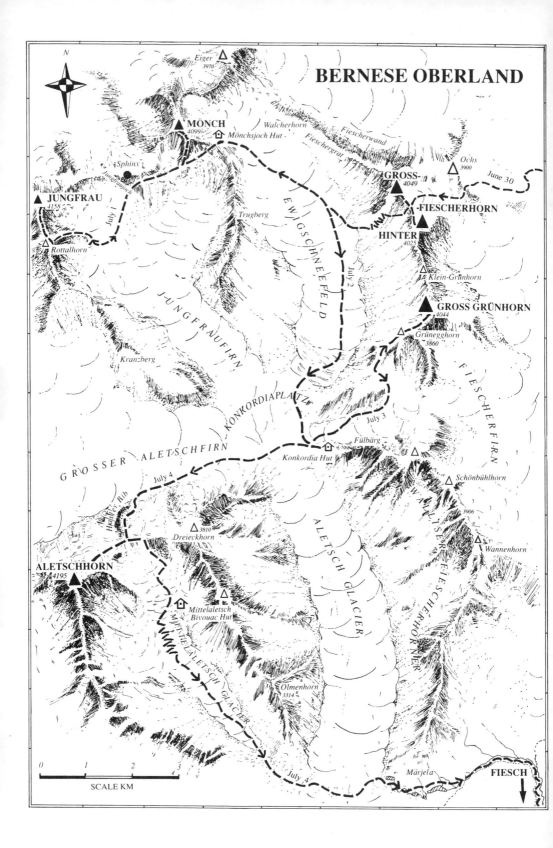

BERNESE OBERLAND

N

Eiger △ 3970

▲ **MÖNCH** 4099

Walcherhorn

Fiescherwand

Fiescherarat

⌂ Mönchsjoch Hut

Ochs △ 3900

June 30

Sphinx ●

Jungfraujoch

GROSS- ▲ 4049

▲ **JUNGFRAU** 4158

July 1

Trugberg

E W I G S C H N E E F E L D

July 2

FIESCHERHORN

HINTER 4025

⌂ Rottalhorn

J U N G F R A U F I R N

△ Klein-Grünhorn

▲ **GROSS GRÜNHORN** 4044

Kranzberg

△ Grünegghorn 3860

F I E S C H E R F I R N

K O N K O R D I A P L A T Z

G R O S S E R   A L E T S C H F I R N

Fülbärg △

△

July 3

⌂ Konkordia Hut

July 4

Hasler Rib

Schönbühlhorn △

3906

△ 3810

Dreieckhorn

A L E T S C H   G L A C I E R

W A L L I S E R   F I E S C H E R H Ö R N E R

△ Wannenhorn

ALETSCHHORN ▲ 4195

⌂ *Mittelaletsch Bivouac Hut*

△

M I T T E L A L E T S C H   G L A C I E R

Olmenhorn 3314

0   1   2   3   4

SCALE KM

July 4

Märjela

FIESCH

long diagonal glide. Simon watched my progress with more than usual concern.

> *As Martin starts the traverse, the saturated snow beneath his skis begins to cut away in a continuous slice. At first only a small glide, the avalanche gains momentum and size until it is clearing all the visible slope of a third of a metre of snow. I stand so transfixed at the spectacle of tonnes of snow releasing that I forget to reach for my camera. Half-way across Martin stops, turns and looks back at me, uncertain whether to be thrilled or terrified by his self-made avalanche.*
>
> *'That looks interesting,' I shout. As long as the snow is avalanching below and not above him I suppose he is safe, but I'm still glad I'm not in his boots. After 200m he turns and skis after the hissing slide to its terminus on the flat glacier below. I wait until he is well clear before I follow.*

Down on the glacier we turned to review our handiwork. A slope some 200m in width had been stripped down to bare ice and a sizable cone of avalanche debris was left at its foot. There remained 4km of gentle climbing up to the Mönchsjoch Hut at 3629m. The snowfields glowed indigo in the evening twilight as we skied towards the noble silhouettes of the Mönch and the Eiger. In spite of, and perhaps because of our exhaustion, that last trek was the perfect consummation of the day.

Close on 10pm we stamped up the last slope to the dark outline of the hut, reluctant to believe that it was closed. The Mönchsjoch Hut stands just 2km from the Jungfraujoch railway and is the best high-level base for climbs at the head of the Aletsch basin. On this the last day of June we fully expected it to be doing business, but no, the inside entrance was firmly locked. I was considering the prospect of sleeping on the lobby floor when Simon tried a side door and almost fell into a snug winter room, complete with wood-burning stove and a good stock of fuel.

Recent visitors had even left bread, cheese and spaghetti with which we could supplement our meagre rations. I was too tired to be bothered lighting the stove, but Simon persevered and for the next two hours we luxuriated in its enveloping warmth while a steely frost settled on the mountains outside. I felt distinctly privileged that we had that wonderful place to ourselves. Whatever the vagaries of the weather, there are important rewards in climbing or ski-ing out of season. Some time after midnight we finally fell captive to sleep.

After consecutive days of 13, 16 and 12 hours' sustained effort, we were in need of a shorter outing. For some reason we regarded the ascents of both the Jungfrau and the Mönch as a relatively easy day. This delusion was fostered by our high starting altitude. These great mountains together with the Eiger make up the famous Oberland trilogy, but their challenge has been muted since the completion in 1912 of the Jungfraujoch railway, which can whisk climbers up from Grindelwald to a height of 3475m between the two peaks in less than two hours. As a result, the peaks are regularly mobbed by day-tripping climbers throughout the summer.

Expecting to have wide trails to follow and plenty of company, we were not particularly perturbed to be starting as late as 7.15am, especially since the morning was wonderfully clear. We skied down under the observatory of the Sphinx and across the Jungfraufirn on crisp hard snow. We left the ski gear at an altitude of 3350m at the base of the subsidiary spur which drops from the Rottalsattel on the mountain's South-East Ridge. Thus we had a climb of 800m to the 4158m summit. This itself constitutes a substantial outing, even ignoring our intention to add the Mönch later in the day.

There was a series of old tracks on the ridge, but nothing which could be called a beaten trail, and the snow was unpleasantly crusted even in the prints. By treading daintily, I could just stay on top of the crust, but Simon continuously broke through close to knee depth.

'It's that extra weight again,' I suggested.

'Well, not entirely,' he countered. 'The tendency to break through also depends on shoe size and the moment of leverage about the knee.'

I realised that Simon had more than a passing interest in this problem and felt slightly guilty that, as the smaller footed and shorter legged of the two of us, he was disadvantaged in every respect when it comes to trail-breaking.

As we rested on the Rottalsattel at 3885m we expected to see a following horde of climbers who had caught the morning's first train from Grindelwald, but there wasn't a soul to be seen on the glacier below. A steep convex slope rises above the saddle perilously exposed above the mountain's South Face. Many fatal accidents have occurred here, particularly later in the season when the slope can be very icy. Even today, with a layer of unstable crust on a harder base, I felt a little insecure, but there were no particular technical difficulties and we were on top by 11.15am.

Some 400m north of the summit lies what appears to be a significant forepeak when viewed from the Jungfraufirn. This is the Wengener top and since Richard Goedeke had credited it with a 40m height differential in his listing of the '4000ers', we were obliged to make a visit. Therefore we dropped 100m down to the linking col. Here Simon set his altimeter and we trudged up the little snow ridge to the top. We were just a bit miffed when Simon declared that the altimeter had only risen 20m and, looking back, we could see that the height gain did not nearly approach the required 35m. The Wengener Jungfrau was thus deleted from our list. The extra effort it had exacted was rewarded by a stupendous view straight down to the Lauterbrunnen Valley 3000m below. However, I began to feel very weary as we climbed back over the main summit.

Clouds now boiled around us and the heat became suffocating. We could still see the Mönch on the far side of the Jungfraufirn, but my thoughts now focused only on the contents of our support team's rucksacks. I'd been promised half-a-dozen fried eggs, Simon a whole roast chicken, and pleasant anticipation turned into a desperate craving as we descended. Two or three times my crampons balled up and I slipped alarmingly on the exposed section of slope. Accumulated fatigue was overwhelming my powers of control and I remembered the immortal words of Edward Whymper: 'A moment of negligence can destroy a lifetime of happiness.' This was the time to stop and I decided to be resolute even if Simon suggested doing the Mönch.

In the face of fast deteriorating weather, Simon was as little inclined as I to risk it that day. We stuck on our skins and commenced the laborious 3km trek back to the hut. My mind was entirely empty save for the thought of that hut, fresh food, hot sweet tea and tin after tin of cling peaches. Would they have arrived? Could they have missed the train? The tension was rising to an unwonted pitch when we spied the lanky frame of Ian ski-ing towards us.

Sandra and Craig were already firmly installed inside and the stove was burning merrily. We were seated at the table and handed the first of several brews while Ian stripped to the waist and, with a devilish grin, produced frying pan, a dozen eggs and nigh on half a kilo of mushrooms. Despite Sandra's jibes that he never did this sort of thing at home, Ian was determined to be the *maître chef*. Craig was employed full-time as bread cutter and butterer while we were alternately fed an egg and mushrooms each. After five eggs Simon was too full to speak coherently, but I kept my promise and polished off the sixth. We then devoured a couple of cans of fruit and slumped down on our bunks with all the contentment of salvation gained.

An hour later a prolonged clumping of boots was heard outside, together with a mêlée of British accents. Snatches of conversation such as 'Where's the galley?' and 'Get out your snap' indicated that the Royal Marines had arrived. The leader was a blond version of Arnold Schwarzenegger and most of his men were fair replicas. They were up to mount a climbing and rescue demonstration for a visiting colonel, and future funding for their alpine training programme was at stake. With Simon and me out of sight under the bunks, the boss scanned the pages of the hut logbook and announced:

'Moran and Jenkins; that'll be them; here's the boys who got killed on the Jungfrau last week.'

We emerged to vouch that we were, in fact, still alive, but we were sad to hear that two English Venture Scouts had died on the mountain just a few days previously in snow not dissimilar to that which we had encountered today.

Luckily the Marines found another dormitory that had been left open and they proved most courteous. Much to Ian's chagrin, they even invited Sandra over to their base in Lauterbrunnen for a game of volley-ball while he and Craig were engaged on their forthcoming attempt to climb the Eiger's North Face. Three Italians joined us in our room and silently chewed on the contents of tiny cartons of pot noodles while we tackled another gigantic meal in the evening.

At 1.30am Simon and I left the Mönchsjoch Hut and headed up the Mönch groaning with mild indigestion. My craving for fried eggs had been effectively cured. Rising just 460m above the hut, the South-East Ridge of the Mönch is a genuinely short climb of PD standard, and we planned to be up and down before dawn. Then we might be able to ski down the Ewigschneefeld and climb the Gross Grünhorn before the morning was too far advanced, which would keep us abreast of schedule.

Since the previous afternoon the weather had stayed misty with continuous gentle snowfall, and in the night the temperature had fallen to just below zero at 4000m so that the snow was semi-frozen. Our torchbeams picked out the ridge ahead through dancing veils of ice grains and, despite the prevailing mist, we could sense the growing exposure as the crest rose to the summit apex. Throughout the climb there was barely a breath of wind and when we returned to the hut at

4.15am, our clothes and rope were evenly coated in fog crystals.

We stopped only for a cup of tea and while the Drings prepared to follow our steps up the Mönch, we strapped on skis and commenced a 6km run down the Ewigschneefeld towards the Grünhorn. Below the hut the snow was horribly crusted. We passed an ascending party who were struggling up to their knees and beyond and felt thankful that we were not on foot. Dawn revealed a morning devoid of colour or inspiration. Thick cloud shrouded the mountains and in view of the bad snow we decided to miss the Grünhorn and descend directly to the Konkordia Hut which we had planned as our last base in the Oberland.

We skied a delicate passage through the icefall at the foot of the Ewigschneefeld, slid gently over Konkordiaplatz and ended our day climbing the long flights of stairs to the hut at the unseemly hour of 8.30am. The main hut was still closed, but we found three British lads in residence in the winter room. The warmth of its stove induced a soporific trance and we were soon fast asleep in our bunks.

Konkordia is one of the wonders of the Alps. Its name was first suggested by the Reverend J.F. Hardy who toured the Aletsch Glacier in 1857 and wrote of it thus:

> The position which we had now attained commands one of the most magnificent views in the whole range of the Alps. From it the spectator looks down on a vast sea of ice, the confluence of three glacier streams, which, uniting here, pour down their frozen waters along the mighty highway which we had trodden the day previously. It is the Place de la Concorde of Nature; wherever you look there is a grand road and a lofty dome.

The hut stands on the sole island of vegetation in this sea of ice. When the first building was constructed in 1877, mountaineers could walk off the glacier straight to the front door. Such has been the diminution of the Aletsch Glacier in the last century that one must now climb 100m up a series of ladders and stairways, which are bolted on to a vertical cliff-face, in order to reach the portals. There are currently 237 rungs and steps to climb and they pose a sore trial at the end of a hard day. Additional ladders will be required should the glacier level continue to fall. Yet despite the current glacial recession there remains a 900m thickness of ice in the centre of Konkordiaplatz.

A second hut was built in 1907 and still houses overflow dormitories and the winter room, while the third and latest was opened in 1976. Their increasing size mirrors the growth in popularity of mountain touring, as we were soon to be forcibly reminded. Simon and I only stirred when Ian, Sandra and Craig arrived at 1pm, and an hour later as the clouds began to clear we heard the buzz of an approaching helicopter. Within minutes it had unloaded the summer guardian, Werner Kaufmann and his family, plus the first batch of supplies for the season. From now until mid-September they would stay up here save for essential visits to town like dental appointments, for which a helicopter service would be available. Their life may sound idyllic, but it can't be easy keeping a young family amused when confined to a play area of 200m square.

'I'm sorry but you must all move out of this room,' announced Werner. 'We have a party of 120 people coming tomorrow night and I think there will be no beds for you.'

With this cheery news we were shaken out of our peaceful repose and forced to submit to the regulation and regimentation which is inevitable in huts during the holiday season. The only consolation to our team was the ready availability of cool Swiss beer from the vaults of the main hut.

In 1988, on their '4000ers' attempt, Paul Mackrill and John Rowlands had twice walked up the Aletsch Glacier to Konkordia in the early days of June with massive loads of 30kg, intending to make a prolonged assault on the Bernese tops. Both times they were rebuffed by bad weather and forced back down to the Rhône Valley. Only on their third visit on 20 June did they finally reach their first summit in the area, the Gross Grünhorn. Thereafter, they picked off the other peaks of the Aletsch skyline so quickly that a mountain of unused provisions remained at the hut, and ironically they made their final descent carrying by far the heaviest loads of the expedition.

The Gross Grünhorn (4044m) is an attractive peak without possessing any exceptional qualities save for the wonderful view which is afforded by its central position in the Bernese wilderness. I had climbed it two years previously via the traverse of its forepeak, the 3860m Grünegghorn, and this route is a fine high-level traverse of PD+ standard, which has become the *voie normale*. It was good fortune to be granted equally fine weather for this return visit.

Night fell with more cloud and drizzle, but dawn came crisp and clear. For the first time in a week I had slept the sleep of a child and skied up the Grüneggfirn in a dreamy stupor. Ian and Craig joined us and we made lengthy halts on the approach to the Grünegghorn so that they could film first the retrospect of the Aletschhorn and then a spectacular sunburst on the ridge ahead. Despite these delays we were on top by 9.10am and back to the hut at 11.30am. The brevity and simplicity of the outing showed us how much energy we could save in good conditions.

Ian and Craig arrived somewhat later, having tested their tempers by ski-ing roped back down the Grüneggfirn. At every turn the rope had extended like a piece of well-strung elastic and sent them crashing into the snow. They were quite aggrieved when Simon told them that such precautions were hardly necessary on a smooth and gentle glacier. Unless the party possesses excellent co-ordination, the pull of the rope can serve to increase the risk of an unwanted tumble into a crevasse. During a descent its use is best reserved for patently dangerous stretches or else in bad visibility.

Weather permitting, we were now only one day away from completion of the Oberland peaks, and Joy and Carole had moved down to Fiesch in the Rhône Valley to await our arrival. Back at the Schreckhorn Hut we had given Ian a message that Joy was to go up the cablecar to the Eggishorn on Saturday the 3rd and await a radio call from us either at midday or 2pm. Carole would then walk up to the edge of the Aletsch Glacier to meet us with shorts and soft shoes on our descent from the Aletschhorn on the following day.

So at midday on this the 3rd I turned on our set expecting to hear Joy's voice, but to our surprise it was Carole who answered:

'Where are you lot? I've been waiting two hours up here for you, and Joy spent three hours on the Eggishorn yesterday waiting for your call.'

'We're still at Konkordia; we thought we were calling Joy today.'

'Well, we were told that you'd be down today,' came Carole's implacable response.

'Oh dear; there must have been some misunderstanding; I'll pass you over to Simon,' and I quickly excused myself.

The mix-up had resulted in Carole walking 1200m up to the glacier from the Fieschertal and in Joy wasting 90 francs and half a day standing in the freezing cold on the Eggishorn trying to amuse the children. Even now Joy was sitting at the Fieschertal roadhead waiting for us to arrive. There would be some explaining to do when we got down.

It was an indication of Ian's magnanimous personality that he accepted full responsibility for getting the days mixed up when he relayed the message. We consoled him by suggesting that expert research scientists regularly have difficulty remembering the days of the week and that he shouldn't feel too bad about it!

As we sat outside pondering the implications for base camp morale, I spotted two long black snakes emerging from the Jungfraujoch. Even at our distance of 7km, their sinuous forms were clearly visible with the naked eye. The 'charge of the one hundred' had begun. Two hours later, after my afternoon sleep, they were still distant specks lost in the vastness of the glacier, but soon the Kaufmanns would be doing a roaring trade. An outside drinks bar had already been laid out in preparation. The trekkers were on a weekend excursion organised by the Swiss National Railways. Their route followed the whole length of the Aletsch Glacier and, save for the Konkordia ladders, every step of it was downhill. No wonder 120 of them had booked the trip.

Despite the influx, Simon and I managed to hang on to our bunk spaces and we focused our thoughts on the mighty peak which lay across the shaded gulf of the glacier. The Aletschhorn (4195m) has few peers in bulk or isolation in the Alps. From all quarters it involves a long approach and a tiring climb. From Konkordia the classic route is the Hasler Rib (AD+), named after the indomitable Gustav Hasler who climbed it in winter in 1904. This spur of 600m in height and 45° in average angle debouches on the mountain's upper North-East Ridge and reputedly has all the atmosphere of a big north wall without the technical severity. From the summit we planned a ski descent of the Mittelaletsch Glacier which offered the most direct return route to the lower Aletsch Glacier and the green pastures of Fiesch.

Big snow routes like the Hasler Rib require a brutally early start so as to ensure safely frozen conditions throughout the ascent. With our reveille set for midnight, we weren't slow in getting to bed and snatched three hours' sleep before the resonant chimes of my watch-alarm shook us into action.

We eat our breakfast of semolina and porridge surrounded by trekkers who are still partying on the hut veranda, and are glad to leave them to their revelries as we head out across the moonlit expanse of the Aletsch. Our rhythm is interrupted by a series of glacier streams which we cross gingerly. Entering the shadow of the mountain I realise the scale of the climb and steer a wide berth to the base of the rib which is flanked on either side by seracs. Stopping to strap skis to the packs, sweat that has formed from the steady exertion quickly cools. We decide to split the lead and Martin takes the first stretch. Gauging a line to the left of the rib to avoid a steep rock-face, we weave to avoid hidden crevasses and reach the snow-slope adjoining the rib. The snow is crusted and I find myself working hard to stay with Martin as I erratically drop through to my knees.

After 75 minutes I take over the lead and find that by balancing my knees on the crust I can stay on the surface and keep momentum without excessive effort. Resting occasionally, I afford myself a glance back down the slope. The exposure has increased, though little detail can be seen in the darkness. I count out steps to sixty, then beyond if my breath lasts. We join the rib at a point which seems to be near the top, but 'near' turns out to be a good 200m. Once there, I turn to photograph Martin as he finishes, framed by the initial glow of twilight way below on the glacier.

The sun's rise over the eastern Oberland horizon was uninterrupted by a single cloud and we quickly felt its radiance on the long plod to the mountain's 4086m forepeak. The slope seemed interminable. At times I closed my eyes and tried to think of other things, but the body was working too hard to allow my mind to wander. From the forepeak, the sight of a steeper finale perked me up a little, but I was thankful to reach the summit cross. The Aletschhorn was a peak long sought by us both and we felt a tremendous achievement to stand on its crest.

Yet across the Rhône Valley to the south, the Pennine Alps were formidably arrayed and I realised that all our hard efforts in the Oberland had merely laid the foundation stone of Alps 4000. Had we then dared to imagine a successful outcome to our journey, there, 110km away on the western horizon, floated the snowy cap of Mont Blanc in mocking salute. It would be yet a month before we would stand at its threshold.

Our early arrival on top proved to be a mixed blessing. Unwilling to wait an hour for the full fledging of the sun, we skied down hard rutted névé into the Mittelaletsch basin. Below us a convex slope curved away towards an angle far beyond that at which a tumbling skier might hope for a reprieve. My knees burned with the pressure of holding two juddering skis together, first across a traverse of 800m and then down a 40° incline which ended in a band of crevasses. This was no place for a shaky skier after an eight-year lay-off, and I side-slipped and kick-turned until the angle eased. With the release of tension we enjoyed a marvellous run down the lower slopes, and in a series of short swings and jumps pursued the snow to its lowest extremity at a height of 2650m.

The Mittelaletsch Glacier appears to have only recently parted from the main Aletsch iceflow. A retreat of 89m in the glacier was recorded in the year 1990–1. Below its snout we found small patches of nascent meadow already established among the rubble. The Aletsch Glacier itself continues to grind a powerful course past the former junction, its surface a storm-tossed sea of ice waves as it turns south-westwards towards the Rhône.

We had to cross the Aletsch Glacier directly in order to reach the side valley of the Märjela where we hoped to meet Carole. However, transverse progress was impeded by a series of meltwater troughs full of charming pools and channels which continually led us downstream. Eventually, we strapped on crampons in order to make more determined progress across the

The Märjela is a perfect example of a glacial overflow valley, a relic of the Ice Age when the Aletsch bulged at its seams and shored up a great lake which drained into the neighbouring valley of the Fieschertal. Even in recent times there was a sizable meltwater lake here, the Märjelensee. In 1861 the Irish mountaineer John Tyndall visited the lake and described 'crystal precipices and floating icebergs, snowy white, sailing on a blue green sea'. Due either to glacial shrinkage or to some unfathomed shifting of the passing ice, the plug has since been pulled on the lake and the Märjelensee has drained to nought.

Several freshwater tarns remain in the valley and Carole was waiting by the largest together with her friend Julie who was out for the next fortnight, plus Ian, Sandra and Craig who had walked out direct from Konkordia. Carole did not spare our consciences in her tale of epic walks and fruitless waits. I sensed that Joy was upset when Carole told me that she had decided not to waste a second day waiting at the roadhead and instead had stayed at a campsite some distance up the Rhône Valley. After a couple of cups of jasmine tea, hunks of wholemeal bread and a switch to shorts and well-cushioned training shoes, the pain of the last 1200m of descent no longer preyed on my mind. Its inclines were all but eliminated when the Drings insisted on shouldering our gear, despite having considerable loads of their own.

The heady scents of herbs and pines on the walk down to the

Fieschertal were overpowering after our week in sterile climes. Despite a heat haze, the alps of Fiesch looked lovely on this Sunday afternoon. Having completed the Oberland peaks without a hitch there was cause for us to rejoice.

4

INTERLUDE IN SAASTAL

Fiesch to the Saastal – Weissmies and Lagginhorn

From Fiesch we were ferried 12km up the valley in the Land Rover to a campsite at Ritzingen. After a fourteen-hour day fuelled by only three hours' sleep, I felt the sort of desperate fatigue that overwhelms civility and impairs logic. Neither a shower nor Joy's magnificent pizza supper made an iota of difference. All I desired was sleep. Yet this was just the moment when Joy needed my love and attention. In addition to the frustration caused by our failed rendezvous, she had endured a lonely week at Grindelwald. With no real involvement in our activities on the mountains, she had ample time to question her purpose in being here.

> *This was certainly not going to be like the winter Munros traverse in 1985 when I had been able to accompany Martin up nearly half of the peaks. With two young children there was little chance of my being fully active on the hills and still less hope of achieving any of the summits. I couldn't feel easy about asking Carole or any of the support teams to take the kids for more than an hour or two. On busy campsites I found it hard enough to keep an eye on them and I wasn't prepared to lumber others with the responsibility.*
>
> *So what was I doing here driving around the Alps from camp to camp, and why had Martin spent our savings to pursue this dream? Was it even fair to the kids for Martin to be continually leaving them for days on end? When he came down off the Oberland peaks and could barely be bothered to talk to me, then I really saw red.*

Alps 4000 was something I had talked about for several years, but it was only the previous autumn that I had declared a serious intention to attempt the traverse. There comes a point in one's life when one sees a dream slipping away unless one acts decisively. I was 38, at the prime of physical strength and with a degree of financial security from my climbing school which had been running for seven years. In Simon I had the right partner. If I left the challenge any longer, either my fitness or motivation would wane, or else someone else would come along and do it. Despite my family responsibilities, I felt that it was to be 'now or never', and could sense the regret and frustration that would haunt the rest of my years if I denied the inner urge.

For me, the presence and support of my family seemed essential to sustain the enormous effort of the climbs. I just don't perform at my best if I'm away from them for an extended period, and with some naïvety I had assumed that Joy would prefer being out helping in the Alps rather than seeing me go off on my own for two months on some Himalayan venture. But she saw the choice in rather different terms. If I didn't attempt the '4000ers', then I could spend the summer full-time with her and the family.

We had argued the issue repeatedly over the previous months, but Joy had never been wholly won over to the idea. Meanwhile, the momentum of planning had accelerated to the point where I couldn't back out, even if I had wanted to cancel the attempt. I had been clinging to the hope that the experience of the trip would prove a good deal more favourable to Joy than its prospect. Now my worst fears were being realised.

While the expedition caused Joy and me strain in our personal relationship, Simon and Carole faced problems of a financial nature. We were lucky enough to have savings to spend on the venture, but they were scraping an empty barrel. Simon had only just started his own mountain guiding business and was struggling on the brink of insolvency, while Carole was midway through a degree course in planning.

Carole and I had thought long and hard about the commitment and knew that we couldn't justify it on financial grounds. My fledgling business would have to be put on hold and without a sponsor I'd be spending the whole of next year's income to do it. A visit to my accountant had produced the somewhat dry advice, 'I would not be taking a prolonged holiday in your situation', but had he ever been bitten by something as powerful as climbing? I think not. Whatever doubts and questions the venture raised, my answer was still, 'Yes, I want to be part of this improbable traverse.' The decision boils down to the simple fact that this is an opportunity which comes only once in a lifetime.

I went to bed that night at Ritzingen hoping for a brighter dawn and a chance to redress the balance over the next three days, which were planned as something of a respite for us all. We knew that a hell-bent dash for the '4000ers' would only end in injury or tragedy. Even within our 48-day minimum schedule, there had to be two or three interludes where we could recover our strength. With the great traverse of the 35 summits of the Zermatt watershed now looming large on our horizon, this was the appropriate time to pause. Our next day's itinerary was light: a 52km cycle-run to Saas Grund, the lower of the two main resorts in the Saastal. Over the following two days we would climb the Weissmies and Lagginhorn, two easy '4000ers' on the east side of the valley, before preparing for a fortnight's assault on the Zermatt skyline.

I emerged from ten hours of deep sleep to a warm clouded morning, which threatened a thunderstorm. We bade farewell to the Drings who were now returning to Grindelwald for a spell of 'Eiger-watching' and at 10am remounted our bikes at Fiesch. My knee muscles were bruised and sore from their battering on the Mittelaletsch ski-run and I was glad that our first 18km were downhill. By the time we were down on the busy streets of Brig, we were well warmed to the pending ascent of 940m to Saas Grund.

Brig lies at the meeting of the upper Rhône Valley with the road and rail links from Italy over and under the 2005m Simplon Pass. A further 9km down the valley lies the smaller town of Visp. This is the entry point to the Saastal and Mattertal, the easternmost of the five great valleys which run south to the frontier peaks of the Pennine Alps. Here we left the rushing traffic of the Rhône axis and set our wheels and gears to the long climb.

We stopped for a cup of tea just past Stalden at the junction where the road for the Mattertal and Zermatt branches to the right, then enjoyed a gruelling ride up to Saas Grund. It became clear that Simon was determined not to fall back as he had on the Furkapass. We seemed possessed by a mutual fear of giving ground and thus maintained a pace that had my heart pulsing close to its maximum. Our competitiveness in the saddle was something of a release of the individualism which we had to suppress when climbing. A spirit of teamwork and sharing was imperative on the mountains, a bonding that was reinforced by the linking rope and the ever-present dangers. On the bikes we could break loose from those restrictions and test our personal fitness, while having a bit of fun at the same time. We entered Saas Grund at a fair old lick at 1.15pm.

A storm broke soon after our arrival and the afternoon of family relaxation was hindered by continuing rain. While Simon could spend the remainder of today in recumbent posture, I was pressed into action by eager children and the heaviest downpour caught me half-way round a game of miniature golf at Saas Almagell, still dressed in my cycling shorts and top.

My time with my family was further compromised by the arrival of our support teams. Suddenly we seemed to be overwhelmed by people who were all dependent on our direction over the next week. Roger Coppock and Bruce Taylor were from my local area in Wester Ross, and both worked for Forest Enterprise. Bruce is a tough and wiry character, a member of the local mountain rescue team with many years' experience of technical climbing. By contrast, Roger was an enthusiastic initiate into the sport and his 90kg frame did not hinder him in the least, whether it was traversing the Cuillin Ridge or seconding an E2 rock-climb. This, however, was to be his first taste of alpine mountaineering and the scale of the big peaks can be daunting, even to the strongest and most able of novices. Bruce and Roger were to assist us on the first third of the Zermatt skyline and had two days in which to acclimatise before we would need them.

Our second team, Martin Welch and his brother-in-law Graham Forshaw, had come out primarily to commence film and camera work on the traverse. Although Graham could only spare a fortnight away from his roofing business in Germany, Martin was planning to stay out until the finish of the attempt and hoped to film some of its most exciting moments.

We had nurtured hopes of getting a professional film team to cover the journey, but no commissions were forthcoming. This was of no great matter to Simon or me. Indeed, we had serious misgivings about over-commercialising the enterprise. However, once we had decided to use the expedition to raise funds for charity, the need to have a regular and efficient despatch of video film and pictures for news purposes was essential. Without a good publicity profile, any charity appeal would fail.

*

Our chosen charity was Blythswood Care, which is based in my home village of Lochcarron. Beginning as a purely Christian organisation distributing Bibles and literature, since 1990 Blythswood has been sending aid convoys to the post-Communist countries of Eastern Europe as part of the drive to ease their desperate poverty. In particular they respond to the plight of orphans, the sick and the victims of war. Their example in translating the teachings of Jesus into direct action to help those who suffer has captured the imagination of the people of the Scottish Highlands.

Volunteers from both within and outside the Church have put in a magnificent effort in fund-raising and donating aid supplies. Most impressively, many truck drivers have given up holiday or else taken unpaid leave from work to take lorry loads of food, clothes, medicines and tools on the long and often perilous journey to Romania, Albania and the war-torn countries of former Yugoslavia. Each journey can take up to a fortnight and one of their drivers was killed in 1991 when a vehicle crashed on a mountain road in Romania. In 1993 Blythswood sent out their 200th vehicle-load of aid, but the charity's continuing survival depends solely on the generosity of the public.

Since the Alps lie midway between our home in Scotland and Eastern Europe, it was an appropriate cause and one where we knew that any funds we raised would go to a specific project. I had approached Blythswood's President, the Reverend Jackie Ross, with the proposal the previous December, and where many charities would have steered clear of an involvement with so risky a venture, Jackie had whole-heartedly backed our plans. We printed brochures, sponsor forms and sent hundreds of Alps 4000 appeal letters to companies. We set the ambitious appeal target of £50,000, in expectancy that we would get some backing from companies, but so far we had not received a single penny of corporate sponsorship.

Nonetheless it was a Press Officer, Bill Shannon, who was appointed to co-ordinate media coverage from Scotland, and Blythswood were funding Martin Welch's expenses while he filmed the traverse. Martin lives close to me on the Applecross peninsula of Wester Ross and has been a good friend for several years. Although always a talented amateur photographer, this was his first film assignment. Martin had hitherto been a perennially impecunious vagabond with the warmest of natures and a love of the wilds. If successful, Alps 4000 could provide for him an opportunity to start a professional career, but there were those who suspected that he would never settle down.

The publicity and film work involved a considerable commitment of the charity's funds. Lacking a major sponsor to cover these expenses, we were facing a task to produce a profit, still less raise our £50,000 target. Everything depended on our ultimate success. The pressure this placed on Simon and me was not altogether unwelcome. We knew that at least one of us had to battle through to the end and dared not be deterred by our own struggles, knowing that millions in Eastern Europe faced a far greater struggle every day of their lives.

My preparedness to fight and suffer in the mountains was in some part sustained by the example of those who endured unending oppression or poverty. I had the freedom to choose my own struggles in the hills and the incentive of lasting spiritual reward if I overcame them. Millions did not. In my youth I despised the complacency with which so many people in rich countries seem prepared to fritter away the gift of life, and how they fail to appreciate the health and freedom that is denied to so many others. The hills offered me a sure way of realising that gift, however selfish the activity of climbing might seem to others. In the mountains the cup of life is filled to its brim, but one must give one's all in order to fully savour its brew. I'd long known that I'd be wasting my own life if I didn't respond to my opportunities and drink from that cup.

Nevertheless, the principle of assisting a charity through the achievement of a personal climbing goal has a definite ambiguity. When I had asked Will McLewin, who completed the '4000ers' in 1988, if he would become a patron of the appeal, he had suggested in typically blunt fashion that the whole charity tie-up was essentially just a big 'ego-trip' designed to gratify the participants as much as to help others. Subsequently he did agree to become a patron, but his critique struck a chord of conscience. After all, Simon and I knew that all the publicity created by the charity would benefit us as much as it would help Blythswood. Yet I could not feel happy to undertake the traverse as a purely selfish enterprise when it could do something for a wider good.

On our first evening in Saas Grund my commitments to charity and conscience made a heavy burden. As the storms continued to reverberate around the valley, Joy was facing a crisis which made all my altruistic notions seem quite irrelevant.

The feeling of being trapped without a purpose had not lifted. All I could
think of was getting back home to house, garden and the peaceful hills of
the Highlands. Martin seemed adamant that he had to continue, but
suggested that for my own good I should go home at the first opportunity.
My nephew, Graham Walton, was due out for a fortnight's holiday. At the
end of his stay I could take the van back to Britain with his help and
Martin would finish the trip with support from the others.
I hated the idea of deserting him. I had always encouraged Martin's
climbing challenges, but with his preoccupation over the planning and mine
with the family, we had grown apart in recent months. Eventually, I
decided I would have to go at the end of that fortnight. We called Simon
and Carole in, and I broke down in tears when I told them my plans.

In fact I felt anything but adamant. To lose Joy's respect and confidence overshadowed all other considerations and I turned over every
possibility that sleepless night. If I truly valued Joy as I ought to then
perhaps I should have given the trip up there and then? Yet how could
Simon finish if I quit so early and how many people who had made
such great efforts on our behalf would we be letting down? Would a
total retreat help Joy and me in any positive way? The pain of the trip
had already been inflicted. Failure would only deepen that pain
without any eventual reward. Perhaps we would have to be apart. I'd
feel easier knowing that she was happier back home and surely we
could still love at a distance. Yet it was going to be hard to cope without
her organisational skills at base camp.

The next morning was cold and showery and we all decided to go up
to Saas Fee for an indoor swim before my departure for the Weissmies.
When we discovered that a Swiss family swim costs nigh on £20 we
backed away, but the children were insistent, and of course it was their
Dad whom they most wanted to join them. Eventually I went in with
them and Joy walked back to the camp. This incident in itself seemed
to sum up all our problems.

Uncertainty ruled my thoughts when Simon and I set off for the
Weissmies Hut at 3.30pm. I was happy to follow in his steps on the
1100m climb from Saas Grund and wondered whether he sensed that
my resolution was wavering.

Martin and Graham were joining us on the Weissmies to take advantage of its wide vista over to the Mischabel and Monte Rosa chains
which formed the first part of the Zermatt traverse. Kindly they offered
to take all our gear and boots up to the hut in the nearby cablecar, so

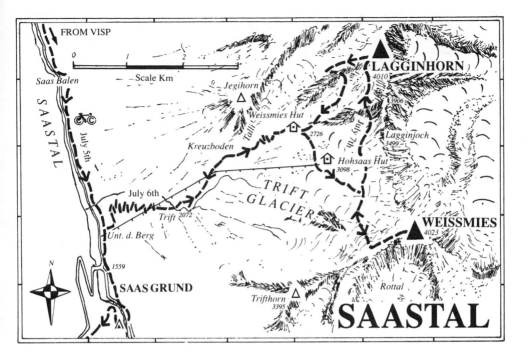

we were clad in just shorts, training shoes and thermal vests. The weather was rapidly clearing with the promise of a really cold night to come, and as we followed the zigzagging path up to the hamlet of Trift we were offered glimpses of the Mischabel peaks through breaks in the pine forest.

Above Trift we entered an open valley of green pastures. The Hohsaas cableway climbed up its middle, its cabins gliding gently up and down in tune with the peaceful rhythm of the grazing cows and strolling trekkers. Above we picked out the snowy shoulder of the 4023m Weissmies, the craggy ramparts of the 4010m Lagginhorn and the shapely final tower of the 3993m Fletschhorn. The Fletschhorn was once the object of a bizarre scheme to construct a 7m summit tumulus in order to raise its height over 4000m and thus ensure its greater popularity.

We passed the midway cable station at Kreuzboden, then followed a steeper line through screes and moraine to the hut at 2726m. Although the two '4000ers' are very popular on account of their ease of access, the hut was virtually empty save for a guided British party. There seems to be an aversion among continental climbers to go up to huts either during or just after a storm, whereas the British are thoroughly used to chancing the capricious weather of their home mountains and will often be found on the heights when everyone else stays down below awaiting a settled spell. By taking the chance they are assured of a pleasant hut stay and might be granted a magnificent clearance of the skies such as we enjoyed tonight.

As we chatted to the British guides about our plans, some of their clients were deluded into thinking that we were tackling the Weissmies in little more than the shorts and trainers in which we had arrived. This was surely taking the lightweight ethic to its absolute limit. Their estimation of us visibly plunged when our two 'porters' arrived from Hohsaas at 7pm carrying all our gear.

'So you climb all these mountains, and then say "Look what we've done",' jibed one rather self-assured young lady.

The services offered by alpine huts often leave a great deal to be desired. All goes well if you keep to the rules and observe the timings of dinner and reveille to the minute, but there is no room to accommodate individual impulse. We needed to be up at 1.30am in order to get both peaks done before the sun did its damage, but the Weissmies Hut knows not of such radical behaviour and our request for a Thermos of hot tea to be left overnight was met with puzzlement. After a considerable search the staff reported that not a single vacuum flask could be found in the establishment and left our morning brew in a jug.

At 2am we considered how the problem might be solved.

'McDonald's restaurants should make a takeover bid for these Swiss huts,' mused Simon as we supped our iced tea by torchlight. 'We'd have a 24-hour service then; a "Big Mac" breakfast at any time of night.' I knew that Simon had a partiality for hamburgers, matchstick chips and such other fast food as McDonald's offered and could see the yearning in his eyes.

'Aye, and flashing yellow neon signs outside every refuge,' I protested.

'But they'd be great for finding your way off the mountain in the dark,' suggested my partner, who was not to be deflected from his dream.

We stole away at 2.15am, climbing up to the Hohsaas cable terminus where Martin and Graham had bivouacked for the night. The station and its adjoining hut were deserted.

'They'll still be fast asleep,' we laughed. 'Perhaps they'll catch us on our descent.'

We crossed the Trift Glacier towards the silent shining dome of the Weissmies. In the shadows of its *bergschrund* we espied an unmoving beam of light. Thinking that some other party had gone ahead of us and were resting there before the summit climb, we approached without undue interest, but as we drew near, the light magnified in strength and amplitude and we found ourselves plunged into the glare of a film set.

'Can youse lads just hold it a second?' The Glaswegian patois was unmistakably Martin's. He and Graham had confounded our expectations and got on the mountain before us. Eager to try his new video camera and accessories, he filmed us walking back and forwards across the *bergschrund* three or four times while Graham manoeuvred a hand-held floodlight. If this was an example of Martin's enthusiasm for his task, we were promised a good deal of attention over the coming month.

We continued up long open snow-slopes into the twilight, crossed the 3820m forepeak and hurried up the final ridge to greet the dawn at 5.30am. The silhouetted skyline to our east included the Bernina Alps, while we could see down the length of Lake Maggiore to our south. A week of coming effort lay dimly illuminated to our west, from the Nadelgrat over the Dom and Täschhorn, across the skyline of the Fee Glacier and over to the massed tops of Monte Rosa, a dozen summits and just a third of the Zermatt skyline. Did I really have the heart for it all?

Martin had chased after us on the Weissmies and met us just below the summit for more filming and chat. We then dropped back to the glacier at 3350m and pondered on possible routes to the Lagginhorn. There was no sense in attempting the linking ridge between the peaks which is highly graded at D, and rarely climbed. However, we needed a traverse line which would save us from dropping all the way back to the hut.

A prominent snowband girdles the west face of the Lagginhorn at 3600m and we worked a line through the loose rock wall which defended its right-hand side. The face was angled at 40° and separated from a higher snowfield by a steeper rock step. We cramponed under the step with our ankles flexing awkwardly sideways to give maximum grip on the hard snowcrust. At only one point was there a break, and by 50m of verglassed slabs and grooves we gained the upper field.

Now we could take a diagonal line to emerge close to the summit, provided that we met no ice on this steeper incline. We were acting on intuition, making our own way unfettered by a guidebook and pressured by the need to be off the mountain by mid-morning. I was enthralled and absorbed by the challenge, and all the troubles of the valley were forgotten. Climbing can be an all-consuming pastime – therein lies the greatest strength and attraction of the sport, but also its greatest danger. It will consume everything that gets in its way unless you occasionally apply the brakes.

We popped our heads over the summit ridge at 9am and sat panting in the sunlight enjoying the view down the forested gorge of the Laggintal to the Gondoschlucht where the Simplon road descends to Italy. In fact our speed had outpaced our best expectations and the physical benefit of that easy day in the valley was self-evident. We were now gaining an enviable level of fitness which needed only to be matched by motivation.

The descent of the Lagginhorn's West Ridge was steeper than that from the Weissmies with a section of PD rock scrambling, but we were still back at the hut by 10.30am, having achieved 2000m of ascent and descent in a little over eight hours. We savoured the day's first hot drink, then headed down to Saas Grund.

On rounding the final bend in the track above the valley floor, I saw Joy, Alex and Hazel leaving our van at the cableway station. Suddenly desperate to see them, I rushed down and caught them just before they boarded the Kreuzboden lift.

'Give me ten minutes and I'll come up with you,' I gasped. Thanks to our haste on the mountain, an afternoon with the family was salvaged. We went back up to Kreuzboden and spent two wonderful hours paddling and dam-building by the little tarn next to the cable station. A calm seemed to have settled on our family life. No longer was Joy accusatory or resentful.

> *Having made my decision with Martin's encouragement a cloud had lifted. With the freedom to go home early I no longer felt a prisoner.*

The Zermatt skyline formed the centrepiece of the '4000ers' traverse and contains by far the greatest concentration of high summits in the Alps, including the great peaks of the Matterhorn, Dent Blanche and Weisshorn. This 80km watershed rings the Mattertal from the Dürrenhorn round to the Brunegghorn and is entirely at altitudes in excess of 3500m save for a short section between the Breithorn and Matterhorn.

In February 1986, the two great Swiss climbers, André Georges and Erhard Lorétan made a non-stop traverse of the skyline over twenty days, so achieving the longest *enchainement* yet made in the Alps. Simon and I hoped to emulate their magnificent achievement in large part, not just because of its aesthetic beauty but also because it offered the quickest and most efficient means of linking the thirty-five 4000m summits of the area. We could, if necessary, make detours to avoid particularly difficult bits of the watershed, but in essence the skyline was our aim and we had set a target of fourteen days. With the glorious weather on the Weissmies and a favourable immediate forecast, the anti-cyclone that we needed to execute the plan appeared to have arrived.

Preparations were therefore well underway for the support operation on the first section of the traverse across the Mischabel range. Roger and Bruce had returned from a crystal-hunting expedition on the Leschaux Glacier above Chamonix, and Carole was packing loads of food for them to take to our first support point, the Mischabeljoch Bivouac Hut up at 3851m between the Täschhorn and Alphubel. In expectation of fine weather, Simon and I decided to travel light. Tomorrow we would walk up to the Mischabel Hut, then on Friday the 9th would traverse the four tops of the Nadelgrat and bivouac on the Lenzjoch at 4121m, ready to make the short but difficult link across the Dom and Täschhorn to meet our support the following day.

The turmoil of the past three days had subsided. My decision to continue and Joy's to go home at the end of the month had settled the basic issues, but more significantly I sensed a moral support from her that previously had been absent. Joy had done some thinking and realised that this venture was much too important for me to abandon. I drew new strength from her tacit assent and at last slept at peace with my conscience.

Simon and I decided to separate on the walk up to the Mischabel Hut, and I set out at midday with Alex to walk up the old path from Saas Grund to Saas Fee. Few tourists who drive up the motor road to the multi-storey car park at the upper resort would even guess that this cobbled track exists. So much of Saas Fee has been swamped by clinical tourist development, none of it particularly grotesque but somehow lacking any soul.

The old path is different. It breathes of a life and culture now lost from the Saastal. At every bend stood a whitewashed stone shrine in which beautifully painted sculptures told the ascendant story of Christ. My six-year-old son was fascinated by the imagery of the white doves, the eye of God in the heavens and the suffering of Jesus on the cross.

'Who are those men on the other crosses next to Jesus?' he asked.

'Oh, they're just robbers – bad men,' I replied.

'Did they come back to life like Jesus?'

Clearly I wasn't getting away easily with just one answer.

'No, but Jesus died with them because he belongs to everyone, even bad people.'

'So why is Jesus still living?'

'Well,' and I thought carefully, 'because he is the spirit of life. We only have one life, but there will always be the little ones left when we pass on, like you and Hazel. So we must use our lives to the best and care for the children.'

Alex's face pictured wonder and thoughtfulness. I thought I'd acquitted myself pretty well. Yet, knowing full well the tenuity of my own existence in the coming weeks, tears filled my eyes as I finished.

The path ended at a church nestled in the hillside with the snow ridges of the Mischabel as its backcloth. I knew then that those mountains were my destiny and that over the coming weeks I must tread that path. It was as if I'd reached a crux in my life, beyond which calmer pastures lay. I simply had to see this through and for the sake of my family I must come back safely. Alps 4000 had become far more than a series of climbs. It was a battle for life itself. Quite stealthily a steely determination possessed me. I would make this succeed come what may. With that thought the last piece in the psychological jigsaw was laid in place.

We met Joy and Hazel in the town and picnicked in the shady woods beyond. It was hard to say goodbye to innocent children who appreciated nothing of the coming dangers, but Joy and I fixed a rendezvous at the Schwarzsee beneath the Matterhorn in one week's time, and with a fond kiss we parted happy. Above me the path twisted endlessly upwards on its 1500m climb to the hut in mimicry of the greater task ahead, but I bent my back to the climb with a resolve that would surely ride the roughest storm. That resolve was to be tested much sooner than I imagined.

5

A BLAST OF WINTER

Nadelgrat – Mischabel – Allalin – Strahlhorn

At 3.45am Martin and I stand at the edge of the Hohbalm Glacier under a clear star-filled sky. To our left is the smooth white sheet of the Lenzspitze North Face and a dozen other climbers are heading off in its direction. Our path soon diverges and we head towards the 3850m Windjoch on the North-East Ridge of the Nadelhorn. From this saddle our route continues its traverse under the peaks of the Nadelgrat and across the upper plateau of the Ried Glacier.

We go down under the sweeping north face of the Hohberghorn, skirting uncomfortably close under a band of seracs to gain a couloir dropping from the Hohbergjoch. A ladder of steps neatly laid by yesterday's visitors takes us quickly up to the col. Here we turn north again and the sunrise catches us on the final scramble to the 4035m Dürrenhorn. The rocky finish is a welcome stimulation after the plain strides of the glacier below.

At 6.15am we reach its crenellated summit which is just sufficient distance from any hut to keep this northernmost of the Mischabel giants peaceful. The Dürrenhorn gives us our first foothold on the Zermatt watershed. Directly west, just 10km across the Mattertal, rises the pyramid of the Weisshorn, yet it will be nearly a fortnight before we can expect to be there.

The Dürrenhorn was the first of four '4000ers' which are collectively known as the Nadelgrat. The traverse of this ridge is a classic expedition which typifies the *assez difficile* grading, but it is complicated by awkward approaches. We were lucky this morning that the approach couloir was filled with snow. Later in the season it can be a runnel of hard ice raked by stonefall from the bounding walls.

We reversed our route to the Hohbergjoch and climbed a steep mixed ridge to the second peak, the Hohberghorn (4219m). Here we could see directly across the Hohberg Glacier to tomorrow's first objective, the Dom. We could pick out the tiny dots of climbers weaving up its North

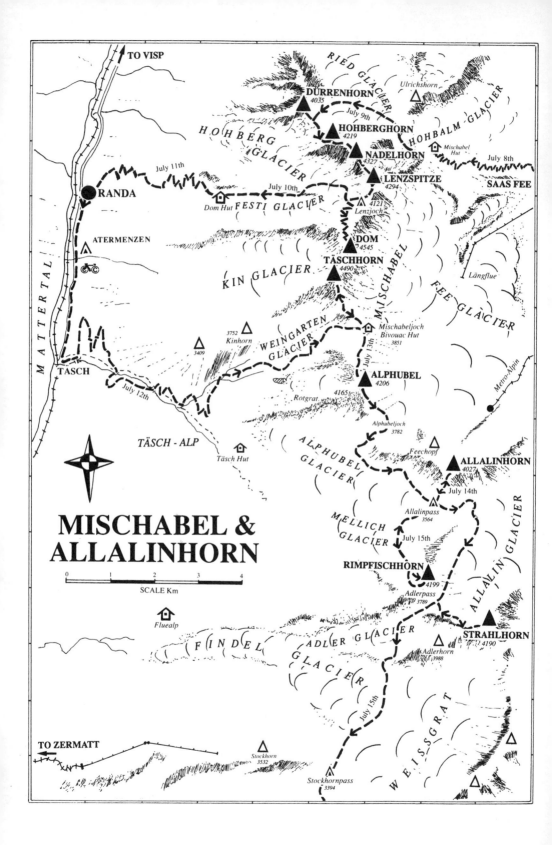

MISCHABEL & ALLALINHORN

TO VISP

RIED GLACIER

Ulrichshorn

DURRENHORN
4035

July 9th

HOHBERG
GLACIER

HOHBERGHORN
4219

NADELHORN
4327

HOHBALM GLACIER

Mischabel
Hut

July 8th

LENZSPITZE
4294

SAAS FEE

July 11th

RANDA

Dom Hut

FESTI GLACIER

July 10th

4121
Lenzjoch

ATERMENZEN

DOM
4545

MISCHABEL

Längflue

TÄSCHHORN
4490

KIN GLACIER

FEE GLACIER

3752
Kinhorn

3409

WEINGARTEN
GLACIER

Mischabeljoch
Bivouac Hut
3851

July 13th

TASCH

July 12th

ALPHUBEL
4206

Metro-Alpin

4165
Rotgrat

Alphubeljoch
3782

TÄSCH - ALP

Täsch Hut

Feechopf

ALLALINHORN
4027

July 14th

MELLICH
GLACIER

ALPHUBEL
GLACIER

Allalinpass
3564

July 15th

ALLALIN GLACIER

RIMPFISCHHORN
4199

Adlerpass
3789

STRAHLHORN
4190

Fluealp

FINDEL
GLACIER

ADLER GLACIER

GLACIER

Adlerhorn
3988

TO ZERMATT

Stockhorn
3532

July 15th

WEISSGRAT

Stockhornpass
3394

0   1   2   3   4
SCALE Km

Flank on the normal route from the Dom Hut. Our day's destination, the Lenzjoch, lay to the left of the Dom, and even from 1¹/₂km away, we could see that it was a sharp and exposed col which would offer little opportunity for a secure bivouac. Therefore we expected to have to drop down to the upper Hohberg Glacier and find a suitable snow hollow for our night out.

There is undoubtedly a tendency among mountaineers, and certainly with me, to envisage a coming climb in the rosiest light possible. The snow is crisp, the sky is clear and the rocks are warm to the touch. The sack seems light, nothing chafes or irritates and the pace feels unhurried. How else could one be sufficiently motivated to get up from warm blankets in the middle of the night? However, such pleasant anticipations rarely materialise. Sweat and toil on fast-rotting snow against a racing clock is the more usual experience of an alpine climb. Yet in the three hours it took to traverse from the Hohberghorn to the Lenzspitze, our progress for once matched our best imaginings. This was how Alps 4000 was meant to be. We virtually glided along the Nadelgrat.

There was a short section of sharp loose rocks on the climb to the Stecknadelhorn (4241m). This rock spike is often considered as a '4000er', but in fact has no more than 20m height separation from its parent peak, the Nadelhorn (4327m). The North-East Ridge of the Nadelhorn (PD) offers the only easy access to the Nadelgrat and several of those who had stayed with us at the Mischabel Hut were climbing its final rise when we arrived at the top.

The descent from the Nadelhorn was by far the most exposed piece of the traverse. A series of abrupt gneiss steps looked highly intimidating from above, yet proved to be furnished with holds the size of dinner-plates which made zigzagging lines through the overlaps However, this part of the traverse would be far more enjoyable in reverse, and indeed we met three of the Lenzspitze parties who had successfully scaled the North Face and were now using the Nadelhorn link as a finale to the climb. We could see their steps down on the face and concluded that the Lenzspitze *Nordwand* makes a relatively safe and simple route to its summit when well plated by snow, as it was today.

On gaining the Lenzspitze (4294m) at 11.40am, our period of grace ended. We faced a blind descent to the Lenzjoch and immediately encountered loose rock with big exposures. The guidebooks give this South Ridge the lowly grade of PD, but the route was clearly in a state of disuse and needs an upward revision to AD–. We were heading towards a bizarre gendarme, shaped like a banana, midway towards the col, but after 100m of nervous meanderings Simon ended our worries by taking us off the ridge and directly down 45° snow-slopes to the Hohberg Glacier.

We found a sheltered wind-hollow on the glacier at 4050m and made our bivouac at 1pm. A few hundred metres to our west the Dom parties passed by on their return journey, which involves a 3100m descent past the Dom Hut and down to Randa on the floor of the Mattertal. In his climbing guide to the 4000m peaks, Richard Goedeke identified the Dom as requiring the greatest physical effort of all the '4000ers' in terms of height gain from the highest point of road or cablecar access.

By contrast, we faced only 500m of ascent from our bivouac to its 4545m summit in the morning. Beyond it we would traverse one of the finest high-level arêtes in the Alps, the Domgrat, which links the Dom to its Siamese twin, the 4491m Täschhorn. I had guided the Domgrat in the reverse direction with my regular alpine client, David Litherland, in late September 1989. Despite wonderful weather we had been hindered by fresh powder snow and had taken eighteen hours from the Mischabeljoch bivouac shelter to the Dom Hut.

The memory of razor-sharp arêtes, crumbling towers and the sense of extreme isolation on that day had left an indelible mark. We had used a magnificent photograph taken from the Dom back across the ridge at the end of that climb in our Alps 4000 appeal brochure, of which nearly 20,000 were currently in circulation all over Britain. I had captioned the picture, 'The Domgrat, a crucial link in the Alps 4000 traverse', knowing that it required clear weather coupled with good snow conditions.

Now we had that ideal combination. Since the day on the Weissmies we had enjoyed brilliant weather with cool northerly breezes to hold the air temperatures down and to keep the snow firm. If this continued we could be on the Matterhorn within a week. We spread out our rucksacks and their foam-backing pads for ground insulation, pulled up our lightweight down sleeping-bags and Gore-tex bivouac sacks, and sat happily brewing and feeding until 3pm. A rising wind was blowing vapour trails off the top of the Dom, but we were snug and sheltered in our hollow. Tired after a restless night at the hut and a good day's work, we were fast asleep by 4pm.

As we slept, our support teams were making their way up from

Täschalp above the Mattertal to the Mischabeljoch Bivouac Hut, Martin and Graham by the direct route up the Weingarten Glacier, and Bruce and Roger by the Rotgrat (AD–) of the Alphubel. We had suggested the Rotgrat to Bruce as offering an excellent introduction to alpine climbing for Roger and from the summit they could drop quickly down the Alphubel's North Ridge to the Mischabeljoch. Yet we had neglected to consider that they would have sacks of some 25kg packed with our supplies. After problems looking after another climber who was off route and slowed by their loads, it was early evening when they found the crucial couloir linking the Rotgrat to the Alphubel's broad summit. Roger was also suffering increasingly from the altitude:

The day, which this morning had seemed so endless, is sliding away and ominous clouds have bubbled up behind the Matterhorn. Exposure, anguish and altitude are beginning to take their toll. Bruce suggests we stop for a bite, the first for twelve hours. Two mouthfuls and it comes back up. Every crest is surmounted by another. Will this bloody ridge ever end? After what seems an eternity, Bruce shouts that we are through. Only a gentle ramp to the summit.

Suddenly the weather closes in menacingly. The first flakes of snow fall with a rising wind. Then Bruce lets out a high-pitched shout.

'Christ, it's lightning! Ahh . . . my gear is burning.' I look at Bruce dancing madly on the slope above.

'Can you hear it buzzing? Can you hear it buzzing?' he yells. 'Get rid of your gear and head for the top.'

We leave everything, even our axes, and the rope which is too wet and dangerous. The summit, must get to the summit; get off the rocks on to the snow. There's no fear now. It will happen so quickly I'll know nothing about it.

We are punching holes for our hands and kicking steps up a 45° slope. No axes, crampons or rucksack. Lightning flashes every few seconds; where is it hitting? This is insane. Bruce stops; we've got to go back for the gear, back across that horrific snow ramp. Leave the hardware, grab the rope and sacks, then head up again. It's so much easier with an axe. We reach the top in darkness. Bruce suggests a snowhole, and we dig like madmen with the adzes of our axes.

Under the Lenzjoch I stirred briefly from a warm sleep. It was 9.30pm and only just dark. I poked my nose out and noticed it was snowing gently. Seeing a distant flicker of lightning I imagined a brief local disturbance in the weather, buttered myself a few oatcakes then drifted back off to my dreams.

We woke independently some time after 3am. I felt an unusual warmth, considering we had slept in the open and registered a definite compression of my bivouac sack. I fumbled my fingers up to its zipper, opened a narrow aperture and a mass of powder snow fell on to my face. We were, in fact, half-buried by an accumulating snowdrift and a blizzard was raging. We sat for an hour silently contemplating the implications for today's 'crucial link' and spent another thirty minutes summoning the willpower to relinquish our warm couch.

At 5am a move has to be made. The snow is steady and blowing. I suffer bouts of claustrophobia struggling into my waterproofs while still inside my sleeping-bag, and eventually emerge from my chrysalis to survey the grey swirling clouds. Martin soon materialises complete with his rucksack which he had packed while still inside his bivvy bag. His clever strategy backfires when he realises that somehow he has left a mitten inside his sleeping-bag and has to empty the sack completely to find it. Cooking is impossible in the wind and spindrift. We search the drifts for our hardware and struggle into harnesses with our hands alternating between numb cold and burning hot aches.

We were so surprised by the sudden change in weather that we had no contingency plans, but we could at least struggle up the Dom which is a simple snow climb broken here and there by crevasses. Yet even that short climb took over two hours as we toiled through crusted old snow and dry fresh drifts. Close to the top ridge I triggered a small windslab slide and we edged along to the summit cross, trying to split the risk of falling off a cornice to one side and triggering an avalanche on the other. A gale of 60km per hour was blowing on the very summit and visibility was under 100m.

The implication was clear. We couldn't hope to traverse the Domgrat and were left with only one option – a retreat to the shelter of the Dom Hut, which lay 1600m below. From there we might be able to tackle the Täschhorn direct by its North-West (Kin) Face if the weather relented overnight. Simon took out our radio and tried to call up the lads at the Mischabeljoch, but at that moment Martin and Graham were less worried about us than the non-arrival of Bruce and Roger, who had spent the night in a half-sealed snow cave.

Our burrow lights up as if floodlit with every lightning flash. After four long hours the storm slowly moves away. I lie there dozing fitfully with the small of my back in a little pool of water while Bruce brews continuously.

Every time I take a drink I'm forced to rip my rucksack out of the doorway and stick my head outside to throw up. At dawn we have to move. There is no future in this icy coffin. Bruce navigates brilliantly along the featureless summit ridge and gets us on to the North Ridge. Some way down he shouts that he can hear cowbells below. We descend to the col to find that the noise isn't cowbells, but the scraping of Martin and Graham's crampons on the metal hut ladder as they come out to look for us. My relief is total when we meet them. It's been some introduction to the Alps, but at least we've got the supplies through.

At that moment Simon and I were retreating back towards the Hohberg Glacier, knowing that we would take at least one or possibly two extra days to reach those supplies. At 4200m the clouds cleared enough to indicate a possible short-cut through bands of ice cliffs. We were lured ever further by steepening convex slopes until at the very bottom a 5m *bergschrund* barred our passage to easy ground. We could have jumped, but nothing was worth the risk of a broken ankle, so we had to reclimb 130m through deep drifts to regain the normal route. Our route passed close to our bivouac site, then steered a long westward curve towards the Festijoch which provides a bridge from the Hohberg Glacier to the Festi Glacier and the Dom Hut.

A thunderstorm caught us descending icy rocks beneath the Festijoch without crampons, which we had removed earlier when our boot soles were balling up with snow. There was no choice but to stop and we refitted the crampons sitting precariously on the slope while volleys of *graupel* blasted across us. Once on the glacier we fled 700m down to the hut, trying to suppress our frustration at so cruel a twist of fate.

The Dom Hut's guardian seemed to think that the weather might be reasonable tomorrow, although there was no evidence he ever bothered to get a radio forecast for us. At 6pm we tried to radio the Mischabeljoch. Since the Täschhorn lay squarely between us and the col, we did not expect any contact, but much to our amazement we heard Martin's voice and were reassured to be told that the supplies were in place. All we could do now was to sit and hope for an overnight clearance. Even if that did happen the Kin Face of the Täschhorn would be a risky proposition with so much fresh snow on its slopes.

My alarm sounded at 3.30am and I peered through the window shutters at a silent world of thickly falling snowflakes. I went outside and to my horror saw that nearly 15cm had accumulated on the hut balcony over the past six hours. The Kin Face option disappeared in that instant. At 6.45am we got up and Simon reported that his altimeter had fallen 90m overnight, a definite sign of a serious and prolonged degradation in the weather. The guardian seemed little bothered by the total inaccuracy of his weather prediction. The 92 francs we had paid for dinner, drinks and breakfast seemed all that really mattered to him.

Over breakfast we got talking to a Swiss guide who had hoped to take his client up the Dom. Without our confiding anything of our plans to him, he suddenly said:

'You know there are some crazy people. Last month I met some British guys over at the Längflue who were trying to climb all the 4000m peaks in one summer.'

Our ears immediately pricked to attention. We had read that a six-man team of Scots Guards planned to start an assault on the '4000ers' in early May, but after initial contact with their leader in April we had heard no more of their activities. It came as a shock to be told not only that they had already started but that they had achieved a tally of seventeen summits a month ago, a total that we had only achieved with yesterday's ascent of the Dom. On our telling him that we were after the same goal, the guide was perplexed that suddenly a flood of British climbers seemed to want to race around the '4000ers' when he climbed them on most days of his working life. We knew that the Scots Guards were using motorised transport and doing the peaks in haphazard order so that their expedition did not strictly compare with our own, but the scent of competition made us just a little more miserable about the days we were now losing.

There would be no sense in waiting here another day. We had no food, money or radio battery power left. The only sure way to get to the Täschhorn would be to descend to the Mattertal where our base camp was now sited and go up to the Mischabeljoch Bivouac Hut tomorrow. Then we could tackle the mountain up and down by its safest route, the South-East Ridge, on the following day. For an extra 3100m of climbing we would be losing three days on our schedule. You have to be phlegmatic to accept such a statistic, but that was the thought with which we left the Dom Hut at 10.30am.

Snow lay thick on the path down to the upper edge of the valley forests at 2000m. Although the morning was bright, a huge swirl of white cloud over the Weisshorn warned of further cold and unsettled weather to come. In less than two hours we were striding through the pretty cobbled streets of Randa and up the valley to the campsite at Atermenzen. The 1500m descent took little toll on our kneejoints, thanks to our each having a ski stick for support, and we were relieved to reach the valley floor even though we would have to start again from scratch.

Joy has an uncanny ability to guess my movements on the mountains and was not in the least surprised to see us. I sensed that her attitude was still supportive. The events at Saas had created a cautious truce in our relationship and now she was looking forward to the arrival of her nephew Graham.

Late in the afternoon the support group arrived back from the Mischabeljoch, battered but not beaten. Martin Welch played back some harrowing video footage of Bruce and Roger staggering across the windswept col to the bivouac hut. They recounted their epic as they unwound over steaks and beers in the campsite café that evening. All four had returned over the Alphubel in another white-out in order to retrieve the gear abandoned during the electric storm. Their brush with death worried me greatly. It was one thing to ask support teams to put in great efforts on our behalf but quite another to entice them into situations where their lives were put at risk. I decided to ensure that our next support pair, Martin Stone and Mike Walford, were not subjected to any over-ambitious planning on our part. If it meant our walking a bit further or going hungry for a day, then so be it. The one thing we couldn't contemplate was a serious accident.

Monday 12 July dawned cold and raw. The campsite manager became a supporter of our cause and sought out the best available weather report on his radio.

'Two more days of cold weather,' he said, 'but getting slowly better.'

Our mood at breakfast was gloomy. Our progress seemed stymied, yet we had to get back up to the skyline today and I had to relive the wrench of parting from the family. This time my anguish was heightened by the sure knowledge that we were going back to dangerous and difficult conditions on the mountains.

We were lucky to be able to cycle the first 700m of the 2400m climb to the Mischabeljoch. From Täsch, where the public highway to Zermatt terminates, a narrow road weaves a twisting route up the hillside and into the side valley of Täschalp. We set off at 10.15am and Martin, Graham, Carole and Alex tailed us by car. For 6km the climb averages 12 per cent in gradient and the only way I could dispel my unhappy mood was to get my head down and go hard.

A cold sweat covers my brow as the bends and angle of the single track road take their toll. Martin is as strong as ever. I feel confident in my stamina but not in the sprint pace that Martin seems to want to set. It takes a mere 45 minutes to get to the hamlet. Up here it is snowing a little and there is no sign of an improvement, just the vague promise from past years as to the reliability of the season. I kiss goodbye to Carole again, then we shoulder the packs and head for the hut.

The first hour of the walk was spent recovering from the bike climb. My stomach had tightened with the effort of the ride and my leg muscles were flaccid with fatigue. Yet by the time we had gained the base of the great lateral moraine of the Weingarten Glacier at 2540m, my body had regained full strength and my spirits had revived. The slopes of Täschalp are one of the few places in the high Western Alps where edelweiss can be found, and a few were poking their flowered heads through the fresh snow by the Rotbach torrent.

The Täsch Hut lay just 2km to our south-west and offered a more circuitous route to the Mischabeljoch, as well as being a good base for doing the Alphubel and the Allalinhorn traverse. Despite several visits to the hut, I had never taken this route up into the Weingarten cirque. The guidebook made the route sound fairly serious, so we were treating it with due respect.

We lunched close by a tarn of turquoise-blue meltwater at 3053m, then climbed into deeper snowdrifts under the western ribs of the Alphubel. Occasional clearances gave us impressive views of the Rotgrat on which Bruce and Roger had so recently fought for their lives. We worked a route through rock slabs defending the leftmost of the Alphubel ribs and thus gained the Weingarten Glacier above its steepest and most crevassed section.

The Täschhorn now lay directly opposite us, but we saw nothing of its South-West Face and only intermittent glimpses of the lower parts of its South-East Ridge which we had to climb tomorrow. We toiled through knee-deep powder and thick mist on a compass bearing for the Mischabeljoch wondering whether we should perhaps have reverted to skis for glacier travel after so much fresh snow. All the crevasse fields mentioned in the guidebook were well buried: 1993 was clearly going to be a snowy year.

There was no real steepening at the col, but we were met by a sudden blast of spindrift with a whistling wind. Up at 3850m the cold was bitter and our supplies of bread and vegetables had frozen solid during two nights in the hut. The shelter was in need of refurbishment, but even at sub-zero temperatures it was a welcome haven. Its construction in 1966 enabled the popularisation of the South-East Ridge as the safest route to the Täschhorn at a reasonable AD grading. Prior to that there were few who possessed the fitness to complete the climb from the valley in a day. Yet the route's original pioneers, the Reverend James Jackson and the guides Christian and Ulrich Almer, did the whole climb to the summit on foot from Randa in a little under twelve hours in August 1876. They then descended by the Kin Face to re-enter the village at 8.30pm after a nineteen-hour expedition.

We did all in our power to keep warm that night. We cooked a great repast and gave thanks to the efforts of our support team. I went to bed fully dressed under four blankets with a Sigg bottle of water boiled for tomorrow's drink warming my feet and my boots wrapped in a blanket under my head to stop them from freezing. Outside the wind continued to boom around the hut.

> At 3.30am we are up. I begin to shiver as soon as I leave my cocoon of blankets, but the porridge which we had soaked the night before warms me a little. As we depart the wind begins to drop and the sky is clear. The morning is bitterly cold, certainly below −10°C, and climbing up the first snowed-up rocks of the ridge my hands turn wooden.

Simon's mittens were in a state of disintegration and his woes were compounded when his camera rewound unintentionally just as we stopped to capture the livid dawn on film. Daylight revealed the ridge ahead as a corniced serpent which snaked gently upwards for a kilometre to the Täschhorn's final tower.

This ridge, which I had climbed with David Litherland en route for the Domgrat in 1989, was totally unrecognisable. Then we had ambled along without crampons and I never felt a moment of insecurity throughout the ascent. On that day the difficulties had only started beyond the Täschhorn on the Domgrat. The contrast in conditions illustrated the impossibility of assigning a single grade to a route. Today, this modest assez difficile was going to be as testing as a fluted Andean arête.

Once we left the initial rocky towers, our greatest concern was the lack of protection. Normally, one can achieve a measure of security when moving together on a snow ridge simply by having 10 or 12m of rope between the climbers so that they are able to keep on different sides of the arête during tricky sections. Large cornices on the Saas side of the ridge prevented any such tactics. We were forced to make long traverses on harder wind-blown snow on the west side, each knowing that we would be unable to arrest a slip.

To our left rose the 900m South-West Face, which consisted of a mass of featureless slabs cut by two diagonal faults to form a diamond-shaped headwall. The two best teams of their generation, Valentine Ryan and the Lochmatter brothers, and Geoffrey Young and Josef Knubel, combined forces to make an epic first ascent of the face in 1906. At its conclusion Young turned to Franz Lochmatter, who had led the crux, and said:

'You will never do anything harder than that, Franz!'

Lochmatter, who was just nineteen years old, thought reflectively.

'No,' he replied, 'man could not do much more.'

Viewing that snow-plastered face and knowing that Lochmatter had led it without pitons, I wondered whether climbing standards had really advanced so very much in the last ninety years.

Occasionally, our own way was barred by patches of unstable drift which had no apparent anchorage to the slope below. Just before the final tower we met a particularly nasty snow meringue on the crest.

> Ahead is a vertical mass of snow some 3m high. On both sides are inconsistent windslabs at an angle of 55°. I toy with the idea of traversing one or the other side, but the consequences of a fall when Martin has no belay forbids that decision. So I choose to bulldoze my way through the slab and chop away at the ridge for 4m or so, working down to a firmer base below. I feel a certain embarrassment at the tactic, for force should generally be rejected as a mountaineering technique. Had the section been any longer, my strength would have been severely tested.
>
> On the steeper final tower, loose snow, which is already melting in the morning sun, keeps us thinking and the summit is reached with relief at 10am. Martin seems unusually slow on this ground. I realise that it is not to his liking. This is a rare view of him, as he so often seems mechanical in his ability to climb, showing no weaknesses. Strangely, this gives me confidence and I feel more of an equal.
>
> The views of the Zermatt peaks are stunning, but they are not wholly appreciated. We have spent five hours on a white tight-rope and the descent will be equally taxing.

Although our tracks greatly facilitated the descent, it still took four hours to get back to the hut. I was thankful that we hadn't climbed the Täschhorn by the Kin Face and then been forced into a blind descent of the South-East Ridge when it was in this dangerous state. Even in good conditions, the Täschhorn ranks as one of the hardest of the fifty major '4000ers'.

A support camp was being set up for us that afternoon on the 3564m Allalinpass, the central of the three great glacier crossings between Zermatt and Saas Fee. This would enable us to stay as high as possible while traversing the four '4000ers' which form the skyline of the Fee and Allalin Glaciers. To reach camp that evening we had to traverse the first of the four, the Alphubel, and if time allowed we wanted to cross the Allalinhorn as well. After mugs of sweet coffee and a meal of soup, bread and fried vegeburgers, we cleaned the bivouac hut as best as we were able, packed up the spare food and rubbish and trudged up the Alphubel's North Ridge. The summit plateau was caked with thick wind-drifts which subsided slowly under each step. The tracks of our support team from two days ago were visible here and there.

From the top of the Alphubel there were two options for reaching the next pass, the Alphubeljoch at 3782m. We could either drop down the east slope on to the Fee Glacier and traverse a kilometre to the pass which is little more than *facile* in standard, or else take a more direct route down the steeper South-East Ridge which is PD in standard. In order to minimise the labour of trail-breaking, we chose the shorter ridge, but even this was plated with wind-driven snow. There was undoubtedly some degree of slab avalanche risk and intermittent mist didn't help us to pick the best line.

On reaching the pass at 6pm, we were so sapped of energy that all thoughts of traversing the Allalinhorn were abandoned. We could, however, still reach our camp by dropping west down the Alphubel Glacier for 200m, then traversing south on to the Mellich Glacier which leads to the Allalinpass. We joined the tracks of our support team on the descending traverse to the Mellich Glacier. Down below Simon spotted a mother chamois and her foal trotting across the wide expanse of ice without any obvious purpose or destination.

After another hour slogging up the glacier we gained the camp which was perched in an enviable site right on the crest of the pass. The evening sun was just beginning to slide down through bands of cirrus and alto-stratus cloud out to the west, its light diffuse and hazy. The temperature was already dipping sharply and we shivered as soon as we stopped.

No fewer than six folk were installed in camp – Martin and Graham,

Bruce and Roger, and Carole and Julie — yet no one had thought to prepare us a brew or have some hot food ready. After fifteen hours of sustained effort I hardly felt capable of eating, let alone cooking, and found it difficult to suppress my annoyance. Eventually, we contented ourselves with a quick tuna and pasta mix, thoughts of tomorrow pressing hard on our patience.

We were now four days behind our base schedule and unless we could climb the Allalinhorn, Rimpfischhorn and Strahlhorn together tomorrow, we would lose another. Our next support point was the Stockhornpass, midway between the Strahlhorn and Monte Rosa, and Joy was briefing Martin Stone and Mike Walford to set up a camp there the following night. At 10pm we settled to sleep, our alarms set for 3am. A cold wind was blowing from the west. The weather signs were ominous, but we couldn't truly believe that another storm was on its way.

I slept through my alarm, but when I did awake at 4.30am the sound of spindrift driving against the tent fabric killed my hopes of getting to the Stockhornpass that day. At least we had a secure base so there would be no repeat of our predicament on the Lenzjoch. The Allalinhorn's South-West Ridge offered our sole crumb of comfort. Climbing just 470m above us and only PD in difficulty, it would take no more than three hours up and down even in a storm. Yet it seemed ironic that we were stuck in the middle of four of the easiest and most popular '4000ers', which we had originally planned to traverse in a single day all the way from the Mischabeljoch to the Stockhornpass.

At 10am Bruce, Roger, Carole and Julie went down, leaving Martin and Graham to support us with our four-man dome tent and enough food for one more night. Bruce and Roger were now departing for Britain. Understandably, they had taken their fill of the prevailing weather, and with this new storm their plans to climb the Matterhorn as the culmination of their holiday had finally disappeared. They had given so much without gaining their just reward of some decent weather. So why should I have been disgruntled with their lack of attention to us last night? I tried to realise that help should be appreciated, not expected, and hoped that this trip wasn't turning us into a pair of prima donnas.

The storm was in no way as severe as that on the Dom, yet thick cloud and steady snowfall made the Allalinhorn a trial. The usual route up the South-West Ridge scrambles under the steepest steps of the crest. As soon as we tried to follow this traverse line we found ourselves wallowing thigh-deep in snow. Further progress was impossible, so we extricated ourselves and thereafter kept to the ridge, which provided a steep step of sporting mixed climbing.

> *This is much like a winter's climb at home, clearing excess snow off the rocks and packing it under our feet sufficiently to support our weight. Our midday radio call is due on the summit. We have to get in touch with Martin Stone to stop him going up to the Stockhornpass today. Fortunately, he has climbed up the hillside above Zermatt and opened his set. They are within minutes of catching the Gornergrat railway up towards the Stockhorn, so we can spare them a fruitless journey. We request a couple of Swiss beers to be included in tomorrow's rations as just at this moment we are feeling particularly human.*

On the 4027m summit we could hear the dull drone of engines, and when the clouds briefly parted we spotted piste-ing vehicles and a few skiers on the grey expanse of the upper Fee Glacier 500m below. Visitors to the Saastal have been able to enjoy dependable summer skiing high on the Fee Glacier since the construction of the underground Metro-Alpin railway in the mid-1980s. With its terminus at an altitude of 3456m, the Metro has also made the Allalinhorn the most accessible of all the '4000ers' except for the Breithorn. Thankfully, schemes to extend cableways to its summit ridge have been stopped. Those skiers were doubtless riding back to the hotels of Saas for a late lunch while we ploughed our lonely furrow down to the Allalinpass.

Our underlying mood became pensive as the afternoon passed without any sign of the snowfall stopping. There was no longer a certainty that we could even get to the Stockhornpass the next day in these white-out conditions. Fortunately, we had excellent tent companions in Martin and Graham who did their best to stem the downward tide of our spirits.

Graham gave us a droll recital of the tourist guide to Goms, which was the only reading material he had brought up. If he was trying to make us yearn for the pleasures of the valley he signally failed, since the visitor attractions of that district of the upper Rhône seemed to consist solely of wine and strudel evenings, folk dances and karaoke nights. Then we all simultaneously decided to brush our teeth and sat facing each other with teeth clenched in ridiculous grins and our mouths covered in foam. For several minutes we became helpless with mirth. An indulgence in juvenile humour seems to be a uniquely British way of enduring adversity and it kept us sane on the Allalinpass.

At 7.30am on Thursday, 15 July, we left camp and traversed south towards the upper slopes of the Rimpfischhorn. The weather had barely improved. Our visibility was no greater than 100m and snowflakes were still falling gently from the clouds. By the time we returned from the Rimpfischhorn, Martin and Graham would have packed up camp and gone. Today we were out on our own. With just snacks for the day and a near-empty gas stove it was imperative that we climbed both the Rimpfischhorn and the Strahlhorn and reached our next camp on the Stockhornpass by nightfall.

The conditions had forced us to choose a most circuitous route between the two peaks. We had originally hoped to climb directly down the Rimpfischhorn's precipitous eastern ramparts and across the Adlerpass to the Strahlhorn. Instead, we would have to retrace our steps to the Allalinpass, drop east down to 3300m and then climb the full length of the upper Allalin Glacier to gain the Strahlhorn. Thus we faced an extra 400m of ascent and 5km of glacier-slogging to link the pair.

We were also resigned to missing out the 4108m gendarme on the Rimpfischhorn's North Ridge. Goedeke's list of the '4000ers' had given this top a 30m height differential. Since we doubted several of Goedeke's estimates, we were trying to climb all the tops which came close to our 35m requirement. Due to our lack of time and the patent difficulty of the North Ridge which is a good AD in the best of conditions, we would have to miss the gendarme. We just prayed that on this occasion Goedeke's estimate of 30m was correct.

Three long stretches on compass bearings took us close under the *bergschrund* of the mountain's North-West Face at 3900m. Here the snow became more than knee-deep and we were still 500m from the Rimpfischsattel where the normal route from Zermatt is joined for the final climb. I completely despaired of progressing further on these loaded slopes and turned to Simon.

'Why don't we just go straight up the North-West Face? It's got to be quicker.'

On the 55° face the fresh snow lay only a few centimetres thick over old bare ice and in places had been blown clear altogether. Progress was undoubtedly faster, but equally was more precarious, especially since we had just one ice axe each. We moved together 5m apart on the rope and stopped every hundred steps or so to rest our calves which burnt with the effort of cramponing solely on our front points. At 4100m we reached a shoulder and then followed mixed ground over a forepeak to an obvious top.

It was four years since my last visit here and two years since Simon's. Was this really the summit? If only there was a metal cross. I took a few steps northwards. The cloud was dense but I could definitely sense a pronounced drop. Meanwhile, Simon checked his altimeter. Over a couple of hours its calibration can be displaced 10 or 20m by changes in the prevailing atmospheric pressure. However, it was now reading 4210m, giving a safe margin of 11m above the actual summit height of 4199m. We therefore declared the mountain climbed.

A brief look over the misted void of the East Face confirmed the hopelessness of attempting a direct descent to the Adlerpass. We kept to the usual route down the West-South-West Ridge to the Rimpfischsattel. These final 200m should be treated with respect. Icy couloirs of 50° in angle and slabby rock steps put it at the upper limit of the *peu difficile* grade. Even at PD+ it is still perhaps undergraded. A covering of rime ice made the descent of the rocks particularly awkward.

From the Rimpfischsattel we ploughed across to rejoin our ascent tracks at the point where we had taken to the North-West Face. Although half-buried, our steps speeded the passage back to the Allalinpass, which was now deserted. It was 1pm and as arranged we radioed Martin Stone and gave him the go-ahead to establish the Stockhornpass camp. With the cloudbase now lifting up to 3800m, we felt confident if hardly thrilled by the prospect of traversing the 4190m Strahlhorn that afternoon, and continued round to the Allalin Glacier.

Simon led the first stretch of the long pull to the 3789m Adlerpass. The air was warming rapidly and the snow deteriorating to a heavy mush. To our right we were treated to a side-show as cascades of thawing ice collapsed down the Rimpfischhorn's East Face.

At 3500m I took over and to my delight found a line of old tracks leading towards the pass. They gave the most slender passage of solid footing, but as we climbed higher they were increasingly obscured by fresh drifts. My eyes scanned the blank white snowfields ahead of me for slight surface ruffles which indicated the tracks. Whenever I lost the steps I found myself knee-deep in snow which had the consistency of wet cement. That vague trail was my life-line for over a kilometre, but it disappeared altogether 120m below the pass.

'This is the toughest thing I've ever done or am ever going to do,' I told myself for the first time. 'Or ever want to do,' I whispered after a couple more steps.

With this admission I began to wonder whether Alps 4000 might, in fact, free me from the urge to push myself to the limit in the mountains. If not a permanent cure, then it would certainly quell my energies for a considerable period of time. I was glad of that thought. After all, if a trip like this couldn't give a lasting fulfilment nothing ever would.

I could have let Simon take a turn, but I wanted to spare his remaining strength for the 400m climb from the pass to the summit. A blast of wet hail greeted our arrival at the crest and Simon headed up into a complete white-out. I prayed he would hold the lead, but like me he was close to the end of his tether. He was additionally hampered by wearing spectacles which became steamed on the inside and spattered with ice on the outside. After 150m he turned to give me a beckoning look and we swopped lead regularly thereafter. Sometimes we fell blindly over unseen banks of soft drift, at others we stared uselessly into the enveloping fog looking for corniced edges over the South Face.

A final steepening took us on to the rocky edge of the summit at exactly 5pm. The conditions of driving sleet would have done justice to the worst of days on the Scottish mountains. We cowered over our map. Realising that a direct descent to the Stockhornpass over the Adlerhorn would be impossible, we decided to retrace our steps to the Adlerpass and take a lower level route across the Findel Glacier.

We descend with care since our tracks are no longer visible, frustrated that not even a simple summit like the Strahlhorn is straightforward. At 6pm we radio Martin and Mike without success. Yet incredibly there is reception down to base at Täsch, even though it is 10km away across several ridges. Base confirms that the camp is being installed, and we catch sight of three figures crossing the Stockhorn from the top cable station towards the pass. We cross the Findel Glacier for 3km, a seemingly endless plod. We have been going for twelve hours with no respite from the deep snow. I have the lead on the final climb of 200m to the pass. My back twinges with pain throughout and the climb drains any remaining reserves.

The convex slope seemed to go on for ever, but slowly eased until at last we saw the two tents 100m away. It was hard to believe that rest and security were that close. We walked over trying to regain composure before the meeting and flung down our sacks at the tent door. It was 8pm, and the most depressing day of the journey so far was finally done.

6

BREAKING THE NOOSE

Monte Rosa – Liskamm – Breithorn

We lay stretched out in our sleeping-bags at the back of the tent listening to the hum of the gas stove and the cheery banter of our new companions. One thing was immediately clear. We wouldn't have the strength to go over Monte Rosa tomorrow, whatever the weather. With that decision made, the layers of stress lifted from our brows. The menu was tea, fresh patisseries, beer, pasta and tuna stew, and the ever-popular tinned peaches. The stoves were still going strong as midnight approached, but Simon and I had already slipped into a comatose state.

Our support team needed no telling that their efforts were more than ordinarily appreciated. The knee-deep slog from the cable terminus across the snows of the Stockhorn had taken them over two hours, and Martin and Mike had been thankful for the help of Joy's nephew, Graham Walton, in ferrying the loads.

Graham had just qualified as a dentist in Glasgow and was a virtual novice in mountaineering. Nevertheless, he possesses such practicality and common sense that far from being overawed by the calibre of his companions he was actually keeping them in order, especially when Martin's attention to the cooking was temporarily diverted in the telling of some anecdote.

Martin Stone is a mountain runner of tremendous enthusiasm and his 24-hour solo unsupported run over 26 Munros around Lochaber in 1986 still stands as one of the most remarkable exploits of its kind. Undeterred by recurrent knee trouble, he has travelled the world in search of exciting mountain marathons over recent years. He recounted his most recent venture, a running race from Alagna up and down the 4554m Signalkuppe on Monte Rosa. He had competed in this without

MONTE ROSA & BREITHORN

WEISSGRAT

Stockhornpass 3394

Stockhorn 3532

Jägerhorn

July 16

MONTE ROSA GLACIER

July 17

NORDEND 4609

MONTE ROSA

DUFOURSPITZE 4634

ZUMSTEINSPITZE 4563

Margheria Hut

SIGNALKUPPE 4556

PARROTSPITZE 4436

CORNO NERO 4321

LUDWIGSHÖHE 4341

Balmernhorn Hut

July 18

PIRAMIDE VINCENT 4215

Gnifetti Hut

Lisjoch

Quintino Sella Hut

GRENZ GLACIER

Monte Rosa Hut

LISKAMM 4527

IL NASO

LIS GLACIER

ZWILLINGS GLACIER

POLLUX 4092

CASTOR 4226

Val d'Ayas Hut

GORNER GLACIER

Gornergrat

Riffelhorn 2927

SCHWARZE GLACIER

Schwarztor

BREITHORN GLACIER

BREITHORN 4164 C. SUMMIT

TWINS 4106

Roccia Nera 4075

July 18

VERRA GLACIER

July 19

Breithorn-plateau

UNTER THEODUL GLACIER

Trockenersteg

Klein Matterhorn 3883

Gobba di Rollin 3899

ZERMATT

Schwarzsee

THEODUL GLACIER

3467

Theodulhorn 3469

Theodulpass

July 19

Testa Grigia 3479

July 20

N

SCALE Km
0 1 2 3

any acclimatisation during a weekend trip from Britain just a fortnight previously.

Weather conditions had deteriorated during the race and Martin had reached the summit hut in a state of severe cold. Fortunately, the young guardienne of the hut massaged some life back into his arms and feet before he commenced the plunging 3400m descent back to Alagna. Despite this untoward delay he was still among the first twenty finishers.

Like Martin, Mike Walford is the sort of athlete who doesn't consider himself fully warmed up until a race has passed the 20km mark. In his mid-forties he is enjoying a new lease of life running in the veteran category of races, many of which he could hope to win. He has an architect's practice in Kendal, Cumbria, yet still manages a phenomenal amount of training, racing, Munro-bagging and alpine mountaineering. Like most fell-runners he possesses an appetite to match his deeds and he was dismayed that Simon and I refused a third plateful of his stew. In the Rottal Hut on the Jungfrau the previous year, Mike, Martin and their partner had wagered with a doubting guardian that they could eat a kilo of dry spaghetti they had asked him to cook. This amounts to fully three times a normal large portion each, but the guardian was forced to eat his words as they polished off the whole lot. The threesome then proceeded to climb the mountain in a fast time the next day.

Although neither Martin nor Mike are technically minded climbers, we knew we were in good hands over the next week as long as we did not ask too much of them. The terrain on the forthcoming traverse of Monte Rosa, Liskamm, Castor, Pollux and the Breithorn was ideally suited to their temperament, giving fast tracking over long snow ridges at a continuously high altitude. In good conditions we could cover all seventeen 4000m tops on this lofty watershed in two days. Geoffrey Winthrop Young had once set out to complete them all in a single day and would have succeeded but for the complaints of his guide.

Yet under the present weather system the traverse could be a series of white-outs and unstable snow arêtes – indeed, a continuation of the conditions we had endured on the Rimpfischhorn and Strahlhorn. We were no longer heeding the hopeful forecasts which still emanated from Zermatt. Our mood of buoyant optimism a week previously had swung through a phase of realism to a resigned acceptance of the present adversity. We knew that no alpine summer could be as continuously bad as this last week, yet for the moment we felt trapped in a slowly tightening noose.

The morning of 16 July dawned bright and clear, but high clouds scudded over the northern buttresses of Monte Rosa, indicating high winds on the tops. I remembered our original plans and chuckled to myself. Today our schedule envisaged us on the far side of the Matterhorn climbing the great East Ridge of the Dent d'Herens. Yet we were stuck here unable to do more than move our camp 5km south to a position adjacent to the normal route to Monte Rosa.

Our idea of keeping to the watershed traverse as followed by Georges and Lorétan was no longer relevant. The Nordend of Monte Rosa offers a direct but difficult route up its North-East Ridge which is known as the Santa Caterina Arête. From the Stockhornpass we might have been at its base within two hours, but we couldn't afford to get into trouble on a route of TD– standard. Reaching the summits was all that mattered now and, for the sake of a few extra kilometres in distance, we could place ourselves safely on the PD approach to the mountain from the Monte Rosa Hut.

Mike Walford came with us while Graham and Martin cleared camp and went back over the Stockhorn. Graham had to return to the valley, but Martin was to pick up a cache of food at Gornergrat, then cross the Gorner Glacier and climb up past the hut to our planned campsite at point 3303m beside the Monte Rosa Glacier. As these arrangements were proceeding, we received a radio call from Martin Welch who was himself on his way up to join us.

'Am on Gorner Glacier; need assistance with load,' was all he could gasp. We guessed that Joy and Carole had burdened Martin with another load of fresh food in addition to his camera gear, and could only hope that Martin Stone would catch him up.

The upper slopes of the Findel and Gorner Glaciers form the biggest glacier field in the Pennine Alps. Our route from the Strahlhorn made a 7km traverse across its widest expanse. The Stockhornpass forms an intermediate shoulder where the two ice flows are divided. Since no great summits lie in immediate proximity, these long slopes are rarely visited. Tramping towards the terminal buttress of the Nordend, we saw that same lonely beauty in the scenery that we had sensed on the Bernese glaciers.

Simon and I enjoyed a miniature piece of guiding as we looked after

Mike on the steeper ground rising from the Gorner to the Monte Rosa Glacier. With no clear guidebook description to follow in this little-visited corner, we had to apply all the elements of our working skills, selecting the route, adjusting rope lengths, getting an occasional belay and chopping a few steps on an icy section. However, Mike's sense of security was shaken a little when Simon led us across tongues of ice debris which had fallen from seracs on the Monte Rosa Glacier. Inevitably, even guides have to take calculated risks, but with someone as fit as Mike between us, we didn't have to linger in the danger zone a second longer than was necessary.

At the exact site of spot height 3303m we set up camp. Our promontory commanded an extensive view of the ice-planed declivities of the Zermatt alps. The ring of surrounding peaks remained partially clouded and a persistent breeze cautioned against any optimism for the coming weather. Nevertheless, this had been much the warmest and, save for the Täschhorn, the finest day in the last seven.

In late afternoon the two Martins arrived within half-an-hour of each other, each loaded with over 35kg of food and gear. While we all enjoyed the fresh melon, fish fingers and fresh vegetables which had been packed, there were murmurings of discontent from the load carriers. Martin Welch admitted that he had come close to hurling the melon into a crevasse on the Gorner Glacier. We had made it a rule that all food parcels would contain one day's worth of surplus rations in case we were storm-bound, but clearly that prudence was being taken too far.

Tomorrow we would have to streamline our operation. Our team was to climb the full length of the Grenz Glacier, cross the 4151m Lisjoch and set up camp at the Balmenhorn to meet us after our traverse of Monte Rosa. If the next day was fine, Simon and I would try to do the whole traverse from the Liskamm to the Breithorn and then drop down to meet our families below the Matterhorn at the Schwarzsee. Beyond the Liskamm we would have to rely on the two huts on the Italian side of the frontier ridge if anything went wrong.

Monte Rosa is the biggest 4000m massif in the Alps, far surpassing Mont Blanc in areal extent. Its eight tops protrude from the surrounding ice cap like arctic nunataks. The highest, the Dufourspitze, is a wholly rock summit, and the technical difficulty of the final scramble to its top keeps the crowds at bay. Normally, 30 or

40 climbers might set off from the Monte Rosa Hut towards the Dufourspitze on a fine night, compared to the 200 who daily toil up the Gouter Ridge of Mont Blanc. Were it not for the siting of the Margherita Hut on the summit of the neighbouring Signalkuppe, Monte Rosa would also rank as the wildest mountain in the Alps.

The traverse of the eight tops formed a substantial challenge whatever the weather. We woke with the alarm at midnight, charged with pent-up energy.

> *Martin puts in his contact lenses and peers outside. The sky is black, the air is warm and there are no stars. Still, we have breakfast and get dressed. As Martin prepares to go outside rain starts, drumming heavily on the tent. I groan with disbelief that the weather could be packing in yet again. Knowing it will be a foul, sleety night on the mountains, we go back to bed for a couple of hours. At 3am I am roused again. Martin says he can see a couple of stars in the sky, but by the time I look out they are gone. The sky remains heavily clouded. What can we do but continue this waiting game?*
>
> *'We'll stay put till dawn,' suggests Martin. Again I turn over, this time knowing there will be no more sleep.*

I drew the hood of my sleeping-bag tight around my head in a search for comfort and lay back, my eyes wide open and my thoughts racing. We were six days behind schedule and on the brink of a seventh. How could we climb out of this hole? The giants of Zermatt stretched across the western horizon on that inky night, all of them plastered with snow and out of condition. There were so many mountains yet to climb, perhaps too many for us to manage now.

As a grey twilight filtered into the tent I was startled to hear shouts outside. People were coming up from the Monte Rosa Hut. Perhaps the weather had improved. I went out for the third time. Yes, there was a clearance in progress. The skies were turning a cautious shade of blue as the clouds dispersed. There was still a chance to save the day. I shook Simon and he sat up looking pale and drawn.

'I don't think I've slept a wink all night,' he said. For the first time his spirit seemed to have deserted him.

'Come on,' I remonstrated, 'we can't throw this away after coming through so much already.'

I reckoned that a brew of tea would make all the difference to Simon, but no sooner had I laid his mug at his side than I knocked it over in my rush to get dressed. The ensuing silence marked a new low in morale. No amount of encouragement on my part could replace that cup of tea. Eventually, Simon emerged and at 6.45am we set off on the long plod up the Monte Rosa Glacier. Even if the weather held fair we were once again guaranteed a long day and a late finish, but any action was infinitely preferable to the torment of waiting.

I deliberately allowed Simon to take the lead for the first hour. I didn't want to appear to be overbearing, frantic though I was that we made some progress. I also knew that he was dogged and would respond to the challenge of trail-making. Sure enough, he took up the pace without a further word. There were five or six parties up ahead and a reasonable trail up to 4000m, but the way was long and the prospect of the coming days' effort weighed on my shoulders.

As so often on a hard trail I turned to music for comfort, humming as we climbed. On this morning the words of 'Bridge over Troubled Water' were much too close to the bone, so I changed to the Beatles and got half-way through the *Sergeant Pepper* album before it was my turn to go in front. When times got better I might manage a snatch of Bach or Beethoven, but simpler rhythms sufficed today.

Gradually, the twin tops of the Nordend (4609m) and the Dufourspitze (4634m) emerged from the distant horizon and grew into peaks of independent stature. At 4200m we traversed leftwards into the silent cirque between the summits. All the other parties were heading direct for the Dufourspitze, so now we had to make our own steps in deepening snow. Nordend's summit is an attractive rocky turret. Poised on the edge of Monte Rosa's huge East Face, it has an air of defiant isolation when viewed from the Dufourspitze. Few parties climb it, even though the summit can be combined with its higher neighbour with only a couple of hours' extra effort.

Seeing streamers of spindrift blowing off the top, we stopped at the *bergschrund* 100m below the summit ridge to put on overmittens and jackets. These alone proved insufficient to withstand the blast of wind which met us on the crest. A full-blown gale is relatively rare on the high tops of the Alps in summer, but this westerly was tearing over the summit at 60km per hour and hurling ice particles into our faces.

Knowing that we were going to be chilled progressively, yet no longer able to do anything about it, we tackled the final turret. Its rocks were caked in dry rime ice like a miniature Cerro Torre. I scrabbled up little grooves, then swung round out of the wind along a ledge hanging above the East Face. A couple of running belays materialised under the coating of ice to calm the tension of the last moves. Easing myself gently into a standing position on the tiny top I braced myself against the wind while Simon climbed up. A thrill of conquest shook me. We were back in business. Our 24th summit had succumbed after a two-day gap.

We reversed the route and followed the linking snow ridge down to the 4515m Silbersattel. The wind made it impossible to stop on the saddle, so we dived under the cornice on the Italian side in search of shelter. We put on our extra fleece jackets and overtrousers at the very point where Sylvain Saudan must have clipped up his bindings at the start of the first-ever ski descent of the 2400m East Face in 1969. Although boiling clouds prevented our seeing more than 100m down the initial gully, we could sense the exposure of the place. A vast expanse of snowfields, ice ribs and seracs drops over 2km in vertical height at an average angle of 45° down to the Belvedere Glacier and the valley of Macugnaga. Although unsurpassed in height and extent, it remains one of the least-known faces in the Alps. It goes without saying that its climbs are all serious undertakings.

The crest of the Dufourspitze was only 90m above us, but we could see nothing of the PD route that was indicated in our British guide-book. A 50° ice slope topped by steep unweathered rocks gave all the ambience of a TD north face. Wisely, we decided to take belays and considered that the two pitches would rank at the top end of grade III were they encountered on a Scottish winter ascent. The general denudation of snow in the Alps over the last century has stiffened the standard of many routes, and this can leave a slightly over-inflated impression of the abilities of the pioneers. On the first ascent of this short face in 1878 one has to imagine that a thick extra banking of snow reached almost all the way to the crest.

At the Grenzgipfel, the forepeak of the Dufourspitze, the wind quite suddenly died away to nothing. The clouds to the east were now able to drift up and over the summits and the day changed from one of bitter cold to dull warmth. Released from the grip of the gale we thoroughly enjoyed the final scramble to the summit. The snow was untouched, as no one had dared tackle the exposed steps on the West Ridge in the morning's winds.

Height isn't everything in mountaineering, but I took a distinct plea-sure to stand on the second highest of our seventy-five peaks. Nor are numbers everything, but from the Dufourspitze onwards we would also have the satisfaction of adding tops to our tally at hourly intervals until nightfall. First we reversed our route to the Grenzgipfel and then carefully descended a steep but broken buttress to the 4453m Grenzsattel. The ridge now swung elegantly up to the Zumsteinspitze (4563m). Here the day's technical difficulties ended, but the mist chose to clamp down and white-out conditions prevailed on the short passage of the Col Gnifetti to the Signalkuppe (4554m). Although the Signalkuppe is 9m lower than the Zumsteinspitze, it has a greater topographical independence. We had therefore classed it as one of the fifty separate 4000m mountains and had relegated its neighbour to the status of a subsidiary top. Being accessible by a long but simple glacier trek and possessing the dubious luxury of a hut on its summit, the Signalkuppe is also much the most popular top in the Monte Rosa range. Not surprisingly, we had plenty of old tracks to take us up to the looming black edifice of the Margherita Hut. Indeed, we passed a couple of ascending parties who would need no more than a thick wad of francs or lire in order to survive the coming night.

The hut is dedicated to Queen Margherita who celebrated the inauguration of the original building by climbing up from the Valle di Gressoney and spending the night in it on 18 August 1893. Its construction was undertaken by the Italian Alpine Club to provide an observatory as well as a refuge for climbers and involved three years of hard labour. Above the Linty Hut at 3100m all materials for the hut had to be carried up on foot. The present building is vastly enlarged from the original and was completed in 1980. It stands as a monument to modern technological endeavour, but equally as a reminder that we now have the power to defile the most hostile and beautiful places on the planet.

We followed a good trail running down over the Lisjoch to the Italian flank of the mountain and were loathe to leave it at 4300m in order to tackle our next summit, the Parrotspitze (4132m). Groping our way through the fog in search of its final slope, I thought with consternation of Martin Stone and his fellow competitors staggering round this plateau a fortnight ago dressed in thermal tights and running shoes. What on earth would have become of them all if weather like this had suddenly descended?

From leaving the trail to reaching the Parrotspitze took me 1300 hard-won paces. It was already 5pm and time to radio Joy with a progress report. It was wonderful to hear three happy voices sounding loud and clear from the sheltered depths of Täsch.

'I've just bought a jigsaw of the Matterhorn,' yelled Alex.

'Well, then you'll be seeing a lot more of it than we are up here,' I shouted back from our snowy perch.

Leading off the Parrotspitze towards the Ludwigshöhe I came upon a distinct break in the slope and was almost ready to jump down the edge when something told me that I should perhaps consult the map at this point. A brief discussion with Simon concluded that we had been veering too far south of our required bearing and were standing at the corniced lip of the South-East Face. To my relief he took a grip on the navigation from there onwards. Beyond the Ludwigshöhe lay the rocky horn of the Corno Nero (4321m). It looked big enough to warrant an ascent and we measured its height separation as exactly 35m on the altimeter. The Corno Nero was thus confirmed on our list.

One more top lay on the Monte Rosa itinerary, the 4215m Piramide Vincent, but our lack of sleep was now catching up with us. Knowing that our night's rest at the Balmenhorn lay only 500m away, we decided to leave it until the morning. We were surprised to drop out of the cloud beneath the Corno Nero. Just ahead rose the rocky eminence of the 4167m Balmenhorn which was topped by a massive statue of Christ, his arms outstretched and his eyes staring impassively over the wooded foothills of the Valsesia. Beneath the statue was a small bivouac hut and we could see the two Martins and Mike waiting at its doorway.

I felt a wave of relief and weariness. The continuous tension of the day had far outweighed its physical effort. The clean new hut was a surprise. We had no idea that the decrepit old shelter had been rebuilt, and a rising wind and sleety showers during the evening made us glad we were not camping.

We had only three companions. A young Italian sat in one corner. He was hoping to make a solo ascent of the North-East Face of the Liskamm by the Welzenbach route later that night. Behind his affable manner I could sense his fear and trepidation of his self-imposed task as he scanned a guidebook with furrowed brow. I thought of myself a decade ago when solo climbing meant everything to me and remembered the dark hours of doubt before the moment of commitment. Without the experience of a dozen solo climbs I should never have developed the resilience to handle this present challenge. Such ventures had also helped me to put the stresses and strains of everyday life into their proper perspective. I silently wished him luck and hoped he might know the joy of success soon after dawn tomorrow.

A young couple arrived later, probably weekenders from Milan or

Turin. Over-crowding down at the Gnifetti Hut had forced them to climb up to the Balmenhorn and they were clearly in no fit state to spend a night above 4000m. The girl in particular looked deathly white and soon after their dinner she rushed outside to be sick.

With only eight of us in residence the hut was crammed to capacity and the cooker generated a stifling heat that rose straight into the sleeping loft. At 11pm Simon went out to sleep in the porch and I moved my bed down to the kitchen floor. Just when we needed some proper rest it was denied us, and a one-day traverse from the Piramide Vincent to the Breithorn seemed no more than a fond hope.

'It's unbelievable,' said Simon, 'there must be 250 or 300 of them.' 'If they linked hands they could probably stretch all the way to the summit.'

"Thank goodness they're not going our way.'

We were sitting on the top of Il Naso (4272m), a subsidiary summit of the Liskamm, and were witnessing the living proof that Monte Rosa belongs every bit as much to Italy as it does to Switzerland. From the moment we had left the Balmenhorn at 4.20am a continuous stream of headtorches had appeared from the direction of the Gnifetti Hut and we were now in the ideal position to scan the whole route from the Gnifetti up to the Signalkuppe. There was barely a single 100m section of the trail clear of people. The sight was all the more a shock to us after so many days making our own path across deserted ranges. If this was weekend mountaineering Italian-style, it hardly looked much of an antidote to the strains of urban commuting.

The night had ended wild and windy, and we had made a bleary-eyed ascent of the Piramide Vincent with the dread of another vile day in store. As we commenced the Cresta Sella, the ridge which links Il Naso to the East and highest summit of the Liskamm, the gusts abated and the grim clouds which had been massing in the west retreated. The upper Lis Glacier was bathed in soft pink sunlight and the snow crest of our mountain began to sparkle and shine. Suddenly the morning seemed set fair. Perhaps our luck was finally changing. I thought of the frustration of the Italian lad back at the Balmenhorn. He had wisely kept to his bed through the stormy night and would now be waking too late to make use of the improved conditions.

The Cresta Sella gave 200m of interesting mixed climbing at PD+ standard before debouching on the frontier crest 200m east of the top.

We met our support team at the summit cross. Martin Welch was delighted to be afforded some decent conditions for filming after a week of cloud, while all three were enjoying their first ascent of a much-admired mountain. It was also my first visit to the 4527m summit. The Liskamm personifies all the finer qualities of the alpine mountains. Its height, elegance, remoteness and capricious conditions had all combined to make it my most coveted alpine peak for the past couple of years.

As I get older I have come to realise that it is worth possessing a few dreams that are never granted. Experience so rarely matches the purity of conception, but for better or worse the Liskamm was now deleted from my fantasies and entered into the diary. The real quality of the Liskamm experience is held in the traverse between its two summits, a corniced edge a kilometre in length. Martin Stone and Mike debated whether to do the traverse before returning to their loads on the Lisjoch, but concluded that with so much gear to get back to Zermatt they should bow to discretion.

For the first time in nine days Simon and I felt marvellously optimistic. The time was just 8am. The last vestiges of cloud were peeling off the summits, the air was fresh and we knew we had plenty of strength in reserve. Suddenly the Breithorn did not seem so very far away. We radioed base and with some conviction fixed a rendezvous with Carole and Joy at the Schwarzsee that evening. Then we thanked our friends for all their help and bade them a safe descent before turning to our task. Surely we could break that noose at last?

The guidebook suggested two hours for the traverse to the West Summit, but we romped across it in 40 minutes. In places the ridge was wonderfully airy and a couple of steps rising to the West top were undoubtedly delicate, but of the fearsome double cornices for which the mountain is renowned we saw none. The traverse might rank as *assez difficile* only on account of its exposure and commitment.

By 10.15am we had crossed the Felikjoch and stood on the summit of Castor (4228m). We wasted no time in dropping down its western slope to the Zwillingsjoch, then traversed to the base of the West-South-West Ridge of its celestial twin, the 4092m Pollux. If we could make the eastern end of the Breithorn traverse by 1pm, then we felt sure we could be across the mountain and down to the Schwarzsee by nightfall. That would give us the option of taking a complete day's rest with our families before tackling the Matterhorn.

We left our sacks for the climb of Pollux. Simon warned me that there was a sizable rock step on this ridge and we begrudged even the short delay it demanded. Clouds were now massing around some of the tops without looking particularly threatening, but the Breithorn was still clear. We strode across the Schwarztor pass and Simon led us up old tracks to the Breithorn's crest at the 4075m Roccia Nera. The existence of an old trail gave us further heart that the afternoon's work could be quickly effected and we were right on our planned time for commencing the traverse.

While the Breithorn has the general reputation for being the easiest '4000er' of all, it actually forms a complex ridge 2½km in length and sports a North Face of considerable calibre. Only the western end is entirely simple, and the highest western top is visited by hundreds of would-be climbers on fine days, thanks to the proximity of the Klein Matterhorn cable-car station at 3883m. Along the crest we had identified at least three tops with a 35m height separation, and so were committed to its full traverse, an expedition of AD standard with rock pitches of grade III.

As the eastern terminus of the Breithorn traverse, the Roccia Nera has traditionally been considered to be a '4000er' top, but it has no more than 15m elevation above the general level of the crest. The first obvious summit on the ridge was the 4106m East Twin. As we worked along beneath the corniced edge towards it a light cloud descended.

Martin takes over for the short climb to the East Twin. About half way up he turns and says he can hear a faint crackling sound. His ski pole is sticking upside-down out of the top of his rucksack and he asks me to remove it just in case there is some static in the air. Before I can reach him there is an almighty flash and hiss. Lightning has struck the summit just 10m above us. Instinctively, we jump down off the edge on to the south side of the ridge and find a rock spike where we can unload our metal gear which is already getting 'hot'.

As thunder echoes across the mountains, hailstones the size of frozen peas rain down on us, filling every crevice in our clothing and rucksacks. I hope that the storm will pass as quickly as it arrived and that we will then be able to progress. As we wait my body temperature drops quickly and Martin struggles into his overtrousers on the steep slope.

After half-an-hour the hail is still pelting down. I think of Carole and Joy waiting without news at Schwarzsee. We do not dare go back up to the ridge in order to call them at 2pm as planned and we can get no radio reception while stuck on the wrong side of the mountain. Reluctantly, we

take the only choice open to us, to head down the Italian flank and wait for
an improvement. The Val d'Ayas Hut is 600m down and will provide
comfort for the night.

So it has done it again! Our vulnerability to the whims of the weather is
all too clear. I feel a pang of guilt for involving Carole in such a protracted
adventure, yet at the same time a sense of pride in her dependability and
support.

For the first time in the summer I felt blindly angry at the cut of fate.
I kept stopping and looking back at the Breithorn before we dropped
too low hoping for a miraculous clearance, but the mountain remained
storm-bound. So just three hours from success and safety we were
rebuffed again. We tried repeatedly to make radio contact during the
descent. Once I heard Joy saying: 'Yes, we've got a nice campsite just
below the cable station,' but she must have been talking to our support
team and obviously wasn't hearing our message to abort the camp. The
summer seemed to be turning into a series of failed rendezvous as far
as our wives were concerned. No wonder Joy had got fed up with it.

Yet we were lucky not to have been struck by the lightning, for it
had seemed only a whisker away, and we were fortunate that escape
had been simple. The Val d'Ayas Hut was also conveniently placed so
that we did not have to lose too much height. It had opened just three
years earlier, and without it our only shelter would have been the tiny
Cesare e Giorgio bivouac hut under the Roccia Nera, no more than a
four-berth 'sardine can'.

As a heavier burst of rain swept across the Verra Glacier we stepped
inside to the warmest of welcomes from the local guide who runs the
hut. For once there was a genuine interest in what we were doing and
where we had been. The guardian waxed lyrical about the beauties of
the Breithorn traverse and promised to update us with the latest
weather forecast. Did we know the British guides, Mr Harper and Mr
Cliff, who had stayed there earlier in the year, he asked, and would we
take a glass of wine with him before dinner? What a change from the
impersonal atmosphere of so many alpine huts.

'You know, Simon,' I said, as we reflected on the day's events in the
warmth of the dining room, 'it's this Sunday business. Last Sunday we
were beaten back down to Täsch from the Dom Hut; this Sunday we
were nearly struck by lightning. Somebody up there is trying to tell
us something.'

With Blythswood being a Christian charity based in the strict Free

Church tradition of the West Highlands, our intention to climb on the Sabbath had caused some difficulty. I had satisfied Jackie Ross that, just like a sailor on an ocean voyage, we couldn't be expected to lay down our tools at midnight on Saturday, and our contribution to Blythswood's work in Eastern Europe outweighed any lingering scruples. On the other hand, perhaps it wasn't Jackie who had the ultimate say in the matter.

'God only knows what's going to happen to us next weekend,' I concluded.

The forecast for the next day was not good, a rapid cooling with snowfall down to 2000m, and however friendly the atmosphere I couldn't erase my thoughts of Joy and the children at the Schwarzsee. In seventeen years of marriage she had been put through this predicament many times. She had once waited three days in Grindelwald while I'd been stuck in a storm on the North Face of the Eiger, even going to the local police on several occasions to see if any accidents had been reported. Perhaps I should not have been so worried for her.

> After getting the camp at the Schwarzsee set up, I had a chance to relax for the first time on the trip. Up here in the mountains life becomes so simple. I was happy and the children were enjoying the adventure. I did not get over-concerned when Martin didn't come down, but Carole was less used to these situations and became quite perturbed. Three British climbers came past who had climbed the Matterhorn earlier that day and Carole commented:
>
> 'Well if they can climb the Matterhorn in this weather why aren't Simon and Martin back yet?'
>
> After five or ten years as a climber's wife she would learn that there are no simple answers to such questions.

Joy did her best to console Carole who remained despondent:

> I tried to shrug off my disappointment, but this time it wasn't working. I was lying in my tent with the wind and rain buffeting the sides thinking 'What the hell am I doing here?' I hadn't even thought to bring anything to read as I wasn't expecting to have to sit out thirty-six hours before seeing Simon.

We were shaken awake by the guardian's young assistant at 4.30am.

'The weather is a little better. I think you can go.'

We looked outside. The predicted snow had not arrived and although the sky remained largely clouded, there were a few clear patches.

Several cups of strong Italian coffee fortified our nerves for the climb back to the ridge. We weaved back up through the seracs of the upper Verra Glacier and stopped for extra clothing on arriving close under the East Twin at around 3950m.

Here Simon discovered that one of his Gore-tex overmitts was missing. After emptying his sack three or four times the glove was pronounced lost. True to his diligent nature he was carrying a spare, but it was almost as tattered as his woollen inners. He looked annoyed and depressed at the loss. I just hoped we could achieve some momentum once we were back on the ridge.

Thick cloud drifted across the summits and the air was sufficiently cold to deposit a good deal of its moisture as rime ice on the rocks. In these conditions the grade III pitches further along the ridge could become desperately difficult. Before we climbed into the cloud I spotted a gully filled with snow slanting across the southern buttress of the Breithorn's Central Summit. It would neatly avoid the three main rock pitches without more than 150m of height loss.

'That's the line for us,' I said to Simon.

'As long as we can find it if the cloudbase drops,' he cautioned.

We went round to the col between the East and West Twins where we could leave the sacks. I swung off the col along a sensational toe traverse high above the North Face. Whether or not this was the right route, I was soon committed to it.

'Watch me!' I called down, knowing that Simon was not attached to any belay anchor. Then, having placed a runner down to my left, I scraped the snow off the rocks above and made a series of delicate steps up to a wider terrace. One further pitch took us to the top. On the descent we found an easier line and confirmed the East Twin's height separation as 40m.

Easier mixed ground took us on to the 4139m West Twin. Slowly our fears of a repeat of yesterday's thunderstorm receded and as we traversed under the next col towards my snow gully a few shafts of sunlight played on the glacier below. The gully was the last barrier to freedom. Beyond it, simple snow-plodding would claim both the Central and West Summits. Although 50° in angle, the couloir was thickly banked with snow and within half-an-hour we were at its top. Up on the 4159m Central Summit we halved our last remaining choco-late bar and as we sat relaxing, the clouds at last parted to reveal a glorious corniced arête leading over to the highest top. I felt a surge of excitement. By a combination of fine judgement and occasional bloody-mindedness, we had won our passage. It was also a timely moment to remind ourselves that this was our thirty-eighth summit and therefore marked the passing of the half-way point of Alps 4000.

Our arrival on the 4164m West Summit coincided with our midday radio call and at last we made contact with Joy and Carole who were still waiting at the Schwarzsee.

'We'll be down at 2.30,' I called.

'Make that 2 o'clock,' added Simon.

Despite the descent of 1700m and 10km of walking that lay ahead, we felt unstoppable just at that moment.

Within an hour we had crossed the Breithorn plateau, passed behind the Klein Matterhorn and joined the ski-ing pistes on the Plateau Rosa. Thanks to the abnormally snowy weather, there were decent conditions for the couple of hundred skiers who were willing to brave the chilling mists and cutting breeze up at 3600m. Across the Theodulpass a pyramidal wreath of thicker cloud hid the Matterhorn and left no illusions about tomorrow's task of climbing its snowy Hörnli Ridge.

Piste-bashing is no fun when you are on foot and everyone else is sweeping past on skis, and I was fast tiring by the time we reached the lower snowline at the Trockener Steg. Here a dozen pistes, cableways and tow lifts converge at the main hub of Zermatt's ski-ing fields. Bare of snow, the place resembles a giant building-works surrounded by acres of bulldozed moraine. After seeing so much that is positive in the management of the Swiss environment, the desecration of the Trockener Steg brought me down to earth with a bump. Some years previously I'd vowed never again to go piste ski-ing precisely because of its environmental damage. Yet I guess I'll be persuaded otherwise when my children are a few years older.

Continuing down towards Furgg, the sight of beds of saxifrage poking through the flattened gravel gave me some comfort. Perhaps nature repairs the damage inflicted by humans faster than is imagined. From Furgg we had to climb 150m to the Schwarzsee. We could see Graham Walton waving on the ridge crest and he took us over to our camp which was idyllicly sited by the lower of the two tarns at 2530m.

Simon and I split off to enjoy a few hours of peace.

Carole and I share a drink at the nearby hotel and I treat myself to a wash, shave and change of clothes, all in the plush toilets of the cablecar station.

Lying by the tents on the grass of this high pasture, I feel confident that I can cope with any pressures that come to bear on me from now on.

Simon's only problem was a mosquito bite on his ankle, which he had picked up at the start of the trip. It was now quite badly infected and swollen, but considering all that we had survived during the last ten days it was a small burden to carry.

I found it hard to cram all the desired relaxation into the three hours before dinner. What mattered most was that the family was happy here and while that lasted there was no point raising the issue of Joy's pending departure in eight days' time. However, the Matterhorn hung above us like a suspended sentence, still swathed in threatening clouds. For a time it became very windy, suggesting the approach of another storm. As the hours passed the realisation dawned that we faced fully 2000m of climbing to get to its summit, and that sort of effort could never be wished away.

At 6pm Martin Welch arrived at camp. The Matterhorn was pivotal to his film work. It was essential that he joined us for the whole climb. The Matterhorn was one name that would definitely get our expedition featured on the news broadcasts. Martin's relaxed approach to life is one of his most appealing features, but tonight he looked more than a trifle dishevelled.

'I only just managed to catch the last cablecar,' he said. 'I didn't have time to get any food.'

As Simon passed some over to him, Martin opened his sack and swore loudly.

'Damn. I've forgotten my ice axe and crampons.'

With the Hörnli Ridge well plated with snow, his chances of reaching the upper mountain seemed to have vanished. At first I was annoyed and couldn't resist the temptation to tease him:

'I bet this never happens to Leo Dickinson on his film assignments.' Then I thought a little deeper, and a solution appeared. 'Look, why don't you go up to the Hörnli Hut. I'm sure you'll be able to borrow some there, and we'll meet you at 5.30 in the morning.'

He waited a while, perhaps checking that he had not forgotten anything else, and eventually he ambled off uphill. Knowing Martin well, I was confident he would pull himself together come the morning.

An hour later we were roused again by the sound of padding feet and heavy panting on the track outside, and to our amazement there stood

Martin Stone and Mike Walford clad only in shorts and running vests.

'We took the bikes to Stafelalp and thought we'd have a run up to see you,' said Martin, 'and we've got some good news. The Zermatt guides are promising five days of fine weather and this time they say they're not joking!'

7

THE ZERMATT GIANTS

Matterhorn – Dent Blanche – Weisshorn

As we walked sleepily through the fog towards the Hörnli Hut the Matterhorn was suddenly revealed. Bathed in ghostly moonlight, it towered impossibly above a rift in the night mists. I was filled at once with a mixture of reverence and fear, knowing now that we were standing at the foot of one of the world's greatest mountains. The cloak of mists then closed over its contours once more, but that moment of luminescent grandeur had provided the inspiration that I needed for the coming day.

The Matterhorn is all too easily maligned as a vertical slag-heap crawling with humanity. Detached and aloof from the surrounding mountains, the peak displays its wares with a candour that has invited crass and sensational publicity for the past 130 years. There are few secret corners on the Matterhorn, few places where the climber can discover what is denied to the tourist's telescope, and for that reason I had long resisted its brazen appeal.

Yet having at last climbed it in 1991 I realised that there is no summit to compare in the Alps. The Matterhorn could never be my favourite alpine peak, but none elicits greater admiration. I had been impressed by the difficulty of even its easiest route, the Hörnli Ridge. Simon likewise had a great respect for the ridge:

The Hörnli Ridge has been climbed by tens of thousands since its first ascent in 1865 and has been underestimated by a good proportion of that number. The mountain's magnetic attraction has drawn people from across the continents. The climbing on the Hörnli might be described as scrambling, but that gives no clue as to the enormity of the task. The exposure is continuous and route-finding is problematic for the first-timer. The crux is well above the 4000m mark and at that altitude can tax the

best of climbers. Finally, we must not forget the descent, which has to
follow the same line when tiredness has gained a hold.

At 5.20am we arrived at the Hörnli and Belvedere Huts at 3260m. Normally bustling with climbers or trekkers in high season, they were deserted and shuttered on this chill morning, save, that is, for the crouching silhouette of Martin. Being short of money, he had bivouacked outside and was now discovering a want of both stove and water. Nevertheless, he had secured the loan of axe and crampons from the hut guardienne and was keen to go.

At first light we set off, hauling ourselves up the first little step above the Belvedere and then making the first of several traverses across the East Face. The mist rose and fell about us, creating an ethereal atmosphere that lifted the undistinguished climbing of the lower ridge far out of the ordinary. Eventually, we climbed above the cloud to see the sun rise over the Mischabel. To our right the Dent Blanche looked like a tapered iceberg floating above the sea of vapour. The absence of any wind confirmed that at last a stable airmass had settled over the Alps.

We climbed unroped all the way up to the tiny Solvay Hut at 4000m, passing three Spanish lads who had left over an hour before us and were struggling to find the route. Apart from them there was nobody else on the mountain. Quite obviously the Zermatt guides had declared the Matterhorn to be out of condition and would not be taking clients to it, nor advising anyone to attempt the ascent, until a good deal of the snow had cleared.

Up to 3600m the ridge was clear of snow and thereafter footprints from the weekend's visitors gave us firm footing without our needing to resort to crampons. The correct route makes a series of flanking movements on the East Face before meeting steeper rocks 100m below the hut. Here the sun was already softening the snow and I felt insecure soloing up the grade II Moseley Slab to gain the hut platform.

'I'd get the rope out for Martin,' I shouted down to Simon. Martin had already stopped to put on his crampons and he was encumbered by the video camera which dangled from his neck. Although he is a highly able climber, there was no point in letting him take unnecessary risks and we decided to climb as a rope of three from there on.

Martin filmed us perched on the hut terrace with Monte Rosa and the Rimpfischhorn as a back-drop, while we commentated upon the trials of the past week and the challenge of the Matterhorn. I began to feel uneasy. The time was already 9am and the sun was burning down, turning the soft snows of the ridge into unstable slush. Even allowing for the snowy conditions and the delays for filming, we had been slow. I was surviving on just three hours' sleep and still felt the fatigue of the past three days in my leg muscles.

The normal guidebook time from the Hörnli Hut to the summit is 5 hours. Zermatt guides moving with a single unprotesting client might do it in $3^1/_2$, and certain 'supermen' among their number have been known to guide the climb twice in a single day. We were going to struggle to make the top in 6 hours and, applying the rule that the mountain takes as long to descend as it does to climb, we were in for a protracted day.

Not only did we have to get up and down the Matterhorn, but from the Schwarzsee we needed to cross over to our next base by the Schönbiel Hut, where Martin Stone and Mike were setting up a camp for us. Our original schedule had envisaged our traversing the Matterhorn and continuing direct to the Dent d'Hérens, but we were sticking to the rule of minimising risk and commitment until the conditions radically improved, and would gladly take the lower level route to the Schönbiel.

I took the lead as we moved together up the Upper Moseley Slab and on towards the Shoulder, a prominent easement of angle before the crux buttress. At difficult places there were ring pegs or iron 'pig's tails' cemented in the rock and these gave us running belays at most stages of the climb. Here, however, the snow was no longer tracked and the stanchions disappeared altogether under the snowfield below the Shoulder. We kicked our crampons through the slush into hard ice or slabby rock, all too aware that conditions on the mountain were becoming treacherous.

At the Shoulder the conditions changed dramatically. A bitterly cold breeze rushed over our ridge from the North Face to take the place of the sun-warmed air which was rising from the east flank. Until air temperatures around the mountain equalised much later in the day, that wind would persist and we were glad we had kept on our windproof jackets. Hawser-laid fixed ropes some 5cm in thickness adorned the final buttress. With Simon now taking the lead, we continued moving together, but each of us kept a sling and karabiner clipped from our harness to the fixed rope at all times. Even with the ropes, the climbing was gripping. Icy slabs of compact rock led up to a series of vertical steps, each smothered in snow.

Simon and Martin had no qualms about hauling hand over hand up the ropes on the hardest bits. By contrast, I preferred to climb free, partly out of respect for the pioneers of the nineteenth century who managed without them and partly out of distaste for such a disfigurement of the mountain. All the same, considering the numbers of people normally climbing the ridge there would be utter chaos and many more accidents if the fixed ropes were not in place.

With the tiled slabs of the North Face sweeping 1000m down to the Matterhorn Glacier, the final buttress is one of the most austere places I know in the mountains. Without the protection of the fixed ropes it would merit a Scottish winter grade of IV in these snowed-up conditions. When challenged as to the difficulty of the Hörnli Ridge, many climbers respond by saying that of course Whymper's party in 1865 didn't climb the buttress direct and moved well to the right on easier slabs. Looking across to those supposedly easy slabs, I failed to detect any obvious weakness. To tackle that line with no protection and such outrageous exposure seemed to me a frightful prospect.

Edward Whymper graphically described the type of terrain in his account of the first ascent:

> The work became difficult and required caution. In some places there was little to hold. The general slope of the mountain at this part was *less* than 40° and snow had accumulated in the interstices of the rock-face, leaving only occasional fragments projecting here and there. These were at times covered with a thin film of ice, produced from the melting and refreezing of the snow.

Yet he goes on to make light of their passage, concluding:

> It was a place which any fair mountaineer might pass in safety.

Sadly, one member of Whymper's party was not 'a fair mountaineer', the young and inexperienced Douglas Hadow. It was his slip on these slabs during the descent which precipitated the fatal fall of four of the party. Whenever I read Whymper's account, I detect a certain bravado in his style, a willingness to understate the difficulties of the ascent and a sense of intoxication at the conquest of the mountain which had bewitched him for five years. Even with fixed ropes and 130 years of hindsight, no mountaineer should misjudge the final slopes of the Matterhorn.

At the top of the buttress we gained steep snow slopes leading more easily to the summit, which barely protruded above a sea of boiling clouds. Over to the west beyond the cross at the Italian top we could see the summit domes of the Grand Combin and Mont Blanc, but otherwise we were completely isolated. There can be few fine days in the middle of July when one has sole propriety over the top of the Matterhorn.

Martin Welch looked parched and drawn. With his hair all tousled and his clothes scuffed and faded, he was truly the wild man of the hills. 'Could you spare a swig of water?' he asked after completing his summit film. Simon and I exchanged a smiling glance, but we couldn't refuse considering the tremendous effort that he had put in to climb the mountain.

We commenced the descent at midday, swinging down the fixed lines and moving without a halt all the way back to the Solvay Hut. Three is not the best number for rapidity of roped travel, but despite his lack of sustenance, Martin soon slotted into our pace. Simon and I had become increasingly confident of his aptitude for this sort of mixed terrain. The rising clouds were protecting the snow from further deterioration and our tracks of the morning were actually hardening as we descended, much enhancing our sense of security.

Just below the Shoulder we met two of the three Spanish boys whom we had passed at dawn. They were still ascending with great loose coils of rope hanging dangerously below their knees and to our amazement were still without crampons, despite the icy base under the snow. I wondered what to do or say. They seemed totally out of their depth and were far too late to reach the top and descend safely to the Hörnli Hut by nightfall.

One part of me said that we had a duty of care to climbers who were obviously inexperienced and should tell them to retreat. Yet this would risk giving offence and I equally realised that climbers value the freedom to make their own decisions in the mountains. Eventually, both Simon and I took the course of mild persuasion.

'You need crampons now!' I said, tapping my own cramponed boot.

'At least two hours to the top; the route gets more difficult,' warned Simon when they questioned the way ahead. They did not seem deterred, so we left them to continue and I admit that I was relieved when they were out of sight.

Their companion had stayed down at the Solvay Hut. A couple of other parties were just arriving with the deliberate intention of spending the night there. If discovered, they risked the wrath of the Zermatt guides and commune, since overnight use of the hut is explicitly prohibited save in cases of emergency or benightment.

Having safely negotiated the descent of the Moseley Slabs we unroped at 3700m. Simon and I were now pressed for time. We wanted to see our families before they left on the last cablecar back to Zermatt and then needed three hours for the walk to the Schönbiel. We therefore agreed with Martin that we would go on ahead. Leading down to the Hörnli Hut Simon set a tremendous pace which I could not match in total safety. Several times either a foot slipped or my body pirouetted perilously close to the limit of balance as I squirmed down the lower chimneys.

We were back at the hut within 40 minutes and at the Belvedere met three British lads with suspiciously short haircuts who displayed more than a passing interest in conditions on the mountain.

'That might be the Scots Guards,' I whispered to Simon as we passed them.

In our preoccupation with our own struggles we had almost completely forgotten about our potential rivals over the past week. Human competition is irrelevant when you're fighting the mountains tooth and nail. Now we suddenly wondered what they had been up to.

'Sitting in their Swiss Army base at Brig if they had any sense,' suggested Simon.

At 4.45pm we reached the Schwarzsee to an enthusiastic welcome from the children who ran up the hillside to greet us. Joy and Carole had a big meal cooked for us, and Martin Stone, Mike Walford and Graham Walton were all set to escort us to the Schönbiel. An hour later the five of us set off. In warm evening sunlight we stretched our tired legs down the paths across Stafelalp through fields of flowers and stands of gnarled pines.

Down at the Stafel Inn at 2139m three bikes had been secreted together with ration bags for our next four days. Martin and Mike loaded the bikes and handed us back our rucksacks which they had carried down from the Schwarzsee. We were then ordered to mount up and start pedalling in the direction of the Zmutt Glacier while they ran on ahead.

This operation had clearly been planned with minute precision. Martin and Mike were applying the logistical skills which they had

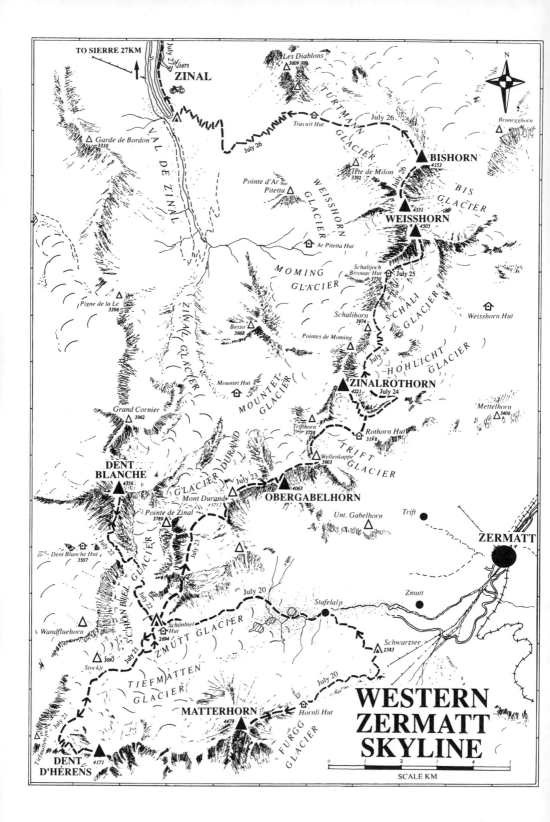

TO SIERRE 27KM

ZINAL
July 27 1675

Les Diablons
3609

Garde de Bordon
3310

TURTMANN GLACIER

Tracuit Hut
July 26

July 26

Tête de Milon
3392

BISHORN
4153

Brunegghorn

VAL DE ZINAL

Pointe d'Ar
Pitetta

WEISSHORN
GLACIER

July 26

4331

BIS GLACIER

WEISSHORN
4505

Ar Pitetta Hut

MOMING
GLACIER

Schalijoch
Bivouac Hut
3750 July 25

Schalihorn
3974

SCHALI GLACIER

Weisshorn Hut

Pigne de la Le
3396

Besso
3668

Pointes de Moming

July 24

HOHLICHT GLACIER

Mettelhorn
3406

ZINAL GLACIER

Mountet Hut

MOUNTET GLACIER

ZINALROTHORN
4221
July 24

Grand Cornier
3962

Trifthorn
3728

Rothorn Hut
3198

TRIFT GLACIER

DENT
BLANCHE
4356

GLACIER DURAND

Mont Durand
3712

July 23

Wellenkuppe
3903

July 23

4063

OBERGABELHORN

Unt. Gabelhorn

Trift

ZERMATT

Dent Blanche Hut
3507

Pointe de Zinal
3789

July 23

July 22

SCHÖNBIEL GLACIER

July 20

Stafelalp

Zmutt

Wandfluehorn

July 21

Schönbiel
Hut
2694

ZMUTT GLACIER

Schwarzsee
2583

Stockji
3091

July 21

TIEFMATTEN
GLACIER

July 21

Tiefmattenjoch

DENT
D'HÉRENS
4171

MATTERHORN
4478

Hornli Hut

FURGG GLACIER

July 20

WESTERN
ZERMATT
SKYLINE

SCALE KM

N

developed in mounting dozens of marathon fell-runs. They preferred
this rapid style of movement to the gruelling load-ferrying to which
they had been subjected on Monte Rosa. We had suggested that they
joined us on the Dent d'Hérens the next day, but they were loath to
carry their boots and personal gear up to the Schönbiel Hut. If it
couldn't be done in a pair of studded running shoes, then they were
quite happy to forsake the opportunity. In many ways fell-runners are
the soul-mates of lightweight alpinists.

Our little cycle ride weaved up through the moraines below the
glacier snout. The outflow of the Zmutt Glacier is diverted westwards
by an aqueduct through the mountains to help feed the Grande Dixence
hydro-electric scheme in the Val d'Hérens. The associated concrete
dams, reservoir and intake channels together with numerous old gravel
pits ruin the scenery hereabouts, yet the sight of the Matterhorn's
North Face more than compensates for any deficiencies in the immediate landscape. Some 600m above the valley floor the terminal serac
of the Matterhorn Glacier draws a cummerbund across the lower mountain. Soaring above this barrier the North Face appears elevated to the
realm of the unattainable.

Simon and Graham drew ahead of me on their bikes. By now my legs
were unable to respond to rotational propulsion. We all dismounted at
the final bend before the road climbed on to the lateral moraine which
bounds the north side of the Zmutt Glacier and which provides a simple
walk up to the Schönbiel Hut. Once again the loads were rearranged
and within minutes we were scrambling up a direct line to the moraine
crest.

I had never been to the Schönbiel Hut or its surrounding basin. The
Schönbiel forms the last staging point on the Chamonix to Zermatt
Haute Route. Ski parties tired by the long glacier traverses south of
Arolla enjoy a magnificent final downhill run from the 3568m Col de
Valpelline down the Stockji and Tiefmatten Glaciers and past the hut.
However, as a summer climbing area the Schönbiel is a backwater.
Although surrounded by four magnificent '4000ers', the Matterhorn
included, all of the routes from the hut are long and awkward, and very
few are climbed. Nevertheless, for us it formed an ideal central base
from which we hoped to pick off the Dent d'Hérens, the Dent Blanche
and the Ober Gabelhorn over the next three days.

The meadows of the Schönbiel also offered a haven of tranquillity
where we could recuperate before the big push north towards the

Weisshorn. Our decision to camp meant that we could make the most of the peace and comfort. We found a beautiful site nestled among huge boulders 500m past the hut. Martin, Mike and Graham helped us to set up the tent and departed at 8pm, hurrying down to reach Zermatt before nightfall.

We wouldn't be seeing Martin and Mike again. They would be off in three days' time to compete in a 50km mountain race at La Plagne in the French Vanoise massif. We were sad to see them go. From here onwards in the expedition we had no guarantee of regular support. Individual friends were coming out to join us for a while and Martin Welch would always do everything he could to help. However, we had no certainty that they could make effective teams in the sense that Ian, Sandra and Craig, Bruce and Roger, and Martin and Mike had formed dependable partnerships.

The Schönbiel support operation had borne us through what could have been an exhausting and protracted end to a hard day. We considered ourselves among fortune's favoured few as we settled into our camp. We were stocked with at least four days of food and sat at the heart of one of the grandest mountain cirques in the Alps. What more could the climber ask?

The 4171m Dent d'Hérens is one of the most remote and more difficult of the major '4000ers', yet it is unjustly diminished in esteem due to its proximity to the Matterhorn. Save for peak-collectors like us, few climbers place it high among their alpine priorities. Nevertheless, it has a fine North Face (TD) climbed by Willi Welzenbach in 1925 and a formidable East Ridge (D).

The East Ridge is a monster of a route, over 2km in length and containing a number of steps and towers consisting of what the guidebook terms 'bad to fair rock'. Ryan and the Lochmatter brothers made the first ascent in their remarkable campaign of 1906, during which they also claimed the Santa Caterina Arête of the Nordend, the South-West Face of the Täschhorn and the East Ridge of the Aiguille du Plan above Chamonix. Simon had guided the Dent d'Hérens East Ridge with David Litherland in 1991, and after a two-day epic on crumbling rock they had returned with a 'never again' look that deterred me from ever wanting to emulate the feat.

Simon and David had descended the easier Italian flank of the peak on that occasion, but after the first ascent of the East Ridge, Ryan and the Lochmatters had made the first descent of the West-North-West Face of the mountain and returned to Zermatt. This narrow and tapering snow and ice face is tucked away at the very head of the Tiefmatten Glacier. Although sometimes complicated by *bergschrunds* and ice walls, the face offered us the quickest route from the Schönbiel Hut. Yet the guidebook time for the ascent is fully six to seven hours. We knew we needed another early start if we were to get back by early afternoon, but equally we yearned for a proper eight-hour sleep.

Martin has set the alarm for 4am, but we hear nothing and sleep on till 6. Already my hope for a gentler day on the Dent d'Hérens seems dashed. We leave in a rush at 7am. The morning is cold and misty. To gain the north moraine of the Tiefmatten Glacier we have first to cross the Schönbiel Glacier. We struggle to find a direct line on to the moraine and end up climbing vertical ribs with the consistency of Weetabix breakfast cereal to gain the safe crest. I make a mental note to seek a lower line when we return.

The upper Tiefmatten Glacier allows quick travel up through a little icefall into a bowl where our face becomes visible for the first time. We see two pairs of ski poles left by a party already on the face. Our time to this point is only 15 minutes ahead of the guidebook. Considering the pace we've been going at I wonder how an average party could ever manage to be on time.

Launching up the face, I take the lead and push the pace to our limit. The undulating slope is broken by crevasses and the occasional serac, and the tracks left by the team ahead give us certainty of the best line. After just 40 minutes we have gained 600m. The slope eases off and we pass the other pair at rocky ground below the final ridge. They are father and son and they have set out from the Schönbiel Hut three hours before ourselves.

Thanking them for their tracks, we push on up treacherous slabs and gain the top at 11.10am, having taken nearly two hours off the guidebook estimate for the upper part of the route. Mist obscures the views and only occasionally do the clouds part to give us a fleeting glimpse of the Lac du Place Moulin down at the head of the Valpelline in Italy. We descend the face easily with the cloud holding the snow firm, avoid the loose moraine at the expense of dropping 100m lower to gain the glacier, and are back in camp at 2.30pm.

The climb had been exhilarating. It is the recompense of a cold and snowy summer that face routes can often be found in incredibly good condition and we had truly mastered the guidebook timings for the first time in weeks.

The Pennine Alps volumes written for The Alpine Club by Robin

Collomb in the 1970s are notorious for their undergrading and over-ambitious timing of routes. The guides are beautifully written and evoke the particular character of each and every route. Yet there are legions of British climbers who have cursed their very existence as they have endured epics on routes much harder and longer than they had been led to expect. Poor Collomb must have suffered the literary equivalent of murder a thousand times!

A guidebook writer faces a difficult task in distinguishing between what is a 'desirable' and what is a 'normal' time for a route. Collomb's guides err strongly to the former. His timings presume a fit, possibly guided, party climbing in good conditions, who can achieve adequate security without any sacrifice of speed. Unfortunately, they remain largely an aspiration for the majority of holiday mountaineers. A new guide of selected climbs in the Pennine Alps is soon to supersede Collomb's volumes. Doubtless, it will be more generous in its time allowances and more clinically concise in its coverage of the routes, but the flowing prose and historical flavour of Collomb's editions will inevitably be lost.

The prevailing anti-cyclone was proving to be a cool and moist affair, and we were kept inside the tent by light snowfall throughout the afternoon and evening. We stretched out, unwound our thoughts and indulged our appetites which had been suppressed during the fast climb. Our bodies seemed to be passing through a series of food cravings, each lasting only a few days. After the excesses of eggs in the Oberland, we had temporarily become a pair of salt 'junkies', but now we were pleading for lashings of fat in everything we ate. Carole had obliged by packing a kilogram of margarine in the Schönbiel supplies and we looked like getting through most of it during our three-night stay.

Each of the peaks ringing the west side of the Mattertal is a giant in its own right. There are no tops or easy connecting ridges here, such as we had enjoyed on Monte Rosa. Each mountain involves a full day's work, none more so than the Dent Blanche (4357m) which lies at the furthest reach of the Zermatt skyline. Certain mountains have such shapely form and poise that they are instinctively designated in the feminine gender. The Dent Blanche is unusual in combining massive size and isolation with its feminine wiles – Maupassant described it as a *'monstreuse coquette'*. Like the Matterhorn, the mountain is pyramidal in form, but its asymmetry of shape and a generous snow cover lend it an elegant beauty that I consider its rival to lack.

From the Schönbiel Hut at 2694m a climb of 1100m is required to gain the mountain's South Ridge (AD) which is the easiest route to the summit. This approach up the Schönbiel Glacier and through the Wandflue cliffs was once fashionable as a feasible means of climbing the mountain direct from Zermatt. However, with the building and recent enlargement of the Dent Blanche Hut at 3507m on the western flank, the Zermatt route to the South Ridge has fallen into disuse. Nearly all climbers now use the Dent Blanche Hut and approach the mountain from Ferpècle in the Val d'Hérens.

Finding the route through the Wandflue posed the first problem for Simon and me. We stood at 3050m at the edge of the Schönbiel Glacier on another damp and chill morning. Again, we had overslept our alarm by an hour and in our haste to leave had forgotten to bring the infamous guidebook. Our worries were compounded by the sight of a layer of fresh snow which covered the cliffs above. We scanned the maze of ramps and gullies on the Wandflue, trying vainly to remember the details of Collomb's route diagram.

A long diagonal snow ramp in the centre of the face was the crucial feature. This looked to give easy access to the snows of the Wandfluelucke at the base of the South Ridge. Two traverse lines gained the ramp. Simon thought we should take the higher, while I plumped for the lower. With dawn already an hour past, we didn't have the time to make mistakes. We only agreed to try the low line because less time would be wasted if I was proved wrong.

We traversed left across my terrace, then moved cautiously through a steep section of vegetated rocks to gain a safe rocky promontory directly beneath the ramp. I was relieved. Nothing is worse than leading your partner up a blind alley. The snow ramp was a godsend. In drier conditions the whole route would consist of loose unpleasant rocks. We put on crampons and within a hour were up above the Wandfluelucke at 3800m.

On gaining the South Ridge we had fully expected to meet tracks coming up from the Dent Blanche Hut, but nobody had ventured out. The ridge was beautifully decorated with soft drifts and fresh cornices from last night's snowfall. With the memory of the Täschhorn still fresh in our minds, we began to appreciate the implications for the route ahead.

The main obstacle on the South Ridge is the Grand Gendarme at 4098m, which is usually outflanked by a slabby couloir on its left. This is often icy and then forms the crux of the climb, but this morning it was thickly banked with snow. After a delicate initial traverse, we romped up the couloir and were soon back on the ridge behind the gendarme. Having apparently solved the key passage, I imagined that our worries were over. On my last visit here seven years ago the rest of the ridge had largely consisted of dry and friendly rocks. However, a series of frosted pinnacles now barred our way, looming impressively out of the mist. We moved together 15m apart, clearing snow off the rocks and placing running belay anchors as we climbed. When the leader's gear was all used, the second man would come through with all the anchors he had collected and take over in front. In this fashion we climbed over one tower, crossed a knife-edge and rounded a second pinnacle by a sensational rightward traverse on huge protruding spillikins of rock. Our rope and our gloves remained frozen despite the occasional burst of sunshine through the enveloping cloud.

Still more pinnacles appeared ahead.

'This is the hardest one; you've got to traverse left,' said Simon who had done the route only a year previously.

This is a notorious place. Three climbers fell to their deaths from the traverse in 1882. Its atmosphere was perfectly captured by Thomas Kennedy in his account of the mountain's first ascent in July 1862, which was undertaken in wintry conditions similar to those we were facing.

> The rocky towers above us were broken into wildly fantastic groups and suggested many an odd resemblance. But the weird and terrible predominated to our anxious eyes: it seemed as though a single thunderclap might have shaken the whole structure to ruin; and the furious wind threatened to bring some overhanging crag on to our defenceless heads.

Simon led the traverse, patiently cleaning snow out of the cracks and placing several runners. The commitment of climbers of the nineteenth century in tackling this kind of passage without any protection was quite remarkable. I led through back to the crest and rejoiced to see that the difficulties were over. An easy-angled snow arête led 60m up to the top and above was blue sky.

For the third day in a row the cloud ceiling lay precisely at 4300m and our arrival at the summit cross was every bit as exciting as that on the Matterhorn. For me, the thrill of breaking trail through virgin snow to a summit, whether it be a Scottish Munro or an Alpine giant, is quite without compare. The time was 12.15pm and we'd been going a little over six hours.

The descent went smoothly until Simon decided to avoid the 'spillikin' traverse by descending a steep rib of snow on the East Face. I was climbing last without any token of protection from the rope and suddenly became frightened as the rotten snow collapsed under my steps. There was simply nothing between us and a 900m plunge to the Schönbiel Glacier if I lost my balance.

'Can we get back to the rocks?' I shouted. 'Surely we're good enough at rock-climbing not to have to risk our necks on this stuff.'

Simon looked surprised. He had not been bothered by the snow and he tends to imagine that nothing that he can do will ever worry me.

Thereafter we kept exactly to our route of ascent and, although gradually tiring, we held a good pace all the way back to camp which we reached at 5.30pm. We reflected that although only graded AD, the South Ridge of the Dent Blanche could rarely be found in more difficult conditions than those we had encountered.

That night I felt more tired than usual and wondered how we could sustain this punishing routine for another three days. We now had to leave the camp, the remains of which would be collected by one of our support team. A traverse of the 4063m Ober Gabelhorn would take us to the Rothorn Hut, then we would make a quick ascent of the Zinalrothorn, traverse the Schalihom and cross the two finest ridges of the Weisshorn to complete our Zermatt circuit. All in three days? There were times when I felt dwarfed by the audacity of our schedule.

For once we rose with the alarm at 3.30am. Thanks to our dozy state, breakfast turned into a messy affair. Mopping up spilt peach juice from the floor with my spare underpants was one of the less savoury experiences of the summer so far. With the tent left in a presentable state for its later collection and a day's worth of food packed in our sacks, we eventually departed at 5am.

Our route to the Ober Gabelhorn first ascended to the Col Durand (3451m), which is the easiest crossing point between the Schönbiel and Mountet basins. After traversing the 3713m summit of Mont Durand, it dropped to the Arbenjoch at 3570m and climbed to the summit by the rocky West-South-West Ridge, which is known as the Arbengrat.

We were pleased to have a perfectly clear morning to tackle this complex approach. The cloud which had dogged us on the Dent Blanche had completely disappeared and the North Faces of both the Matterhorn and the Dent d'Hérens were emerging from their twilight silhouettes as we climbed the screes of the Kumme behind the hut. The trickles of the streams in the coomb were clasped by frost, the petals of the flowers were closed tight awaiting the sunlight and the loose screes tinkled eerily under our boots. The mountain world seemed suspended in silent anticipation of the coming day.

Irrespective of any considerations of safety, it is worth commencing an alpine climb before dawn just to share these sensations. At no time of day are the climber's own hopes and doubts more closely bound to the stirrings of nature.

From the head of the Kumme we crossed a shoulder and traversed loose rocks to gain the Hohwang Glacier. Mont Durand seemed clearly visible over to our right and I was immediately tempted to steer a direct course for the top rather than first going to the Col Durand. After my successful choice of route on the Wandflue, Simon was prepared to defer to my judgement, even though he had perceived the local geography rather differently.

> We curve off to the right well before the col, ploughing into deepening snow. I spy a gentle snow ramp heading out to the left ridge, but Martin takes us right up a steep slope and directly on to the skyline at an obvious top.

When we arrived on the ridge my heart sank to my boots together with a good deal of my pride. The 'obvious top' was only a subsidiary and the true Mont Durand lay over half a kilometre away across a sharp rocky ridge. Had I bothered to look at the map I might not have been so easily deceived by the topography. We had, in fact, climbed the 3672m Hohwanghorn. What a mistake to make on the clearest day for a fortnight!

> We try to follow the rock ridge, but soon meet a smooth sheer drop which must be abseiled. As we only have a single 40m rope we elect to retreat, return to the glacier and gain the summit by the left ramp. Martin seems annoyed by his mistake, but I am able to shrug it off. After all, it has only cost us 30 minutes and it's such a nice day for a change!

The error seemed unbearable at the time, but in the scheme of a fifty-day expedition it was a mere incident. I tried telling this to myself as we crossed the Arbenjoch and slowly calmed my anger. The Arbengrat is a route best saved for the latter part of the season when it becomes a rock climb. Today, it was heavily iced and the steep grade III tower high on the route looked less than inviting. As we worked our way carefully up the lower steps I noticed a line across snowfields on the face to our left which led to the easy final section of the Ober Gabelhorn's North-West Ridge. This would avoid the crux tower of the Arbengrat.

Dare I suggest yet another change of route after the last humiliation? Fortunately, Simon was thinking along exactly the same line, so below the tower we traversed out on to the face. With just one ice axe each and no protection, the success of the manoeuvre depended crucially on the quality of the snow. The angle varied from 50 to 55°. By staying in the centre of the slope, the snow was firm and dependable, although at one point we strayed on to a patch of water ice which fractured into dinner-plates at the blow of the axe.

Alps 4000 seemed at times to have turned into a series of calculated gambles, each of which drew on all our wit and experience. This time, however, the ploy worked perfectly and we were on top by 11.30am. Due to its slightly lower elevation, the Ober Gabelhorn gives an impressive view of the surrounding peaks, particularly the Matterhorn, which stands just 7km away across the Zmutt basin.

The summit possesses an enormous cornice which hangs over the South-East Face. As I edged out on to this meringue on my stomach in order to touch the highest point, I was unaware that the whole mass collapsed under Lord Francis Douglas at the conclusion of the mountain's second ascent in 1865. Fortunately, one of his guides, Josef Viannin, arrested the fall, but Douglas' luck ran out a week later when he was one of the four killed during the first ascent of the Matterhorn.

Our descent route via the North-East Ridge and the Wellenkuppe to the Rothorn Hut has become the normal way up the Ober Gabelhorn, although it was the last of its four ridges to be pioneered. Like the other arêtes, it is *assez difficile* in standard. On so grand a day we had expected tracks, but the reasons for their absence were soon obvious. The first section of the descent drops down a rocky ridge alongside the mountain's North Face. The rocks were so iced that after 50m of hesitant progress, we moved right on to the face and kicked steps downwards until we could traverse back to the ridge at its first saddle.

We then crossed the rocky spike of the Grand Gendarme which is usually the crux in ascent. On its far side fixed ropes allowed us to descend without resort to abseil, and we were soon over the Wellenkuppe and on easier ground, descending into the basin of the Trift Glacier. We reached the Rothorn Hut at 3.50pm, savoured a cool beer and then went indoors for a doze while awaiting the arrival of our next food supplies.

After our three days of isolation, we were now back within radio range of base at Täsch, and we learnt from Carole that David Litherland was bringing up the food. It was to David that Simon and I owed much of our prior experience on the 4000m peaks. In 1986 David approached me with the scheme of climbing all the 4000m peaks over a ten-year period. After an active climbing youth, his mountaineering had lapsed during long spells spent abroad working for Shell.

Once posted permanently back in Britain, his enthusiasm had returned with a vengeance. Being single, suitably affluent and long past the rashness of youth, the engagement of guides for three or four weeks each summer seemed the best means of pursuing his project. He was now two-thirds of his way through the list. Had we not been otherwise occupied this summer, he might have already passed the three-quarters mark. Instead, he was going to help us wherever he could over the next three weeks.

Although Simon and I never doubted our good fortune in being able to share and profit from his dream, we had each endured several epics in helping David to accomplish the harder of his list of routes. My eighteen hours on the Domgrat and Simon's two days on the Dent d'Hérens were the most notable examples. Yet without those and other ascents of the classic *grandes courses* of the Alps, we should never have gained the extensive experience necessary to make our present assault on the '4000ers'.

The walk up to the Rothorn Hut from Zermatt is a 1600m slog and David's laden figure did not appear on the final twists of the path until nigh on 7pm. He was carrying a good 20kg and was clearly unused to acting as a porter for his guides.

'What kept you?' we asked mischievously as he slumped on the hut terrace.

'I want a day's free guiding for this,' he retorted. 'You boys are going to pay for my services this summer.'

So the verbal banter began and it continued throughout dinner.

David's enthusiasm is infectious and he prised every possible detail from us regarding the routes we had so far climbed which remained outstanding on his list. Even though he was late and we were going to be late getting to bed, his presence raised our spirits.

For me, there was only one fly in his ointment. I asked how the family were doing.

'I think they might be leaving for home tomorrow,' he said. I knew that Joy was going to Chamonix to check on our climbing courses which were still running in my absence, but she had planned to come back to Zinal to see me before going home. I asked no more and just hoped that David was mistaken.

Despite the superb weather, the hut was barely a quarter full. We feared that we would have to break trail up the Zinalrothorn in the morning. Nobody seemed very keen to be first up the mountains after so snowy a period and the local guides were conspicuously absent. Eventually, we got talking to another British party and they reported a slow but successful ascent of the normal Gabel Notch route earlier that day. With our tracks laid we went to bed just a little happier at tomorrow's prospects.

The crossing of the Zinalrothorn had always seemed a crucial stage in our schedule. This was not due to any particular difficulties on the mountain itself. The Zinalrothorn is a magnificent rock peak, but because of the high altitude of the Rothorn Hut, the Gabel Notch route is not particularly long, nor is it especially difficult at its grade of AD–. Our problem, however, lay in getting from the summit across a string of intervening peaks to the 3750m Schalijoch, where a bivouac hut offered a night's rest before we tackled the Weisshorn.

The intervening peaks comprise the Pointes Sud (3963m) and Nord (3863m) de Morning and the 3974m Schalihorn. I remembered reading Lorétan's account of traversing the Zermatt skyline. He had come near to reaching the end of his tether on the Pointes de Morning: 'They seemed to go on for ever and were the most depressing part of the whole traverse.' Lorétan was the man who had climbed the North Face of Everest in forty hours, so I knew that he must have a fairly long tether. I therefore dismissed the direct route north from the Zinalrothorn, which would have taken a day in itself and would have left us in no condition for the Weisshorn.

Our chosen alternative was to retrace our steps from the Zinalrothorn almost back to the Rothorn Hut and then take a lower route over the Unter Aschjoch and across the Hohlicht Glacier to the Hohlichtpass. This avoided the Momings and left us with only the traverse of the Schalihorn to reach the Schalijoch. Nevertheless, the descent of the Schalihorn was reputedly loose and difficult, and even Collomb suggested that anything up to five hours might be needed for that one section alone.

We rose at 2am and left David to his slumbers. With growing confidence in the weather, we pared our loads to the minimum and carried just one night's worth of rations plus snacks for two days. We left our sacks at a height of 3450m. With the snow firmly frozen and good tracks to follow, we fairly raced up the Schneegrat, traversed under the Kanzelgrat and only stopped to put the rope on when we reached the Gabel Notch on the South-West Ridge. The climb above the Notch up the Biner Slab and over the Kanzel was short but exhilarating. Despite some ice on the rocks, we were not slowed as we had been on the Ober Gabelhorn and a golden sunrise saw us scrambling up to the summit cross.

We were back at our sacks within $4^1/_2$ hours of leaving the hut and soon after 8am crossed the Unter Aschjoch. The sun was already hot. We had to maintain our rate of progress in order to get over the Schalihom with any margin of time or safety. Traversing the Hohlicht Glacier and under the Zinalrothorn's East Face, Simon took over and put in a determined stint of pace-making which got us up to the Hohlichtpass while the snow-crust remained frozen. We radioed Carole from the pass.

'How is the weather?' we asked anxiously, hoping for an update on the forecast.

'It looks good from down here,' came the reply.

'Well, it looks pretty good from up here, too.'

Simon and I exchanged a wry smile as we imagined Carole commencing a morning's sunbathing down on the campsite. She was just 5km distant, but 2500m lower and effectively a world away.

'We should be over the Weisshorn and down to Zinal tomorrow, so you can move camp whenever you want. And can you tell me where Joy is?' I asked.

'She's coming back from Chamonix today and we're meeting at Zinal.'

The pleasure of knowing that she would be there gave me new impetus. Simon had his own incentive to keep going. Tomorrow, 25

July, was Carole's birthday and we both thought fondly of reunions down in Zinal as we continued. A week ago on Monte Rosa we had never imagined that we would be standing now at the threshold of completion of the Zermatt circle.

We reached the Schalihorn at 10.30am. Directly to the north the massive wedge of the Weisshorn seemed to fill the sky, confirming that our work was by no means over. The Schalijoch lay only 225m below us and we spotted the aluminium roof of its bivouac hut glinting in the sunlight. In the intervening kilometre lay one of the most contorted and shattered arêtes that we had encountered in the Alps. After an hour of dipping and ducking under and between loose pinnacles, we had advanced only 300m and lost just 20m in height.

The five-hour estimate for the descent no longer seemed excessive. Despite enjoying the intricacies of the route, we both felt an increasing lethargy. The torrid heat brought conditions more typical of late July in recent years. We were suffering equally from lack of sleep and dehydration. Although we tried our best to inject some pace, our movements seemed slowed as if controlled by a greater hand. I even started feeling light-headed and realised that my margin of energy was slim.

The ridge now dropped steeply, but further pinnacles forced us into two abseils and a series of rightward flanking manoeuvres on rotten snow. The descent finished with a fine crest of sound granitic rock, which would be a crowd-puller if relocated to the aiguilles of Chamonix. We finally stepped on to the snows of the col 4¹/₂ hours after leaving the Schalihorn.

If the Liskamm had been my most-wanted mountain before the expedition, then the Schalijoch was undoubtedly my most-wanted col. The approaches from either the Zinal or Täsch sides are serious *assez difficiles,* and the col sits at the base of the Weisshorn's most difficult ridge, the Schaligrat (D). With the added facility of a tiny bivouac hut there can be few finer places to spend a night anywhere in the Alps.

We gladly climbed into the cool interior of the hut and set about replenishing the litres of liquid which we had lost during the day. Glancing at the hut logbook, Simon noted that save for a helicopter visit by the hut guardian, we were the year's first guests. I lay flat on the bunks and only after two brews of sweet tea and a mug of soup did I rise from my stupor.

We kept the door open until sundown and occasionally heard avalanches of wet snow coming off the Weisshorn's East Face. Their passage sounded like the approach of trains in the London Underground, a sinister roar gathering in pitch and momentum. The Schaligrat looked steep, but given its south-facing aspect, much of the snow had cleared from its rocks. We anticipated its grade III and IV pitches with a degree of equanimity, and certainly no prospective climb, not even the Weisshorn, could have delayed our sleep that evening.

We got up at 3.45am and checked the conditions outside. The wind was rising ominously and clouds were spreading from the west. We only needed eight hours to get up the Schaligrat and down the Weisshorn's North Ridge. Perhaps we could beat the onset of any bad weather, so we ate breakfast and packed up. An hour later we stepped out of the door, cramponed, roped up and raring to go.

Immediately we sensed that a storm was imminent. Even to our east the stars had been extinguished by the advancing cloud and mist was already licking the towers of the Schaligrat. The fear of sudden lightning such as had nearly hit us on the Breithorn sent us straight back indoors. At 6am snowfall commenced and the wind blew close to gale force across the exposed col. Our day seemed lost before it had even begun.

We spent the two hours before our first scheduled radio contact lying fully dressed on our bunks, hoping that the storm would be short-lived. At 8am I went out on to the crest of the col, braced myself against the wind and switched on my set. My call was answered by Martin Welch down in Zinal.

'It's to be bad today and unsettled tomorrow,' he said.

Our fate was sealed. We faced a day marooned on the col without food. If the weather didn't improve by tomorrow, we had to consider the prospect of retreating to Zinal without doing the Weisshorn. Like our defeat on the Dom, it would add another three days to our schedule, and could destroy our morale. Then the realisation dawned.

'Of course, you know what day it is, Simon,' I said.

'You don't have to tell me,' he replied.

At least the Lord in his mercy had provided us with a safe and warm haven in which to pass his day. But save for bunks and blankets, the hut's facilities were spartan. Usually a bivouac hut has a good supply of spare food left by other parties: we found only one packet of dried potato and another of dried milk. The day's prospective menu would have looked more appropriate on a weight-watchers' diet plan.

We scoured the place for reading material, but there was nothing except the hut logbook. Because of the paucity of visitors to the Schalijoch, the log went back a decade and was still only half full. At 2 March 1986, I spotted the entry of André Georges and Erhard Lorétan. Georges had written: 'Tomorrow, the Weisshorn; it is windy and foggy, but we are very happy.' They were then just two days from the completion of their traverse. For the previous eighteen days they had kept exactly to the Mattertal watershed, relying on helicopter airdrops of supplies on seven of the cols and climbing several routes that Simon and I had been glad to avoid. The pair had also endured half-a-dozen open bivouacs. Georges had given his all to make the traverse of these his home mountains. This was his third attempt and during the second in 1984 his companion, Michel Siegenthaler, had been avalanched on the Adlerpass. I imagined his euphoria as he stood on the brink of success here at the Schalijoch.

Starved of entertainment, we soon went back to bed, wrapped ourselves in four or five blankets and dropped straight back to our dreams. Over the past ten days we had survived on an average of five hours of sleep a night. We both felt a severe deficit and on the Schalijoch there were no distractions to prevent its recovery.

We stirred at 4.30pm to hear the same wind buffeting the hut and to see the same dense mist and light snowfall through its tiny window. Two brews of tea, mashed potato and a little muesli mixed with the dried milk formed supper, and then we went out for the 6pm radio call.

'Happy birthday!' we shouted over the wind.

Carole's party was proceeding as best it could without Simon's presence. Then Martin came on.

'I'm afraid the weather news is not good. There's to be heavy snow fall overnight, and showers through tomorrow.'

We went back to bed realising that we would have to consider a descent into the Ar Pitetta basin and down to Zinal. By morning our fuel as well as our food would run out. We couldn't stay a second day here. I lay back, thought of the difficulties of the Schaligrat under fresh snow and racked my brains for a solution.

I remembered the Weisshorn's East Face, usually a mass of loose rock in midsummer but now thickly covered by snow. With colder conditions there would be no risk of the wet avalanches that we had heard yesterday and perhaps the fresh snow would have blown off it. If we could traverse down to the Schali Glacier then the face might give us a life-line to the summit. That possibility was my one crumb of comfort as I settled back to sleep.

When we woke at 3am I calculated that we had slept for twenty-two hours out of the past thirty, so we started the day well rested if underfed. Martin's dire forecast had not materialised. There was a sea of cloud below us and stars above. I thought back to the storm I'd endured with Dave MacDonald on the North Face of the Eiger in 1981. After two nights stuck on the Traverse of the Gods the weather had done exactly the same. The clouds had dropped below us to give an eight-hour window of clear weather. It had been just enough to see us to the top of the face before the next storm arrived. Now we had the same chance on the Weisshorn. I suggested the East Face route and Simon's lingering doubts as to the weather were soon dispelled.

After the day of inactivity we set out with a certain trepidation of touching the mountain again. Could we cope mentally? How weak were we due to lack of food? Some confidence returned as we worked our way down a ramp line towards the upper shelf of the Schali Glacier. We gained the shelf at 3630m and so faced a straight 900m pull to the Weisshorn's 4505m summit.

Dawn revealed the remnants of frontal cloud moving away to the south-east. A fine day was promised, but the cold was bitter and again Simon was suffering torment from cold hands. We waded through fresh snow to the biggest couloir which rose to join the final section of the East Ridge, which is the normal route to the summit from the Mattertal.

In trusting to the couloir we felt that we might be pioneering a new line, but unbeknown to us, our route had been climbed by Geoffrey Winthrop Young with Richard Mayor and the guide Josef Knubel in August 1906. Young had called the East Face 'the Shining Wall of the Weisshorn'. The appellation suggests that the face once held a far more extensive snow cover than has been normal in recent times. However, Young's label was entirely appropriate today, for the face was a single sweep of icy ribs and snow couloirs which glowed amber in the morning sunlight.

The couloir was angled at 50° and consisted of a fusion of wind-blown fresh snow with underlying ice to give a firm but slightly yielding climbing surface. There were no complexities or interruptions, just a long tiring slope of Scottish winter, grade II standard. We gained the

East Ridge at 4350m in an hour and reached the summit at exactly 9am, just 4¹/₂ hours after leaving the hut. This was an hour's saving on the guidebook time for the Schaligrat and, looking down on the corniced upper section of that ridge, I knew we had made a smart decision to avoid it.

With the trough of the Mattertal still filled with clouds, the Mischabel and Monte Rosa chains appeared detached from any earthly semblance. Fine though they looked, I was moved to share the opinion of Young regarding the Weisshorn's status.

> Though not the highest, in supremacy of form and of position the summit of the Weisshorn is the snow queen of the Alps and looks out royally on a concourse of lesser princes. The Matterhorn alone stands a little aloof, dissociating its severe and dissimilar supremacy from a homage which it may itself justly claim.

Leaving aside the rather special claim of Mont Blanc, the Weisshorn, the Dent Blanche and the Matterhorn are the finest of the '4000ers'. It was hard to believe that we'd climbed all three during the last seven days.

Our descent first dropped gently down to the Grand Gendarme at 4331m on the North Ridge. Of the three Grands Gendarmes we had encountered in the last four days, this was undoubtedly the biggest and counted as a separate top on our list. Beyond the Gendarme, the North Ridge continued as a spectacular arête of serpentine rock and curved round the head of the Bis Glacier to gain easy ground at the 4153m Bishorn, which formed the final 4000m summit on our Zermatt round. Graded at AD+, the North Ridge is a magnificent but serious route and lies well above 4000m in altitude throughout its 2km length. We were glad we had some time in hand for its descent.

The initial section of the ridge held only one surprise. As we crossed a snowy gap we were hit by an incredible wind which rose from nowhere and blasted ice needles straight into our faces. Clinging to our axes and twisting our heads sideways, we edged over to sheltered ground. Fortunately, these conditions were not repeated anywhere else on the descent.

We barely paused before climbing the Grand Gendarme. Its snowy ramparts looked so simple that we continued to move together without belays. We might have been wiser had we seen pictures of the Gendarme in normal summer conditions. About 20m from the top my crampons started hitting rock. As usual I scrabbled my feet about searching for a ledge, but there was nothing. With my upper body relying solely on the downward pressure of my palms on the soft snow, I realised that I was no longer attached to the mountain.

'This isn't funny,' I warned Simon. He took off some of his rope coils and gave me what at best amounted to a moral belay.

Stretching up I lodged my axe in a crack at arm's length. Then, using the technique beloved of Scottish winter climbers, I torqued on the axe and skipped my feet up to bring my body into an arched position. For a few seconds only that twisted axe held me from making closer acquaintance with the 600m face below. With my other hand I reached up to grasp a wobbly block, which allowed me to extract the axe and mantle-shelf into a standing position on the stone. Above here the snowpack was thicker and the last few metres were easy.

We had been warned. Under snowy conditions the rock ridges of the Pennine Alps become decidedly desperate. Their metamorphic strata are usually gently dipped to give easy-angled but slabby ground. Presenting no particular difficulties when dry and warm, they become close to impossible if iced or masked by soft snow. Now knowing what to expect on the remainder of the ridge, we immediately started taking running belays.

Between ourselves and the easy snows of the Bishorn lay 700m of terrain which most resembled a crocodile's spine. Throughout the next hour we felt that one lash of the monster's tail would surely throw us off. After the experiences on the Lauteraargrat and the Täschhorn, I had thought myself immune to vertigo, but at times I felt giddy looking over the abyss down to the Weisshorn Glacier on our left.

We had saved a few snacks from the Schalijoch, but these were now finished and we were starting to feel the lack of food, both in our ability to concentrate and our energy output.

Descending from the Gendarme I become aware that my muscles are acquiring energy from a different source. My legs ache but are not stiff. Having missed the usual high-calorie meal last night the energy is probably coming from the muscles themselves.

This section is similar to descending the roof of a house with several loose tiles after a wet night! At least the route-finding is not a problem. There is only one way to go on a knife-edge.

Martin goes first and I back up from behind. Belays appear every 10 or 15m, allowing a degree of safety, and where there are none we can usually stay on opposite sides of the ridge. If one slips the other can jump off the other side.

However, mutual trust was our main protection on the arête. I never imagined that Simon would slip, so could apply all my concentration to my own technique. We abseiled a vertical step of grade III in ascent, then continued weaving and edging towards a flat-topped tower. The tower rose in three steep pitches which faced south and were clear of snow. The rock strata were also favourably inclined so that the holds dipped inwards rather than out as they had on the rest of the descent. After the insecurity of the snowy arête, I was so keen to get to grips with those warm dry rocks that I promptly thrust my bare hand into a jamming crack and smashed my watch face.

After the tower there was a sudden transition to easy slopes as we swopped the precipitous Ar Pitetta basin for the gentle Turtmann Glacier on our left. The trial was over. Thank goodness for the few easy '4000ers' like the Bishorn. At 1.30pm we slumped down on its flat top and lay there motionless for five minutes. Behind us the view across the North-East Face of the Weisshorn to the Grand Gendarme was a vision of icy splendour. The Bishorn may be a simple trekking peak, but it is one of the finest grandstands in the mountain world. What a finale!

'I never thought I could so appreciate a piece of level ground,' I said to Simon.

'It's hard to believe we've cracked it.'

After thirty-five summits and eighteen days we had closed the chapter on the Zermatt skyline. Our thoughts jumped an hour forwards to beer, coffee and omelettes at the Tracuit Hut, then down to the forested depths of Zinal and finally over to the distant dome of Mont Blanc. Our way there was clear at last and for the first time we actually dared to think of a finish.

8
FAREWELL TO SWITZERLAND

Zinal to Val d'Entremont – Grand Combin – Val Ferret

Dinner was over and we were sitting in a circle on the campsite at Zinal.

'I can hardly believe that it's taken you five days to send off that Matterhorn film,' I said despairingly.

Martin Welch was seated in penitent pose, realising that we were just a little annoyed.

'Well, yesterday was Sunday and we just missed closing time at the post office on Saturday,' he explained.

'So what about Friday, Thursday and Wednesday?'

'I couldn't do anything until more money came through.'

I fumed with frustration.

'Then surely you could have borrowed some. There's not much point taking the film unless it gets sent straight off. Simon and I have pulled out all the stops to get here. It's pretty depressing to find that absolutely nothing has happened on the publicity front. Unless Blythswood get regular film, they'll never make a story out of this.'

'Perhaps we shouldn't be talking about this in front of everyone,' suggested Carole.

'Well, I don't think anyone should have anything to hide,' I answered. 'We've all got to get together and make a plan for the next two weeks. If we don't do it now we never will.'

The day's triumph had vanished. Valley life was something of a mess and with Simon keeping a diplomatic silence I felt that I had to speak out. With no current job, Martin was dependent on retainers from Blythswood to cover his expenses. Having spent his last pennies on the Matterhorn, he had been forced to wait until his wife Heather brought out another cheque from the charity before he could post the film.

So far only £3,500 had been pledged to Blythswood in sponsorship, which wasn't even enough to cover their expenses in publicising the expedition. Our Press Officer, Bill Shannon, was a genial chap with a genuine desire to help Blythswood's work. His favourite catch-phrase whenever we called him was 'Well, I think it's all coming together now lads.' Ever the optimist, he had even used it after nobody turned up at our pre-expedition press conference. However, when I'd called him earlier in the evening, the phrase was absent and his enthusiasm for our project was audibly waning. He needed material fast or our appeal would lose all momentum.

I looked at the faces gathered outside our camp: Martin and Heather, David Litherland, Angus Andrew and Bob Neish. Tousle-haired, fresh-faced and disarmingly open, Angus was a candidate to enter the British Mountain Guides training scheme. He had travelled out to the Alps with David, hoping to get some routes done to complete the experience he needed to join the scheme. Bob was an old friend of Simon's. As a former racing cyclist and with a mountaineering pedigree that included a ski crossing of Greenland's ice cap, Bob was just the sort of fit and dependable chap we needed; sadly he only had a week to spare.

This assortment of disparate talent could surely be combined into an effective squad. The most pressing need was to find a suitable partner to help and protect Martin during his film work on the Mont Blanc massif. Angus was the obvious choice, especially as he himself possessed considerable photographic ability. David would back up with load carries, car transport, weather reports and financial assistance should Martin again go short of cash. Bob thought he'd be able to help with our first resupply of food in the Mont Blanc range before he had to return home.

There was a little relief for me when these matters were resolved and I turned to my domestic situation. It no longer seemed certain that Joy would be going home. Graham had been forced to travel home early and Joy needed a couple of extra days to sort out problems with the running of our courses in Chamonix. With an end in sight and so much hingeing on the organisation of base camp, surely she would now change her mind and stay to the finish.

Over the last fortnight I'd hardly stopped, what with one trip to Chamonix, another to Geneva, four different support teams to organise, plus the constant demands of Alex and Hazel. However, I much preferred being busy to sitting without a purpose as I'd done in Grindelwald. For the first time I'd felt an essential part of the set-up and began to consider how things could go wrong if I suddenly disappeared. Martin had put in an enormous effort to organise this expedition. Why should the final outcome be left to other parties?

Maybe it was pride or lingering doubt, but Joy was not yet ready to convert her thoughts into action. I went to bed that night feeling upset by the confrontation with Martin and with future plans still beset by doubts and complexities. Not surprisingly, I could hardly sleep. Life seemed so much simpler on the mountains and I longed for the morning when I could get my head down on the bike and cast all these cares aside.

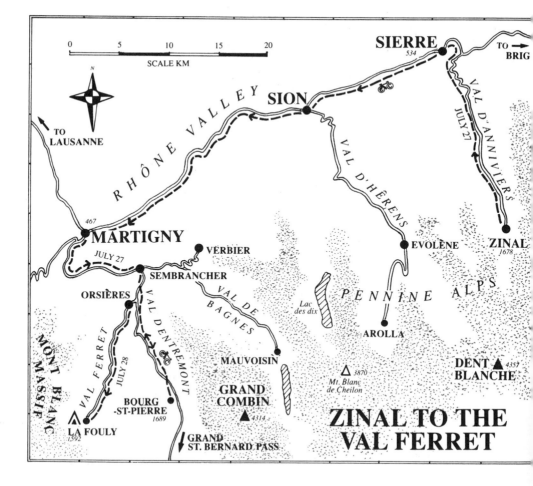

The day spent storm-bound on the Schalijoch meant we had only just maintained our schedule since the Matterhorn and still lagged six days behind our minimum target of forty-eight days. By eliminating a planned rest-day in Zinal and compressing the next three days into two, we could reduce the deficit to four days at the start of the crucial Mont Blanc section. With the weather now forecast to be hot as well as settled, we were keen to make up some lost ground.

Our final Swiss mountain was the 4314m Grand Combin, a mighty mass of ice and crumbling rock which forms the bridge between the Pennine Alps and the Mont Blanc range. To reach the Combin from Zinal, we faced a cycle ride of 103km down the Rhône Valley and up the Val d'Entremont to Bourg-St Pierre. If we had any energy left, we would walk up to the Valsorey Hut that evening and climb the mountain the following morning.

For the first time in the trip we had felt twinges of pain in our knees during the 2600m descent from the Bishorn. We were therefore glad to get back to biking. A walk to the Combin would have followed the line of the Haute Route over three high passes and taken two full days, whereas setting off by road on 27 July at 11am we knew that we would be in Bourg-St Pierre for an early tea.

> *Coasting down the road from Zinal just ahead of Martin I feel that a huge burden has been lifted from us. We have survived the worst conditions that the Pennine Alps could possibly throw at us and are now escaping. The cycling is a joy as it allows us to cover large distances with certainty. We arrive at the switch-backs which drop steeply down to the Rhône Valley and feel cheeky enough to overtake the local post-bus on the steep incline. Ten seconds later at the next hairpin my bike skids sideways without warning and I find myself dumped rudely on the tarmac.*

Following 50m behind I watched his spill with horror. Was this the end of the trip for Simon? No; he jumped straight up and pulled his bike out of the path of the bus. After a quick examination of both himself and his machine he remounted, claiming vigorously that a patch of wet tar had caused his fall rather than any misjudgement of speed. Nonetheless, he was not tempted to overtake the bus again and we reached the valley floor in the wake of its exhaust.

Within an hour our descent had taken us from the pines and pastures of the Val d'Anniviers down to the vineyards and baking Mediterranean heat of the Rhône Valley. On a hot summer's day it is a major trial just to drive down this heat-bowl. With air temperatures hovering at 30°C and strong up-valley breezes, the cyclist faces a particularly arduous task. We passed through Sierre, the first French-speaking town as one moves west from Brig down the valley and the starting point for the annual race up to Zinal, the most famous of all the mountain running events on the Continent. About 15km ahead lay the castellated walls of Sion. For Simon, Sion was not just a centre of culture and history but a city of gastronomic excellence. It had a McDonald's!

Cravings are a part of alpine climbing. Just at the remotest part of your climb you feel a pang for bangers and mash, a long cool drink or any of a hundred other unobtainable treats. Unfortunately, the reality rarely lives up to the image you held when climbing. Your stomach cramps half-way through the first ice-cream, or that first beer gasses up inside and leaves you feeling mildly sick. High on the Weisshorn I had been haunted by the thought of a chocolate 'thick shake', obtainable only at McDonald's. The craving has lingered and only gets worse as we approach Sion. Jumping off my bike I join the queue, hoping that this time the treat will match my expectations.

Beyond Sion there were no more treats, just 29km of level running into a strengthening headwind. We tucked in close to one another, taking turns to shield the wind all the way to Martigny, another fine town of spacious boulevards and classical architecture. Martigny was the lowest point of the entire projected journey, at just 467m above sea level. The significance of that fact lay largely in the realisation that we were 3847m lower than the Grand Combin, or 12,621ft to quote the more impressive Imperial scale. I was just reaching that stage of fatigue where such a statistic is decidedly unwelcome.

The cycle ascent of the Val d'Entremont would gain the first 1220m of the huge climb. This route from Martigny to Bourg-St Pierre and over the 2469m Grand St Bernard Pass to Aosta is Roman in origin. It was established in AD47 by the Emperor Claudius as the Romans tried to gain control of the alpine regions. Since then the Grand St Bernard has become the most famous of all the alpine passes due to its height, strategic importance and the history of its hospice and monastery.

Although the final section of the pass is now tunnelled, the Grand St Bernard has lost much of its traffic to the nearby Mont Blanc Tunnel and it provided us with a relatively quiet ride of considerable scenic charm. The valley first twisted eastwards in a deep wooded defile and then turned to the south at Sembrancher. Here the Val de Bagnes branches off leftwards to Verbier and the Mauvoisin barrage. Having wriggled through huge planed cliffs of smooth shale, the main valley opens and you look directly ahead up the Val Ferret which defines the eastern edge of the Mont Blanc range. This looks to be the line of the pass until the sleepy town of Orsières, where the route makes a surprising left turn away from the Val Ferret and the serious climbing up the Val d'Entremont begins.

On the first long upward curve of the road above Orsières, my legs began to tie up and I quickly lost power. Simon suddenly found himself well out in front.

> *While I find an easy rhythm, Martin has dropped back 500m. I think little of it and imagine that he will probably be snapping at my heels at the next bend, but to my surprise he drops back further. After another 2km I realise that something is up. Perhaps the heat is the problem, so I wait to help him up the final section. Joy passes in the motor caravan and stops to douse him with buckets of water and we ride on towards Bourg-St Pierre at a slow but steady pace.*

After the water a series of shaded avalanche shelters and a slight tail-breeze gave me a small reprieve, but I was relieved we didn't have to ride all the way up the Grand St Bernard. If we had, I might have faded completely, and as it was I arrived at Bourg feeling nauseous and dehydrated. I had plenty of possible excuses for blowing up – the oppressive heat, my lack of sleep or even that 'thick shake' at Sion. In truth, I'd found the sustained pace in the lower valley just beyond comfort and had nothing more to give when the steeper stuff began. Simon must have felt a little relieved that I had finally shown my fallibility and I was secretly pleased that he had gained some measure of recompense for his own torment on the Furkapass.

Once reassured that I'd be fine in an hour or so, he went off up the track to Cordonna at the start of the Valsorey Hut walk, leaving me with the family at the main road. Ideally, I should have gone to bed with a wet towel wrapped round my head, but as soon as I climbed into the van a polite but imploring little voice said:

'Dad, I want to tell you something. We still haven't done the Matterhorn jigsaw and Mummy said you'd be good at it.'

There was no point in protesting. I was cornered and spent the next hour piecing together the intricacies of the Zmutt Nose and Hörnli Ridge, while Hazel did her best to throw all the loose pieces on the floor.

At 6.30pm I re-emerged feeling bloated, vaguely dizzy and not entirely sure of my ability to walk 8km and climb 1350m up to the

Valsorey Hut. I wheeled my bike up the first steep incline of the side road to Cordonna, which itself seemed an admission of defeat. At the road-end Simon was waiting together with Angus, Bob and Martin. We left the bikes with Carole and Heather and set off with $2^1/_2$ hours of daylight in which to complete a hut walk for which 4 hours is prescribed in the guidebook.

The heat of the day had gone and the evening sun was at our backs, casting a rich light on the valley ahead. Despite a 15kg sack containing boots and all clothing for tomorrow, I soon found a sprightly pace. My climbing muscles were working. This was my first visit to the Valsorey. The tantalising views ahead to the northern slopes of Mont Vélan gave me an infusion of new spirit and my difficulties on the bike were forgotten.

The walk developed into one of the finest I've ever done. I could make a list of great hut walks with the same enthusiasm as that of my favourite peaks. Certain factors are common to them all. Length, solitude, changing terrain and atmosphere do count highly, but for some reason a considerable fatigue is the prerequisite to my deepest appreciation of such treks. Beauty, it seems, produces its most stunning response in a tired body. It is this which drives me to pursue the extremes in mountaineering, not some desperate masochism, as some might suspect.

Our path weaved up past waterfalls to the deserted chalets of Amont, climbed steeply through verdant grasses and traversed into the stony coomb of the Grands Plans. Here we saw the brooding hulk of the Combin for the first time. I stopped to photograph Angus who sat barechested on a boulder soaking up the last rays of sunlight. To the west over Mont Blanc the crimson glow of the sunset was traversed by slate-grey lenticulars of clouds throwing darker shadows across the glaciers of the Vélan behind us. Judging by the lack of conversation, I think we were all affected in some way by the scene.

We pulled on some clothes and clambered up the boulder fields into the shade. The temperature had dropped some 10° before we reached the hut at 9.30pm. The Valsorey is a small, traditionally styled hut with wood-panelled corridors, narrow stairways and a convivial dining-room which was warmed by a wood-burning stove. The guardian offered us a correspondingly warm welcome. Although the Haute Route passes through here on its way to Zermatt, the hut seemed to have resisted the allure of modernisation.

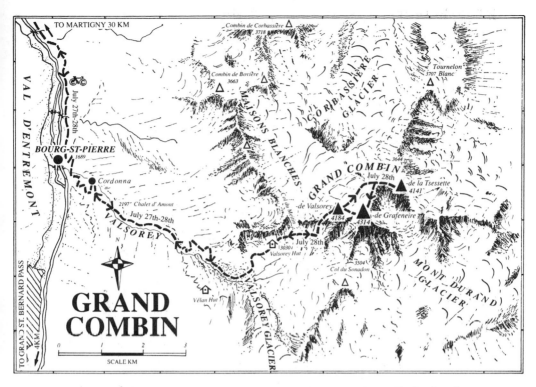

Map labels:
TO MARTIGNY 30 KM
Combin de Corbassière △ 3718
VAL D'ENTREMONT
July 27th-28th
BOURG-ST-PIERRE 1689
Combin de Bovière 3663 △ △
Cordonna
2197 Chalet d' Amont
July 27th-28th
MAISONS BLANCHES
CORBASSIÈRE GLACIER
Tournelon 3707 Blanc △
3644
GRAND COMBIN
July 28th
-de la Tsessette 4141
-de Valsorey 4184 △ △ 4314 -de Grafeneire
VALSOREY
N
GRAND COMBIN
3030 Valsorey Hut
July 28th
Col du Sonadon 3504 △
MONT DURAND GLACIER
Vélan Hut
VALSOREY GLACIER
TO GRAND ST. BERNARD PASS
4 KM
0 1 2 3
SCALE KM

We took some supper after which I headed straight to bed. My sleep was disturbed by a vivid dream that I was climbing the Combin without boots or ice axe. I sat bolt upright in my bunk as I began to slide down the ice slopes. Only the fact that I woke up at that very moment saved my slumbering colleagues from a blood-curdling scream. My heart was pumping furiously and I was bathed in sweat. The nightmare was a sure sign that the day had been altogether too stressful.

We left the hut at 5.15am. The temperature had risen considerably since our arrival the previous evening and thick grey clouds were streaming off the Combin de Valsorey, indicating storm-force winds high up. For the first morning in nearly a month the snowpack was completely unfrozen. Our route first made a long rising traverse of the Meitin Glacier to reach the Plateau du Couloir at 3664m. For spring skiers this is perhaps the crux of the Haute Route due to its steepness and susceptibility to avalanche. As we weaved across loose rock ribs, stonefall was our major concern, and we were glad to be ahead of four or five other parties, including our support team.

Half-way up I heard a yell from below. Turning, I saw a giant 4m boulder which we had passed but a minute ago sliding straight down rock slabs towards the others. There was frantic movement among the people below. The stone crashed into a snow runnel and tumbled out of sight in a rushing avalanche of wet snow. Silence returned. After half a minute of frozen shock, the following parties proceeded towards us. Only then was I sure that no one had been carried away. With acres of similarly shattered rock tilted above us, the place was a potential death-trap. We hurried on, not stopping until we gained the safety of the plateau.

Here we felt the first gusts of the wind and dressed for battle. The Combin de Valsorey's West Face (PD) is usually a mass of rubble after midsummer, and most parties then follow the slightly harder but safer West Ridge. This year it was a continuous snowfield at 45° maximum angle. We romped up the rotten snow and poked our heads over the summit lip at 8.20am. We had expected to be met by a withering blast of wind, but remarkably the gale had died.

From the 4184m Valsorey top we traversed under the Combin de Grafeneire and out to the eastern summit, the Combin de Tsessette (4141m). En route we passed a couple of teams who had climbed the North-West Face of the mountain from the Pannossière Hut. A great sea of clouds billowed in the west, leaving only the south-eastern quadrant of the view clear, out over the Valpelline and down to Aosta.

On the return journey to the crowning summit of the Grafeneire, my arms began to ache with the incessant thrusting of my ski pole and ice axe. The sides of my knees also emitted a constant dull pain. Like Simon on the Weisshorn, I guessed that I was eating into my muscle protein despite having consumed two bowls of cornflakes and four slices of bread for breakfast. I stopped a moment and nipped the side of my stomach. The roll of fat that usually sits there so stubbornly had all but disappeared, confirming the suspicion.

An automatic weather recording station sits atop the 4314m Grafeneire. We joined two young climbers sitting beside it and celebrated our fiftieth top by sharing their supply of chocolate biscuits. On 19 September 1988 Paul Mackrill had stood here at the end of his '4000ers' attempt with the consolation of at least having completed all the Swiss summits. Simon and I now anticipated the pleasure of extending that record.

We met Angus, Bob and Martin back at the Combin de Valsorey for an hour's session of photography and film commentary. The cloud-fringed final dome of the Grafeneire and the green vale of Ollomont provided an ideal backcloth. We did all we could to oblige Martin's requirements, but the moment he was satisfied we departed, for there was much still to do.

We descended the snows of the West Face in a flowing rhythm of giant strides and sustained a sufficient pace below the Plateau du Couloir that no loose stone was given a chance to mark our passing. We were back at the hut seventy minutes after leaving the summit and after another hour's break continued down to Cordonna.

The day's final trial now awaited me. Could I get back on that bike and perform? I had 30km to cycle to La Fouly in the Val Ferret where Joy was camped and a 24-hour rest was promised. The ride was short, but it included a continuous 690m climb from Orsières up to La Fouly. A minute's complete submergence in the icy cool waters of the Valsorey torrent seemed a suitable way to prepare for the heat of the road. I set off ahead of Simon who was happy to chat awhile to Carole and Heather.

Speeding back down the long curves of yesterday's humiliation, I questioned how my quadriceps could possibly respond to the coming climb, for they felt utterly lifeless. Then I wondered if Simon would come powering past me as I wheeled my machine up the steeper inclines. As I entered Orsières, a crucible of stagnant heat in the mid-afternoon, I faced a crisis of confidence.

It was crucial to my morale that I didn't drop immediately to my lowest gear. For a kilometre I held firm in the middle range. Another passed without my legs faltering and by the third I was beginning to enjoy the scenery. The Val Ferret is a pocket of rural tranquillity and although the least exciting, is much the prettiest of the valleys flanking the Mont Blanc range. I was pleased that this was our gate of entry to the roof of Western Europe. Although lying only 15km to our west, the bustling streets of Chamonix seemed a world apart. I pedalled past the black-stained hay lofts of Praz de Fort and inhaled the sweet scent of freshly mown grass. The granite tips of the Clochers du Portalet and then the immense Amône Slab passed by on my right. By the time I reached camp, I was humming Beethoven's Ninth. That sense of triumph, absent since my arrival in Zinal, had returned in full measure.

My rest at La Fouly was marked by one significant event: Joy confirmed that she would stay to the end. The pledge was made in the expectation that we would be on the Barre des Ecrins by 14 August at the latest in order to give us time to travel home for the start of Alex's new school term. I realised the practical and symbolic importance of my meeting that deadline, and immediately it became my new goal. If I were to achieve it, nothing could be allowed to go badly awry in the Mont Blanc massif. The deadline of 14 August would give a completion time of 53 days. We were still 4 days behind the 48-day base schedule, which meant we could only afford to drop one more day.

Simon had no comparable personal pressure to finish so quickly, but he was equally unwilling to relax now that an end was in sight. Having seen nothing of the Scots Guards team, either in person or in the entries in hut logbooks, we were no longer concerned by their threat. There was, however, a record to be set and we wanted to make it a good one.

Having had so rough a passage in the Pennine Alps, I feel that the odds must be weighted in favour of good weather and conditions on Mont Blanc. This is the range that offers the most technical and committed climbing. We are reliant on stable weather. In that event ten days should see us through the range and I find myself looking forward to them. I am ever hopeful that we can make up some more of the lost time and finish within fifty days.

Another fillip to morale during our night's rest at La Fouly was Bill Shannon's confirmation that the Matterhorn film had arrived and had been shown on Scottish television. Martin Welch's funding for the remainder of the expedition was confirmed in another call to Jackie Ross.

'I know that we aren't getting much sponsorship at the minute, Jackie,' I said, 'but please keep faith. Everything will happen when we succeed. Just two more weeks and we can do it.'

We spent the whole of the next day, 29 July, resting at La Fouly. Even at 1600m in the pinewoods, the heat was intense. I prayed for the evening shadows and eventually took the children to cool off at the glacier torrent which drains the A Neuve Glacier. Stonefall and bare ice were our new enemies on the mountains as this heatwave stripped the snow off the flanks and couloirs, and we packed our helmets for the first time in the expedition.

David Litherland arrived from Chamonix at lunchtime with the latest weather forecast direct from the French meteorological office. Despite the growing influence of the Azores high-pressure system over the alpine weather, storms were predicted for the following night which would linger through the 31st. I thought through our planned route. We had envisaged crossing from the A Neuve basin over the Col d'Argentière to the Argentière Hut. Then we hoped to climb the Couturier Couloir of the Aiguille Verte, traverse Les Droites and then drop to our first resupply point at the Couvercle Hut.

In view of the forecast and our uncertainty over the condition of the *difficile* Couturier Couloir, I wanted a surer alternative.

'I think we should go direct to the Couvercle tomorrow. We can sit out the storm there with a pile of food and tackle the easier side of the Verte and Les Droites as soon as the weather lifts,' I suggested to Simon.

He immediately agreed 'It's only a few hours further than the Argentière and it will save us carrying two days of food.'

So, from the Argentière basin we would continue over another high pass, the 3601m Col des Cristaux, to reach the Couvercle.

The plan was sealed. Bob and David would bring four days of food from Chamonix up to the Couvercle Hut by lunchtime tomorrow. Angus and Martin would follow them up later in the day ready to film the sensations of the Aiguille Verte. They all departed during the afternoon, leaving Simon and me to enjoy precious hours with our families before our own departure for the A Neuve Hut at sundown.

The high season and hot weather inevitably bring the masses on to the mountains. Hearing that the A Neuve Hut was full, we decided to sleep out on the alps beneath the refuge. Having so much enjoyed the solitude that had accompanied us through the Pennine Alps, we did not want the Mont Blanc traverse to be spoilt by crowds.

After a steep walk of less than two hours up from La Fouly, we made our bivouac on a grassy terrace at 2600m. Brewing a bedtime drink, we watched the rise of the full moon tinged pink with the sunset's reflection. The air was warm: at 10pm I could lie out in shirt sleeves with my feet resting bare on the grass. Neither the hut nor our sleeping-bags were particularly missed.

In the absence of frost, our safe passage across the two cols could only be assured by a very early start. We rose at 1.20am and left less than an hour later. With no summits beckoning and 1600m of climbing ahead, the day promised much toil for little reward. Yet the traverse of a high unknown pass has a special appeal and I soon understood why the attainment of the most difficult cols was held to be as worthy a challenge as climbing many of the summits in the Golden Age of alpine exploration.

There were both navigational and technical difficulties on the route to the Col d'Argentière. The moon had long disappeared behind the ridges to our west. In inky darkness we found our way up a steepening glacier slope that cuts across the face beneath the col. We weaved through a succession of crevasses until we were stopped by an over-hanging *bergschrund* that seemed to span the whole width of the slope. Simon belayed while I balanced over a bridge of soft snow and chopped steps in the bulge of the *schrund* above. With one delicate pull over the projecting lip I was back in balance.

Immediately we moved left off the slope on to a twisting spur leading directly towards the col. Amazingly, the snow on the ridge was firm and crusted. How could that be when the air temperature must have been close on 10°C? Clad only in vests and windshirts, we were still overheating. I've puzzled over this problem on many occasions and the answer must lie in outward radiation from the snow surface. Provided the night is clear, snow will freeze even though the air temperature is above zero.

The lights of La Fouly twinkled in the Val Ferret below and I thought fondly of Joy, Alex and Hazel asleep down on the campsite. The valleys were heavy with a haze even blacker than the night sky. We hopped in and out of deep melt runnels to reach the col at 3552m. Behind us a pink dawn crept lazily around the brooding mass of the Grand Combin and we turned to bid farewell to the Swiss Alps. They had treated us badly, sure enough, but they had given us an adventure to remember.

Ahead of us the familiar shapes of Les Courtes, Les Droites and the Aiguille Verte were emerging from their night shrouds. We were back on home ground among peaks and glaciers which we knew intimately from years spent guiding in the Mont Blanc massif. We were relying on that knowledge to take us safely through the coming week.

Time was no longer on our side as we strode down the easy slopes of the Tour Noir Glacier and across the head of the Argentière basin. The couloirs leading up to the Col des Cristaux face east-north-east and receive the full power of the newly risen sun. Wet snow avalanches and rockfalls are common in the heat of the day. We took the safest line which lies up a subsidiary gully 100m to the right of the main couloir and then climbs a rib of rotten rocks to gain the col. We took exactly 3 hours and 10 minutes to get from col to col and reached the Cristaux at 9.10am.

The col brought back a flood of memories to Simon and me. In both 1988 and 1989 we had camped here during attempts to make a non-stop traverse of the 50km watershed of the Mer de Glace. This was a shorter but far more intense version of our '4000ers' traverse and a comparable though technically harder undertaking to that of Georges and Lorétan on the Zermatt skyline.

On our 1988 attempt we had arrived at the col in a thunderstorm after climbing for 48 out of the previous 60 hours in order to traverse the Les Drus, the Aiguille Verte, Les Droites and Les Courtes. A year later we covered this first quarter of our traverse in less than two days, but it was here that I fell prey to a throat and respiratory infection. After 24 hours' rest I had not improved, but we pushed on for another two days. I can remember the feeling of total weakness as my condition worsened and Simon forged the pace.

However, by the time we reached the Aiguille de l'Eboulement Simon had himself caught the infection in full measure. Despite perfect conditions and weather, we were forced to abandon the whole project and retreat to the doctor's surgery at Chamonix. It took a fortnight's course of strong antibiotics, plus a complete rest, to get us back to normal health.

The Mer de Glace skyline remains to be completed in a single journey, although fast French climbers have done several large sections of it. With support teams we might have succeeded, but in pursuit of perfection we had placed our own food dumps on four of the cols, including the Cristaux, and had attempted the traverse without any back-up whatsoever. Once something went wrong we had no recourse save retreat. The lesson was well learnt when we turned our attention to Alps 4000. Had I suffered a similar infection this summer we could have radioed down for the necessary drugs and perhaps continued climbing.

Our failure on the Mer de Glace skyline had been bitter, but they had forged our partnership into an unshakable bond. Starting as the younger and less experienced partner, Simon had emerged a good deal older in maturity as well as looks.

As we commenced the descent to the Talèfre Glacier and the Couvercle Hut, I felt heartily glad that we had made the extra effort to come over the Col des Cristaux. Despite the forecast of a storm for the coming night, we felt in control of the situation and were ready to give our best to the next crucial week. The Aiguille Verte, the Grandes Jorasses and Mont Blanc were no longer distant and rather fearful prospects. The three cornerstones of the Mer de Glace basin stood proud before us in the morning sun. The stage was set for a grand finale.

9

FIGHTING ON HOME GROUND

Aiguille Verte – Grandes Jorasses – Rochefort Arête

The Aiguille Verte (4122m) has more closely modelled the development of classical alpinism than any other mountain. Its snowy summit *calotte* stands 3000m above the floor of the Chamonix Valley and, viewed from here, the Verte stands rank with the Dent Blanche or Weisshorn in beauty and grandeur. In its western arm the mountain cradles the most impressive rock spire in the Alps, the Aiguille du Dru. No other '4000er' possesses such a jewel.

All the routes to the summit of the Verte involve difficulties on snow and mixed terrain which leave the climber vulnerable to the caprices of weather and conditions. None is easier than *assez difficile* and in terms of quality and variety they are surpassed in the Alps only by those on Mont Blanc itself. Whymper and Almer, Kennedy and Hudson, and Mummery and Burgener are three of the great teams which made routes on the mountain in the nineteenth century. Few climbers return from the Verte without a good story to tell, and only those possessed of speed and skill will avoid an epic.

I'd climbed the mountain three times previously and had been tested close to my limit on each occasion. Two of those ascents had been on our Mer de Glace skyline attempts, when we traversed the peak's two finest arêtes, the Sans Nom Ridge (D+) and the Jardin Ridge (AD+). The Jardin Ridge drops from the summit over two subsidiary tops, the Grande Rocheuse (4102m) and the Aiguille du Jardin (4035m), before ending abruptly above the Col de l'Aiguille Verte. Beyond this col another long and spiny arête climbs over Les Droites.

Simon and I were all too familiar with the difficulties of the ridge linking the Verte and Les Droites after our experiences in 1988 and

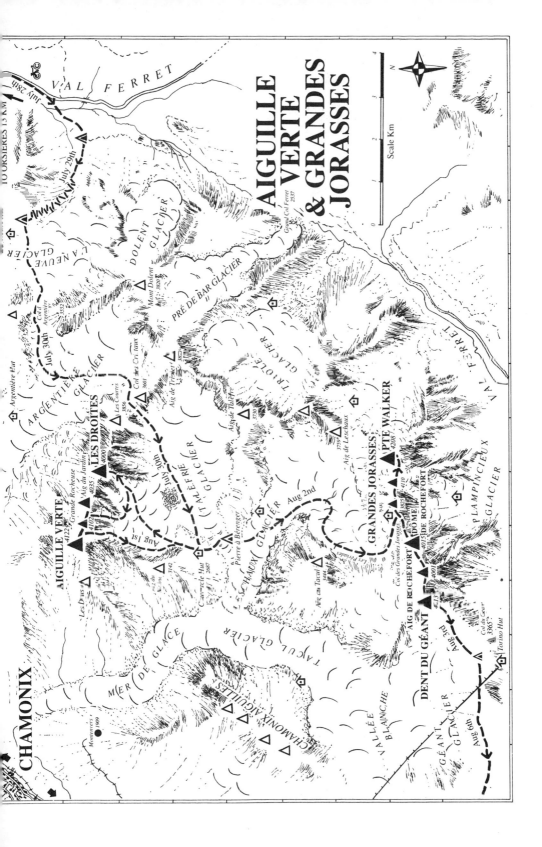

AIGUILLE VERTE & GRANDES JORASSES

Scale Km

Grand Col Ferret 2537

N

CHAMONIX

VAL FERRET

TO ORSIÈRES 13 KM

July 28th

July 29th

L A N E U V E G L A C I E R

DOLENT GLACIER

Mont Dolent 3820

PRÉ DE BAR GLACIER

TRIOLET GLACIER

Argentière Hut

July 30th

Col Argentière

A R G E N T I È R E G L A C I E R

Grande Rocheuse 4102

Grande Rocheuse 4035

Aig du Jardin

Les Courtes 3856

Col des Cristaux 3601

Aig de Triolet

Aig du Triolet 3703

AIGUILLE VERTE 4122

LES DROITES 4000

July 30th

Les Drus

T A L È F R E G L A C I E R

Aug 1st

Aig du Moine 3412

Couvercle Hut 2687

Pierre à Bérenger

L E S C H A U X G L A C I E R

Aug 2nd

Aig de Leschaux

3759

3720

GRANDES JORASSES:
PTE WALKER 4208

4196

3825

DÔME
4015

DE ROCHEFORT

PLAMPINCIEUX GLACIER

VAL FERRET

M E R D E G L A C E

Montenvers 1909

Aig du Tacul 3444

Les Périades

Col des Grandes Jorasses

AIG DE ROCHEFORT 4001

DENT DU GÉANT 4013

C H A M O N I X A I G U I L L E S

T A C U L G L A C I E R

V A L L É E B L A N C H E

Aug 3rd

Aug 4th

G É A N T G L A C I E R

Col du Géant 3365

Torino Hut

1989, and we reckoned that it would be quicker to climb the peaks separately. When the expected storm did materialise during the night of 30 July, we were pinned down in the Couvercle Hut for an extra day. In order to recoup that delay, we decided that as soon as the weather cleared we would try to climb both Les Droites and the Verte in a single night. From the upper fringe of the Talèfre Glacier at 3300m we would go up and down the *voie normale* on Les Droites (AD), then traverse the glacier and gain access to the Jardin Ridge by one of the couloirs on the Verte's southern flanks.

The likelihood of moonlight was a significant factor in the hatching of this plan. All we needed was the clearance that was predicted for the evening of the 31st. After a day of drizzle the clouds began to thin in the early evening. The odd hole appeared in the mists, revealing glimpses of the North Face of the Grandes Jorasses, and then the whole mass of vapour began to subside slowly into the glacier trench of the Mer de Glace as dry stable air resumed control of the weather.

At 7pm we packed our gear in readiness and then ploughed our way through an enormous dinner. As usual, Simon struggled to cope with his plateful. He has the ability to consume snacks at regular intervals throughout the day, but when faced with a really large meal he rarely matched my appetite during the expedition.

'Get it down you,' I said. 'We've got a long night ahead.'

'I'm doing my best,' he replied, stirring his fork through his remaining pile of spaghetti in an effort to look hungry.

We discussed our schedule with Angus and Martin and decided they would get the best pictures if they joined us on the Jardin Ridge just after dawn.

The hut had been filling slowly during the afternoon and at 9.10pm we left fifty or sixty other climbers to their night's rest and set off. The ascent of the Aiguille Verte usually requires a 1.30am reveille and we did not long regret what little sleep we were missing. Even before the twilight had vanished from the great north wall of the Jorasses, a magnificent full moon rose above the rim of the Leschaux basin.

The snow on the Talèfre Glacier was already crisp, and we ascended in an arc above the Jardin de Talèfre towards a thin spur which drops from the higher eastern summit of Les Droites. During the long ascent I remembered the words of Dougie MacLean's song, 'Turning Away', which had become something of a battle-cry for me each time we commenced a climb at night: 'In darkness we do what we can; in daylight we're oblivion'. I stiffened my pace just a touch. We had eight precious hours of darkness ahead and if we weren't on the Aiguille du Jardin at the crack of dawn, we would suffer the consequences on the Verte.

Fortunately, I had guided the normal route on Les Droites just a year previously, so was well prepared for a nocturnal ascent. A snow gully cuts up to the spur, then a mixed face leads up to an attractive snow ridge close to the top. If conditions are good, and provided you keep to the right at the top of the mixed ground, the whole route can be climbed without encountering any moves harder than Scottish grade II. We crossed the *bergschrund* at close on midnight and climbed a deep avalanche runnel for 50m. Not a stone or even a pebble moved on the rocks above. Everything was frozen into silent suspension. This would be a different place come the heat of midday.

With no danger of stonefall, we breathed easily all the way up the gully and the face above. At 1.20am we reached the top, which is at a height of exactly 4000m. We rested just long enough to munch a chocolate bar. On the Argentière flank, long snowslopes dropped away into the mountain's 1200m North Face. This remains one of the touchstones of modern alpine climbing and has retained its *extrêmement difficile* (ED) grading.

Les Droites was my first major North Face route in the Alps and almost my last. Charlie Heard and I were caught in a wild storm on the last 300m of the climb. I looked down to the brèche where we had emerged from the face at nightfall and remembered how I was shivering uncontrollably on the brink of hypothermia. Mountain clothing wasn't quite so good back in 1980. A proofed nylon cagoule, cotton anorak and wool jumper provided nothing like the protection of the Gore-tex jackets and fleece layers which we were now wearing. Despite tumbling the last 100m of the descent couloir on the Talèfre side in an avalanche of powder snow, we had somehow escaped unscathed.

Much of the satisfaction I was now gaining from Alps 4000 lay in doing the routes in fast style with a reasonable margin of safety. There is an enormous pleasure in feeling some measure of control in the mountain environment. The risk can never be eliminated, nor should it be. But good climbing is all about keeping the odds to a reasonable length and maintaining the ability to shorten those odds to your advantage by skill, speed or judgement. So far on this expedition we had rolled the dice many times, but always loaded it in our favour. I was certainly glad to be beyond the phase of youth where I only got up harder climbs like Les Droites' North Face by the skin of my teeth. Such experiences are undoubtedly formative, but they should not be chanced too often.

Descending by the exact line of our footsteps, we were back on the Talèfre Glacier at 2.50am. Simon led the way round the base of the parallel spur which supports the West Summit of Les Droites and then up towards the Aiguille Verte. His pace was strong and I was having a job keeping up with him, when he turned and said:

'I'll just have a minute's rest; I'm getting cramps in my stomach.'

'Small wonder, the pace you've been setting,' I replied.

Lights were now approaching from the Couvercle Hut. Most were going for the Whymper Couloir which provides the easiest and most direct access to the Verte. Two teams were heading up on our right to the Col de l'Aiguille Verte in order to tackle the Jardin Ridge and, as arranged, Angus and Martin were waiting for us at the foot of the South Couloir of the Col Armand Charlet. This couloir, though very rarely climbed, is graded AD+ and seemed to offer a quicker route to the Aiguille du Jardin than the line taken by the two teams to our right. The only cause for doubt was a dark narrow section low in the couloir. If there was no snow there, we could be in trouble.

Angus and Martin followed us up the gully. As we approached the narrows we heard the ominous sound of a waterfall from above. Facing south, this face had been taking the full brunt of the hot sun over the last few days and one cold night had been insufficient to still the flow of meltwater. I led up into the line of the cascade with Simon following 5m behind. The waterfall was fringed on either side by a screen of bubbly ice, formed as its spray froze on the adjacent rocks.

By climbing out on this ice we were able to progress while avoiding a soaking in the fall. Although we had only one axe each, it was always possible to bridge a foot or a hand across the gully to extract the axe pick and place it higher. Three old pitons gave a pleasing sense of security as we moved through the impasse.

Above this pitch a 50° slope of snow led all the way to the col at 3998m and dawn was only minutes away. Our problems seemed over, but for Simon they were just starting.

In the lower couloir I sense my stomach tightening against my harness and feel bloated. Ignoring it I press on, but just above the ice pitch my stomach starts going into spasm. I ask Martin to hold on a minute and double up with cramp. The inevitable is going to happen and I just hope to get it over with quickly. I'm violently sick and the cramps subside.

'OK, we'll go on,' I shout, but just minutes later the spasms come back with a vengeance and I am retching again. I can't imagine what is causing this. All I can do is try to follow Martin up the couloir. I'm oblivious to the route and just concentrate on controlling the cramps.

Our progress towards the col was punctuated by two further stops to allow Simon to be sick. I imagined his misery having to front-point up this endless slope while feeling totally debilitated, but we had no choice but to press on as best we might. We could not give up so close to the summit. I guessed that Simon's problem was probably due to his forced feeding last night rather than any virus. If so, his nausea might soon pass.

We gained the Col Armand Charlet at 7am. This is one of my favourite spots in all the Alps. The ridge here forms a wafer-thin edge of snow which scythes across the head of the couloir we had just climbed. The sheer obelisk of the Pointe Eveline lies offset just to the right of the ridge. Barely 50m beyond, the summit of the Jardin rises in an elegant curl of snow which is poised on a monolith of ochrous granite. This is mountain geometry of stunning perfection.

The col is a worthy memorial to the greatest of all the Verte's pioneers. Between 1919 and 1964 Armand Charlet climbed his beloved local mountain 100 times by 14 different routes, which included 7 first ascents. Charlet was renowned for his acerbic personality and merciless treatment of his paying clients almost as much as the lightning speed of his climbs. He became a legend in his own lifetime and remains revered, even by today's generation, as the greatest of all the French guides.

Fine though it is, Armand's col did not offer the most commodious lodging for Simon's immediate needs. He was now suffering an acute attack of diarrhoea. I belayed him down into a snow trough where he was out of sight and there he attempted to clear his system of its remaining contents. Angus and Martin used this delay to climb up past us on to the Grande Rocheuse which offered a marvellous vantage for the Aiguille du Jardin. By the time we groped up the snowy final steps to the top, they were perfectly positioned to photograph our silhouettes high above the morning cumulus.

When we met them after our return journey across the col, we could sense their thrill in capturing this fabulous scene. After weeks of hard labour Martin had got his reward. If he could now get a technical climbing sequence of us on the Dent du Géant or the Diable Ridge of Mont Blanc du Tacul, then he should have the makings of a successful film.

Simon rallied as we crossed the Grande Rocheuse. The climbing was nothing like as awkward as that to gain the Aiguille du Jardin and within minutes we were down on the final col before the Aiguille Verte. From here a simple but beautiful snow arête led up on to the summit, where we joined four French climbers who had just climbed the Couturier Couloir.

Being poised on the very edge of the range, the summit view from the Verte is one of exceptional variety and its prospect of Mont Blanc at the head of the Mer de Glace basin has no equal. Edward Whymper commented on its special quality after making the first ascent of the mountain on 29 June 1865, just a fortnight before his ill-fated Matterhorn climb:

> Upon the summit of the Verte . . . you see valleys, villages, fields; you
> see mountains interminable rolling away, lakes resting in their hollows;
> you hear the tinkling of sheep-bells as it rises through the clear
> mountain air, and the roar of avalanches as they descend to the valleys;
> but above all there is the great white dome, with its shining crest high
> above; with its sparkling glaciers that descend between buttresses
> which support them; with its brilliant snows, purer and yet purer the
> farther they are removed from this unclean world.

We could not stay long, for the Whymper Couloir must be descended by mid-morning to avoid serious avalanche risk, and it was already bathed in hot sunshine. The couloir is 500m in height and the descent was every bit as tedious as expected. Our progress was complicated by a series of vertical runnels in the snow. These were initially created by snowslides and had been grossly enlarged by accelerated melting in the sun. The couloir had effectively been crumpled into giant corrugations, each 2–3m in depth.

Since our route took a long diagonal line down the left bank of the couloir, we were continually forced to jump in and out of the channels. Finally, we crossed a rocky spur and gained a subsidiary gully which dropped to the *bergschrund*. This develops to monstrous proportions after mid-season and often has to be abseiled. However, we found a sneaky ramp which led down under the lip and had been used by the parties we had seen ascending the couloir before dawn.

Although we were well pleased to have taken only 100 minutes from the summit to the *bergschrund*, our time paled in comparison with the 54 minutes achieved by Charlet with Marcel Couturier in the 1930s. After that incredible descent, Armand had come dangerously close to flattering his client. 'At last, you seem to be learning how to crampon,' was his one, and only, comment.

We took off our crampons and virtually ran back to the hut. Having been out for fourteen hours, we were more than ready to soak up the sun and breezes on the Couvercle terrace. After two brews, a beer and an omelette, Simon declared himself recovered and our happiness was complete. The Couvercle Hut is a pleasant place in which to relax. It is rarely crowded and guardian Michel Tavernier allows you to feel at home while still maintaining an efficient establishment. After Angus and Martin had arrived down and departed for Chamonix, we asked for a dormitory and were able to enjoy a couple of hours' sleep during the afternoon.

On rising at 5pm I felt oppressively groggy and devoid of energy, as though severely jet-lagged. The torpor continued during our short evening walk across the Talèfre Glacier. I could barely put one leg in front of the other. Nor was Simon exactly brimful with energy after his bout of illness. What chance the Grandes Jorasses tomorrow, I thought? To get to the Jorasses we faced a very long climb out from the Leschaux basin and we wanted to be as close as possible to the start of the route. Since the evening was beautifully warm, we decided to make a bivouac under a huge boulder, the Pierre a Berenger, which stands on the brink of the moraine overlooking the Leschaux Glacier.

With a couch of lady's mantle for our bed and a nearby trickle of snowmelt, we set up camp, cooked a quick meal and settled into our bivouac bags at 8.15pm. The usual questions revolved in my head. The next two days were crucial. We were without support and could carry very little spare food. Although the forecast was generally fine, I sensed a risk of thunder in the warm, close air. Neither of us knew the West Ridge of the Jorasses, but it was a route with a reputation. Thankfully, my doubts were quickly submerged by a deep and dreamless sleep.

'Simon! Come on, we're late.'

Sometimes I cursed his reluctance to get up in the morning. Why was the job always left to me?

'Is it time?' came a stifled grunt from beside me. I was beginning to suspect the reason why Simon had not brought an alarm watch along this summer.

'I'm afraid we've overslept. It's half past three.'

That information brought a flurry of activity. We'd planned to be up at 1.30am and a climb for which we had calculated a fifteen-hour schedule was already slipping out of our reach. All the same, I felt wonderfully rejuvenated by the extended sleep. By 5am we were striding up the dry ice of the Leschaux Glacier and I was confident that we could make up the loss of time.

Few mountain approaches have the intense power of that of the North Face of the Grandes Jorasses. The glacier is broad and spacious and there are many other peaks on either side. Yet the 1200m wall completely dominates the scene, drawing the climber into its clasp like a magnet. This morning it lay peaceful and silent. Our eyes followed the West Ridge leftwards from the 3825m Col des Grandes Jorasses over the successive tops of the Pointes Young, Marguerite, Hélène, Croz and Whymper to the crowning top, the Pointe Walker at 4208m.

From the bivouac hut at the col we had to follow the full 1¹/₂km crest of the West Ridge and then reverse the route back to the shelter by nightfall. First climbed in 1911 by Geoffrey Winthrop Young, Humphrey Jones and Josef Knubel, the ridge remains a worthy *difficile* in standard and is climbed only two or three dozen times a year. I was both intrigued and intimidated by its prospect.

Our route to the Col des Grandes Jorasses was a tiring plod with 1400m of vertical height gain. We turned sharp right off the main Leschaux Glacier and climbed up under the little granite spires of Les Périades. The snow crust just supported our weight over most of the trek. From the head of the long glacier only a steep and bare ice-slope 150m in height barred our way to the col. This consumed more than its time's worth in nervous energy.

As we teetered up on front points towards the crest of the col, we became ever more aware of a rising south-westerly wind. The lazy cumulus cloud which had hung around the Chamonix Valley at dawn now boiled up on the mountains in threatening mushrooms amid a pervasive warmth. We gained the col at 9.15am, no longer sure of the wisdom of proceeding up the West Ridge.

On the col the Canzio Bivouac Hut provided a welcome shelter. Its most remarkable feature is a little frozen lake outside the front door. Simon was able to break through the ice to gain a ready supply of water for our morning brew. While he was hacking at the lake, I wandered over to the rock parapet overlooking the southern flank of the mountain and scanned the hazy outlines of the Italian foothills, while trying to decide our best course of action.

Suddenly my attention was drawn by the sound of barking. I looked directly down to the Plampincieux Glacier.

'Jesus . . .'

I had expected to see a smooth crevassed snow-slope, but instead the whole glacier was covered with the debris of an enormous avalanche which seemed to have emanated from somewhere close to the Pointe Walker. Even from my viewpoint 800m above, individual blocks of ice stood out as large as sugar cubes, which placed them somewhere between motor cars and bungalows in actual size. The tiny specks of rescue dogs and their handlers were visible weaving through the sea of fragments.

'Simon, come and see,' I called. 'That serac on the south face must have collapsed. It's wiped out the whole valley.'

Simon stood speechless at the scene.

We didn't need to be told that several people lay dead under the debris. The avalanche had probably occurred in the hour before dawn, just when we were strolling peacefully up the Leschaux Glacier.

'That serac was threatening to go back in 1990. I remember passing it on my way down from doing the Walker,' he said.

'You wonder why it should choose to go just when folk are on the glacier.'

'There could have been dozens going up the normal route this morning,' said Simon

There was no escaping our sense of vulnerability when went back into the hut. We supped coffee and tried to keep the avalanche out of our thoughts, but neither of us felt much like climbing. Nor did the weather give any positive encouragement.

Clouds mask the high tops, giving an air of uncertainty. A lot of 'what if's' are now circulating in our minds. Martin suggests going out to 'have a look' at the rocks on the Pointe Young. This might allow the weather to make a statement of intent without our being too far up the route, but I know full well how quickly we will be committed by our efforts.

However, I can but agree to this foray. This is the point where all chances have to be grasped, since tomorrow could so easily be worse than today and we don't want to get trapped at the hut.

We fumbled around trying to find the line on the first buttress above the hut. Our confidence seemed to have deserted us for the first time in the summer. I felt like a shaky novice. The icy cold rock on this shaded crag further deterred our efforts and the climbing seemed to be grade IV or harder wherever we tried. A random scattering of old pitons across the slabs gave no clue as to the right way.

It was well past midday when we gained a ramp traversing round the north side of the Pointe Young. The rock was now verglassed and increasingly loose. I became committed to a bulging pitch without piton protection and edged nervously in every direction except upwards. Suddenly my exasperation got the better of me. I pulled angrily over the bulge, levered into balance and forged a direct line to reach the crest of the ridge about 80m before the 3996m Pointe Young. This was my moment of commitment and Simon knew it.

> *At this point I realise that Martin will not want to throw away the effort of that pitch and I also know that when I reach his belay on the crest I will agree with his suggestion to go on.*

A drop in the wind and a shaft of sunlight strengthened our resolve. Yet as we edged along the ridge I was continually searching the cliffs on either flank for suitable ledges to which we could bolt should a thunderstorm break. We now faced the crux section of the route. In his account of the first ascent, Young described the crest beyond the Pointe Young as 'a barbaric flame-pointed ridge', and the Pointe Marguerite as an 'insolent upward swirl of impossibility'. Nothing had changed.

To gain the Marguerite we abseiled 20m down the South Face and looked for what Will McLewin had told me was an entirely improbable traverse line across a smooth buttress. I soon spied a crackline which satisfied the requirements and launched into a full-blooded hand traverse. Its grade was irrelevant. With boots and rucksack and only two pieces of protection between myself and Simon, it required every ounce of energy. After a second traverse of similar calibre, my respect for the pioneers of this route had soared.

A loose icy couloir then led up to the 4065m Marguerite. Although we had solved the key passage, there was no prospect of relaxation. The ridge continuing over the Pointe Hélène was a knife-edge. Surprisingly, the greatest exposures were over the mountain's South Face rather than the more famous North Wall.

The sheer crenellations of the ridge are hard to absorb in full. Very aware of the thinness of the edge, I find that our continuous movement concentrates the mind and gives us no time to think of anything but the moves ahead. There is still an underlying pressure from the unsettled weather which lends urgency to our completion of this tightrope.

The Pointe Hélène is too small to count as a top on our list of seventy-five summits, but it marked a transition from the sensational to the merely precipitous. The ridge became snowy, but we were able to find a line along loose rocks underneath the corniced edge and thus avoided the need for crampons until the Pointe Croz. This top has no significant height differential, but it is important as the exit point for the great spur of the same name. The Croz Spur is the most feasible winter route on the Jorasses North Face. Hanging down its last pitch was a full-length rope, half-frozen into the ice. I imagined the epic of some unfortunate party who had lost that jammed rope and faced the descent of the south flank without it.

The ridge now became easy, but the snow was aerated and rotten. We followed some tracks, probably laid down by recent ascensionists of the Croz Spur. A biscuit wrapper was lying in one of the steps. Although this was hardly an appropriate place for a litter crusade I picked it up and discovered that it was full of delicious fig rolls, still sweet and eminently edible. Having consumed these we continued wearily over the Pointe Whymper (4184m) and down into the hollow beneath the Pointe Walker. We were now just 50m above the fracture point of the great serac. All afternoon we had heard the buzz of helicopters which were ferrying rescuers in and out of the avalanche site, so the disaster was never very far from our minds.

At 6pm we stood on the final and highest summit. The Pointe Walker was a special place for Simon, for it is the finishing point of the great Walker Spur, the finest buttress climb in the Alps. In the dry and settled summer of 1990, Simon had soloed the Spur in a single day, leaving Chamonix at 8am, climbing the route in 7¹/₂ hours and descending to the hut on the Italian side just after nightfall. He had no prior knowledge of the upper two-thirds of the climb, which made it a remarkable performance.

We had taken nearly as long to climb the supposedly easier West Ridge and now had only four hours of daylight in which to reverse the route. Happily, the weather had progressively mellowed and the evening was warm and atmospheric with alternating bands of clouds and sunlight drifting across the surrounding peaks. Provided we reached the Pointe Young by nightfall, I felt that we could safely abseil the steep terminal buttress back to the hut by torchlight.

Our ability to recall the intricacies of the route was now put on trial. One mistake would have condemned us to a bivouac on the ridge. We halted only once, when Simon was gripped by a recurrence of the stomach cramps he had suffered on the Verte. This time he was not sick nor weakened by the attack and we continued after a five-minute delay.

The light was fading and the air rapidly chilling when we reached the hand traverses. We were wearing sticky-palmed work-gloves for most of the rock-climbing, but the traverse crack was so thin that they had to be removed. We swung across the crack with haste and aggression lest our fingers should freeze in transit and stuffed our hands back into gloves the moment we gained ledges at the far side. Another bare-handed sequence of moves was required to climb a smooth step on the ridge back to the Pointe Young.

We maintained just enough momentum to keep our bodies warm and prevent our hands from numbing until we were stopped by the final 170m buttress. Here we hoped to find a series of good abseil points with slings and pitons in place. As we cast our torchbeams around in the darkness searching for suitable anchors, an icy breeze attacked, producing involuntary shivers down my arms and spine. We had been going for nearly nineteen hours and our brains were aching with fatigue. Now the cold tried to remove what limited control we retained over our movements. We had to resist it with all our power.

For our traverse of the Mont Blanc range we were carrying a 60m rope of 8.2mm diameter. When doubled on an abseil this gave us only a 30m maximum descent. Keen to get moving, I elected to go first. This gave me the job of finding and securing the next belay point. After the second abseil I could see no suitable anchors. However, we had landed on a terrace and I traversed 20m along to its very end, trailing the ropes behind me. There I fixed one of our own slings around a block and we continued the descent. The next abseil ended on smooth slabs, so I swung from side to side close to the knotted rope-ends until I spotted two old slings tied around a slim neck of granite, which could have been no more than 15cm in diameter.

By increasing the pendule I managed to grab the slings and establish a belay. Reluctant to rely on so slender a spike of rock, we looked for a second anchor as a back-up, but there was nothing within reach. With a little prayer I slid off down the ropes and at last reached a good stance just 50m above the hut.

That tiny aluminium ice-box was as welcome as a five-star hotel. Despite the midnight hour, we proceeded to treat ourselves to a magnificent repast. Our sense of celebration was such that Simon spent a good ten minutes whisking an instant lemon mousse as a finale to the meal.

'I reckon we've earned this one,' he said.

Some time past 1am we turned into our bunks. Sleep was instant, but in my case it was broken an hour later by an agonising attack of cramp in my thigh. This time Simon was not spared my screams of pain, nor an unearthly clattering of pans as I involuntarily kicked over the contents of the kitchen table.

Morning produced the unexpected pleasure of being handed a mug of tea in bed from Simon. We considered the day's prospects. On the Jorasses West Ridge we had been stalked by the sense of ever moving away from our support and safety. Today's traverse of the Rochefort Ridge to the Dent du Géant would take us in the opposite direction towards the security of a camp on the Col du Géant which was being established by Joy and David Litherland. Although the Rochefort is an airy and occasionally difficult traverse of D– in standard, that knowledge lent us a new mood of confidence as we set off at 8.30am.

The weather was unchanged from the previous morning. The same pregnant clouds boiled out of the Arve Valley in France and we imagined the day might be similarly indecisive. In 1989 I had traversed the Rochefort arêtes in the opposite direction starting at the Col du Géant and remembered abseiling a couple of pitches which looked decidedly nasty. The first of these lay at the top of the initial buttress above the hut and today this was partially iced. Having bridged up the ice section, Simon was forced to take off his crampons in a tiny recess before he could tackle the steeper rock moves above.

A second grade V pitch followed soon after. The ridge dropped into a little gap with an overhanging wall on its far side. To get round this, it was necessary to drop 10m down an ice gully on the north side and climb a flake crack to a long slab which led back to the crest. Chris Bonington had traversed this ridge with Ian Clough after climbing the Walker Spur in 1962 and he had commented that this pitch seemed harder than anything they had encountered on the Walker.

I soon found out why. Having removed my crampons at the point of stepping from the ice gully on to the rock, I muscled up the crack only to find that the slab above was half-covered in snow. From a position that might be best described as spreadeagled, I probed under the snow, unable to find any handhold. When friction appeared to be succumbing to gravity, I turned to my last resort, the axe. Reaching up at full arm's length, I hooked the pick on to an edge and scrabbled my feet upwards until I could mantle-shelf into balance. Having rescued me once already on the slabs of the Weisshorn's North Ridge, the axe again provided my salvation.

The slab now offered some protection and gradually eased in difficulty towards the crest, but the two pitches had cost us nigh on three hours. We continued over the snowy Calotte de Rochefort (3981m) where we met two parties coming from the opposite direction. An easy scramble then took us to the first '4000er' of the day, the 4015m Dome de Rochefort. It was already midday and we made our pre-arranged radio call to Joy on the Col du Géant.

'We've just arrived and I've got Alex here. By the way, David is eyeing the patisseries we've brought up. We'll wait to see you. How long do you think you'll be?'

'Say, between 3 and 4 o'clock, and tell David to keep his thieving hands off!'

'We'll see you then. Over and out.'

As the traverse continued in increasingly deep and heavy snow, we began to realise the impossibility of that meeting. Yesterday's effort really started to hurt and glowering clouds gathered around the ridge. We took over an hour to reach the Aiguille de Rochefort (4001m). This is a popular summit as it forms a suitable objective for the majority of parties who wish to make a return journey along the Rochefort Ridge and back from the Col du Géant. However, the morning's visitors had long departed and it was now a deserted pile of shattered rocks.

The initial descent of the Aiguille was bare of snow and lethally loose. I was climbing first when Simon yelled a warning.

Before I could dodge, a sizable stone hit me square on the knee-cap. I winced with the impact and clutched at my leg, but the pain was short-lived. After a short burst of cursing, I put my weight on to the leg and noticed with relief that nothing was broken. Suddenly our passage towards completion of the '4000ers' seemed particularly tenuous. We now scented menace in the air. Given the choice, we'd have wished ourselves anywhere but on this ridge.

The arête between the Aiguille de Rochefort and the Dent du Géant is one of the most beautiful in the Alps, but there was no joy there for us today. With its crest scarred by a deep trail and its curvature lost in the flat light, the ridge was just something we had to get across as quickly as possible.

At 2.30pm we reached the Salle à Manger. This spacious belvedere is an ideal launching-pad for parties ascending the Dent du Géant, which towers above in a single 120m cliff. Dozens of rucksacks lay strewn about, indicating that the rocks above were crowded. We prepared to add our own sacks to the pile when the cloud suddenly thickened and a hailstorm commenced.

'We're an hour too late,' I said, sitting down in despair.

It was immediately tempting to give up the fight and descend straight to the Col du Géant, where at least I'd have the pleasure of seeing Joy and Alex before they left for the last cablecar. And yet the thought of having to climb back up tomorrow, and thereby lose a day, did not appeal one bit.

'We can always sit it out for an hour and see if it clears,' suggested Simon.

We put on extra clothes and watched enviously as several parties completed their descent from the summit.

The *voie normale* of the Dent du Géant is unlike any other on the 4000m peaks. The summit only succumbed in 1882 to elaborate steeple-jacking with iron stakes and fixed ropes after a clean attempt by Mummery and Burgener had failed to make any impression on the planed slabs of the South-West Face. An abundance of fixed equipment remains in place. Were it all removed and the route done free, rock-climbing of sustained grade IV and IV+ with a crux move of grade VI would be required to reach the summit.

Thanks to the ropes and the peak's accessibility from the Pointe Helbronner cablecar station, the Dent du Géant is mobbed in the high season. Today was no exception. After half-an-hour, a brightening of the cloud persuaded us to have a go, but we had barely got off the ground before we were completely entangled in the ropes of retreating Italian parties. A grand confusion reigned with much gesticulation but no discernible movement. If things were this bad on the Dent du Géant, I didn't fancy getting caught in a traffic jam in Milan.

Somehow we threaded a way through the hordes and turned the corner of the face to arrive at the foot of the Burgener Slab, where we were greeted by Angus and Martin. They had waited nearly three hours for us and were beginning to get concerned. They soon prusiked back up their ropes and filmed us climbing the slab. As they did, the clouds closed rank once more and a light snowfall restarted. We realised that no other parties were above us. Everybody was getting off the peak as quickly as possible.

Simon now took over in the lead and I took a belay on a stanchion just below the steepest part of the face. A low distant rumble reverberated across the Vallée Blanche from the direction of Mont Blanc. This time a storm really was brewing.

The mists curled around the tower above. Flurries of hail swept across my stance while thunder rumbled behind.

'Dear God, this can't be happening to us, just 50m from the top. Surely Simon will come down.'

I shrank deep inside my jacket waiting for the buzz of static and the whip-crack of the first strike. Then suddenly the rope began to snake upwards.

'I can't believe it; he's going for the top!'

> Although we can hear the distant roll of thunder, I decide that if we are going to attempt the route, we should do it now and as fast as possible, before the storm reaches us. It is just one more of those decisions which we've been making all the way along this traverse. I can't quantify the risk we are taking, but a gut feeling tells me that we should go. I brace my feet on the wall and swing hand over hand up the hanging rope.

Panic welled inside me and for the first time in the summer I was unable to control my fear. We were climbing the best lightning conductor in the range with a thunderstorm only minutes or even seconds away. In any other situation our predicament would have been described as crazy. Only speed could help us. Our own rope drew tight and I began the ascent, forsaking all pretence at free-climbing and, like Simon, trusting wholly to the fixed ropes. Angus and Martin stayed behind, ready to bail out when the storm arrived. The rope-climbing was brutally strenuous. My arms ached to the point of exhaustion, but I didn't dare stop. I continued past Simon to the end of the fixed ropes 15m below the forepeak.

Somehow I had to free-climb over the forepeak, but my composure was shattered. I groped and lurched to the top, and, but for the tension of the rope, would have fallen off the moves down into the little gap before the main summit. Simon threatened to do the same when he followed, but he had no tensioning rope to steady him. I grabbed his arm just before he pirouetted backwards and pulled him over to the gap.

We raced up the last rocks to the main summit. Almost the moment we reached the crowning Madonna, the clouds swirled apart and allowed a shaft of weak sunlight to bathe the top. We looked behind us in surprise. Black thunder clouds were peeling off Mont Blanc and across the Val Veni, away from us. The air felt strangely soft and warm. Its tension was quite suddenly diffused. We hitched our rope around the statue. The Madonna's head was peppered with shot-holes from past lightning strikes. Nothing needed to be said. I sat down under her, hung my head and for a minute heard nothing but my pulse pounding through my temples. We had been spared.

10
THE ROOF OF EUROPE

Mont Blanc

Mont Blanc is worthy of its claim to be monarch of the Alps. No alpine mountain possesses such majesty over the surrounding ranges in both elevation and scale. Viewed from all sides, the summit ice-cap rises in isolated splendour, far removed from the stains of the lower world. Some two hundred people trample its final slopes on each fine day in summer, but its snows are renewed at the coming of every storm. Mont Blanc always appears inviolable. It sails in a class of its own.

The mountain's dominance is emphasised by the four magnificent ridges which radiate from the summit dome, each of which contains significant satellite peaks. In total, Mont Blanc has twelve 4000m summits and their linkage posed the greatest route-planning challenge of our journey. Somehow, we had to cross all four ridges in a single high-level expedition.

Our original schedule envisaged us climbing Mont Blanc twice in order to achieve this. From the Col du Géant we would climb the Diable Ridge of Mont Blanc du Tacul to a support camp at 4035m on the Col Maudit. Late in the night we would climb over Mont Maudit to Mont Blanc itself and at dawn descend 900m down the Peuterey Arête, the finest of all alpine ridges. This would take us to the Aiguille Blanche de Peuterey (4112m) from where we could traverse under the Frêney Face to the Eccles Bivouac Hut. A third day would see us climbing back over Mont Blanc over the three tops of the Brouillard Ridge, and finally we'd descend to the Val Veni in Italy via the Bosses Ridge and the Aiguille de Bionnassay.

This outing would take us through some of the most savage and difficult terrain of the expedition, at altitudes continuously in excess of

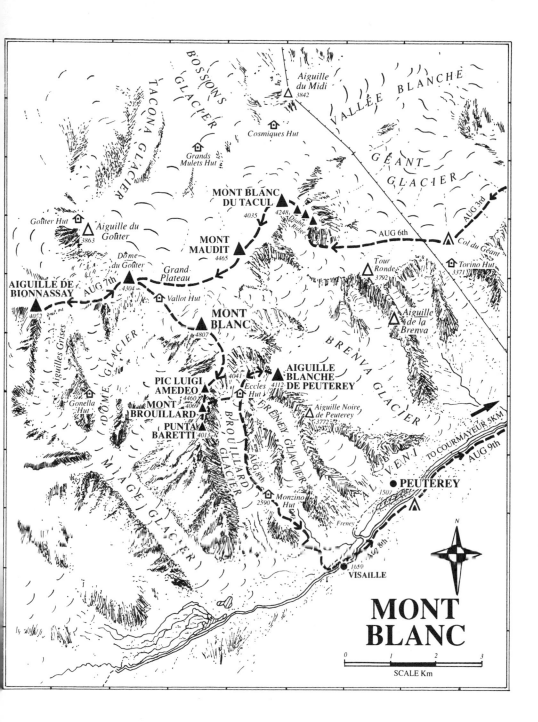

BOSSONS GLACIER

TACONA GLACIER

Aiguille
du Midi
3842

VALLÉE BLANCHE

Cosmiques Hut

GÉANT GLACIER

Grands
Mulets Hut

AUG 3rd

MONT BLANC
DU TACUL
4035   4248
                    Diable
                    Ridge

AUG 6th

Col du Géant

Goûter Hut

Aiguille du
Goûter
3863

MONT
MAUDIT
4465

Grand
Plateau

Tour
Ronde
3792

Torino Hut
3371

Dôme-
du Goûter
4304

AUG 7th

Vallot Hut

Aiguille
de la
Brenva

AIGUILLE DE
BIONNASSAY
4052

MONT
BLANC
4807

DÔME GLACIER

Aiguilles Grises

BRENVA GLACIER

Gonella
Hut

4041

AIGUILLE
BLANCHE
DE PEUTEREY

PIC LUIGI
AMEDEO
4460

Eccles
Hut

4112

Aiguille Noire
de Peuterey
3772

MONT
BROUILLARD
4069

PUNTA
BARETTI
4013

BROUILLARD GLACIER

FRENEY GLACIER

MIAGE GLACIER

AUG 8th

TO COURMAYEUR 5KM

AUG 9th

VAL VENI

PEUTEREY
1507

Monzino
Hut
2590

Freney

AUG 8th

N

1659
VISAILLE

MONT
BLANC

0   1   2   3

SCALE Km

3800m. Above all else, it required settled weather. Mont Blanc stood as the last obstacle to success on the '4000ers'. Beyond lay only the gentle inclines of the Gran Paradiso and the Barre des Ecrins. Having reached the Col du Géant, we could at last focus all our thoughts on that final test.

Wednesday 4 August deserved to be a day of complete repose. Our tent on the Col du Géant was suitably isolated from the main trails and cableways, yet we were only five minutes' walk from the toilets and telephones of the Torino Hut. We had a good stock of fresh food and had even brought some magazines over from the hut to while away the afternoon hours.

But relaxation did not come easily. I was troubled by the risk we had taken on the Dent du Géant. For the first time I felt we had sacrificed a reasonable measure of control and had laid our lives at the door of chance. We had now heard that the avalanche on the Jorasses had taken eight lives, the worst single climbing accident in the Alps for many years. Viewed against that tragedy, our escape on the Géant was unsettling. True, we had already had a close brush with lightning on the Breithorn, but on that occasion the storm was sudden and entirely unexpected.

On the Géant, we had continued upwards knowing that a thunderstorm was likely and had gambled only on its timing. I held nothing against Simon for taking the initiative. Events had placed us in a virtually impossible position, for we were so close to the top and had expended so much effort to get there. Perhaps I had over-reacted and, indeed, Simon saw the decision no differently from many others we had taken through the expedition. Still, the terror of those moments remained in my thoughts.

Looking forward, our plans were seemingly blocked by an unsettled weather pattern. We had just phoned the Chamonix *meteo* office. The immediate outlook was for further thundery conditions with a violent storm forecast for Thursday evening. After our flirtation on the Géant I was not prepared to tackle Mont Blanc with anything less than a settled forecast. Simon was a little less patient.

> *Martin seems willing to sit tight for two days. I see no problem with this if conditions dictate, but I will not agree if there is any chance that we can gain ground on this vital section. Second chances have rarely occurred this summer.*

I sensed that Simon was ready to try to climb the Diable Ridge at the first hint of blue sky in the morning and then retreat to the Cosmiques Hut on the Col du Midi before the storm. That would get the hardest technical climbing and four tops done, leaving the way clear to cross Mont Blanc as soon as the weather settled. Simon was itching to get started, but in the current conditions I didn't want to consider that option.

The Col du Géant offers a magnificent view of Mont Blanc with the full length of the Peuterey Ridge profiled to its left. Today, the summit dome was swathed in a carapace of grey cloud. Mont Blanc's cloud cap is a notorious sign of strong winds and pending storms. Over to the right the Diable pinnacles were barely visible in the pervading gloom. There seemed little chance of improvement until a major storm broke and we awaited this event with growing anticipation.

Our support team – Angus, David and Martin – had all returned to the valley awaiting our decision. David had asked Winky O'Neale, the wife of one of my guiding colleagues, to help him ferry a load to our first support point on the Col Maudit. Joy and Carole were now both camped in the Val Veni. After so much waiting and worrying, they were increasingly anxious that we should get moving.

Thursday morning came without any discernible shift in the weather. Unable to move, we went through the same rituals – a radio call at 8am, breakfast, a walk to the hut to wash and make telephone calls, and then an afternoon of idle waiting. At 4pm I spoke to the Chamonix meteorologist yet again.

'What's going to happen after the storm tonight?' I asked.

'Tomorrow and Saturday will be fine, but isolated storms are expected on Saturday evening and Sunday will be bad all day.'

I walked slowly back to the tent to tell Simon. Even if we left early tomorrow, our route plan would put us somewhere on the Brouillard Ridge in Sunday's storms. Our original schedule just wasn't going to work. I juggled the options. An inspirational change of route and some very fast climbing were needed if we were to fit all 12 peaks into a single 36-hour weather window.

The storm finally broke at 6pm. The thunder was quickly chased away by some violently gusting winds. At dusk we were outside repegging the tent and piling snow on its valance in order to survive the gale. Showers of hail beat against the flysheet. Our mood was solemn. We were meant to be starting for the Diable Ridge at 3am and lay awake in our sleeping-bags with a growing sense of impotence. Could we hold our nerve for another day?

The alarm rang at 2.30am, but the tent fabric still heaved and billowed in the gale. It would have been folly to have left. There was little chance that the cablecars to the Aiguille du Midi and Pointe Helbronner would be working in such a wind, so our support teams would be unable to set off towards the Col Maudit. Worse still, there was a good chance that our tent would blow away before its collection by David and Winky later in the morning.

We couldn't sleep after that. Yet again I reconsidered our route. How could we fit it all in? How could we avoid having to climb Mont Blanc twice? Then an idea began to form. What if we climbed without sleep, and only stopped for a meal at the Col Maudit? What could we safely climb at night? As the grey light of dawn filtered through the tent, I thought I had the answer:

'Simon, listen: I've worked out a much better way of doing it. Let's climb non-stop tonight. We'd never find the top of the Peuterey Ridge in the dark, so why not traverse from Mont Maudit out to the Aiguille de Bionnassay and double-back to Mont Blanc. If we can be on top by dawn on Saturday, we can descend the Brouillard Ridge to the Eccles and even do the Aiguille Blanche before the storm. That way we only climb Mont Blanc once.'

Simon was never the instant enthusiast for sudden changes of plan. He was wise to think very carefully about this one.

> Initially, the prospect of climbing non-stop for two days and a night seems totally impractical, but once we have talked it through I see it as an audacious solution, and the idea grips my imagination. These sorts of tactics have become all too familiar through this unseasonal summer, the requirement of bold answers to difficult problems.

'You know, we've just saved six hours on our schedule without moving an inch,' I concluded.

'It's a pity it wasn't all this easy,' he replied.

By 8am the wind had eased and the clouds were sinking. Patches of clear blue sky began to appear over Mont Blanc. We made ready to leave and waited for David and Winky to arrive to collect the tent and spare gear. This new delay was hard to bear. The Diable Ridge has a guidebook time of 12 hours and it was essential that we reached the Col Maudit in the early evening. We saw 9 o'clock pass without their appearance. The cablecars were now in operation.

'Where have they got to?'

'We can't risk leaving without knowing that they've got up.'

Just as we began to despair, we saw two figures hurrying down from the cable station. David was breathless and apologetic.

'The Midi cable wasn't working, so we had to drive through to Italy and take the Helbronner lift to get to you. Angus and Martin are coming up later.'

At close on 10am we set off, dodging through the slalom course and drag-lifts on the summer ski-ing pistes and then dropping into the wide névés of the Cirque Maudit. I started with a pit of tension in my stomach. We sank to our ankles in the soft snow on the long trek across the cirque, but as the clouds cleared my nerves settled.

The dome of Mont Blanc shimmered brilliantly up to our left and mists shifted across the burnished pillars of the Grand Capucin, Le Trident and the Clocher du Tacul. They finally rolled away into the Géant basin, revealing the clustered spires of the Diable Ridge on the skyline. With the challenge unveiled, the response was left to us alone. The mountains present stark choices. They offer none of the excuses or delusions by which one can muddle through normal life. You either keep faith with your dreams or lose them for ever. In the next 36 hours we had the chance to grasp our ultimate ambition, but there could be no half-measures. I began to feel very excited.

The Diable Ridge is graded D+ and contains several rock pitches of grade IV and V, but we had the advantage of prior knowledge. Simon had taken David Litherland up the route in 1990.

Whenever David mentioned the route, Martin and I would hesitate because we perceived it as a highly technical and complex climb which was committing in every sense of the word. It was with some trepidation that I finally agreed to guide him. To our relief, we found solid towers of perfect Chamonix granite with solid anchors and good abseil points. In short, the Diable Ridge is a delight and a hidden classic.

At 1.30pm we sat at 4047m on the Brèche Chaubert after a 600m climb up broken rocks and ice slopes from the cirque below. The brèche is situated between the first two of the five 'devil's needles', known as the Corne du Diable and the Pointe Chaubert. Since the Corne rises only 17m above the brèche, we were not obliged to climb it and we there-fore immediately turned our attention to the East Ridge of the 4074m

Chaubert which rises as a smooth blade of granite.

On its first ascent in 1925, Armand Charlet had made a human pyramid of his two companions in order to overcome the initial section. Climbed free with a couple of protection pitons, the moves rate no more than IV+. Simon let out a squeal of pleasure as he laybacked up the crest. The carefree climbing and immaculate rock seemed a world removed from the austerities of the Jorasses West Ridge.

The pioneering of the Diable Ridge spanned a period of six years. Charlet was the driving force, leading parties on to the pinnacles from above and below. One by one the spires were climbed and then on 3 August 1928 he made the first integral traverse with fellow-guide, Georges Cachet, and clients, Miriam O'Brien and Robert Underhill. No pitons were placed either for assistance or protection on these ascents. Their use was reserved solely for abseil anchors.

From the Pointe Chaubert, three abseils took us down to the Brèche Médiane. A sombre diedre soared 80m to the top of the Pointe Médiane. The atmosphere here was cold, shaded and oppressive, the climbing athletic, strenuous and sustained at grade IV. We regained the sunshine at the 4097m summit, where a huge block is jammed across a cleft to make a giant needle's eye.

As on the Chaubert we found a bunch of abseil slings and rappelled airily into the Brèche Carmen. We were carefully noting the height separations of each pinnacle and on this occasion one 30m abseil was sufficient to land us safely in the gap. The Médiane therefore failed to qualify on our list of '4000ers' and its place was taken by the next peak, the 4109m Pointe Carmen.

The final 5m of the Carmen formed a smooth razor's edge with no possibility of protection. Simon shuffled up the edge *à cheval,* then swung both legs on to the right wall and boldly laybacked the last moves. These definitely rated grade V. He was able to place a sling on the very top to protect his descent and I followed, thankful to have the benefit of a top-rope.

So far, we had taken three hours to make 300m of horizontal progress. The next gap, the Brèche du Diable, gave a couple of horizontal pitches on snowed-up rock before the ridge rose to the base of L'Isolée (4114m), the final and most imposing of the pinnacles. Our route lay up the shaded east side of the spire and its lower ledges were covered with icy snow. I was concerned by the readiness with which Simon declined the lead at this point.

'You've done this before, so perhaps it'll be quicker if you go first,' I suggested.

'Well, it is your turn. You'll enjoy it,' he countered. 'I seem to remember going left round the corner after 10 or 15 metres.'

I tried to heed Simon's advice to traverse, but the direct cracklines were so compellingly obvious that I ignored the leftward variation and committed myself to strenuous grade V climbing. Having reached a roof, it became immediately necessary to transfer to a parallel jamming crack a metre to my left. It was probably in this very crack that Charlet had wedged his ice axe and climbed up it hand-over-hand on the first ascent. It is hard to imagine the audacity of such a manoeuvre without piton protection. Lacking a metre-long alpenstock but greatly reassured by three running belays, I was forced to use more conventional means of progress, namely jammed knuckles and wedged elbows. With a good deal of thrutching, I made the transfer and gained some ledges Our 60m rope was just running out when I reached the top block.

From L'Isolée a long and comparatively scruffy scramble led on to Mont Blanc du Tacul. As the nearest '4000er' to the Aiguille du Midi *télépherique* and with a simple PD– route up its North-West Face, the Tacul regularly sees over a hundred visitors a day. Now it was deserted. From the summit we strolled down the easy snow shoulder to the Col Maudit where Angus and Martin were waiting at a tiny bivouac tent. We had taken just nine hours from the Col du Géant and were brimming with confidence.

'That's got to be the best route of the summer,' I concluded.

David and Winky had brought the gear and food up at 2pm, and Angus and Martin had spent the afternoon on the col filming our acro batics through telephoto lenses. We squeezed into the tent and commenced a two-hour cooking session with the stove wedged between my knees. After successive courses of tea, soup with fresh bread, pasta, tuna and cheese, we emerged at 9pm.

The rich light which had bathed the col was now paling into a pink alpenglow. The sun sank blood-red behind bands of slaty cloud, leaving the jagged peaks of Aravis standing proud in the twilight. We stood for a moment in mute admiration of the spectacle, then turned to work. The coming night now held no fear, only the sense at last that our time had come.

We pulled on every stitch of clothing, checked our headtorches and reorganised our gear, handing a stove, pan and some food to Angus and

Martin, who planned to meet us at the Vallot Hut at 4am. Martin persisted in filming our preparations, despite the bitter cold. When we left at 9.10pm, they dived inside the tent for three hours' rest before setting off to make our rendezvous.

The climb to Mont Maudit was taken slowly out of respect for Simon's digestion and it was 11.15pm when we mounted the distinctive little tower that forms its 4465m summit. Mont Blanc itself lay only 2km away across the Col de la Brenva, but our revised route now made a long traverse under its North Face by the glacial shelf known as the Corridor. This would lead us out to the Dôme du Goûter at 4304m where our detour to the Aiguille de Bionnassay commenced.

From Mont Maudit we trekked into a chill and windless night under a canopy of a thousand stars. In the west, faint neon glows marked the distant cities of Geneva, Annecy and Chambéry. We lost the moonlight as we dipped into the Corridor. Although Simon and I had each climbed Mont Blanc over a dozen times, neither of us had been down this route. All we knew was that the line is complicated by crevasses and threatened by seracs. When we lost old tracks under fresh snowdrifts, we became a little concerned and edged nervously down a steepening incline. At each crevasse we had to guess whether to go left or right in search of a snow bridge. We dreaded the thought of getting into a cul-de-sac and having to climb back up, but our intuition served us well. We were soon striding across the Grand Plateau and up a long convex gradient to the Dôme du Goûter.

It was 1.15am and we were still moving quickly. From the experience of doing a 24-hour fell-run in Scotland, I guessed that we would be hit by a sudden fatigue just before dawn. This is usually the time when the body's clock realises that it is out of phase and makes its loudest protest. For the moment, our strength was holding, buoyed by the thrill of walking the roof of Western Europe in the dead of night.

We left our sacks on the ridge descending from the Dôme du Goûter. Casually I said: 'We may as well leave the rope as well; the Bionnassay was no problem when I did it last year.' In fact, the Aiguille de Bionnassay has a reputation for a razor-edge on its East Ridge, but this had been absent when I'd guided the mountain in 1992. On that occasion we had followed the normal route towards Mont Blanc from Italy via the Miage Glacier and the Gonella Hut and turned westwards to the Bionnassay at a little shoulder known as the Piton des Italiens.

We now descended easily to this shoulder and bore steeply down right to the Col de Bionnassay. Here the real excitement began. Our torchbeams picked out a wafer of snow heading towards the Bionnassay and I immediately realised my folly in leaving the rope behind. A track the width of a single boot weaved from side to side of the edge in a manner somewhat akin to a motorway contra-flow system. On the north side of the ridge, a 600m ice face plunged to the Bionnassay Glacier. The narrowness of the trail enforced a dainty heel-to-toe walking style that made us feel like a couple of ballerinas coming on stage. With a few coils of rope between us we could have relaxed, but we had to proceed in the knowledge that if we missed a step and tripped, there would be no reprieve.

Near to the summit we passed an enormous meringue-shaped cornice which projects 10m from the ridge and is one of the finest of its kind in the Alps, being clearly visible from the Col de Voza 2500m below. The Aiguille de Bionnassay possesses an aura similar to the Liskamm It is in every sense a classical peak with no simple routes and a particularly fine snow climb up its North-West Face. This was Simon's first visit and with its ascent he completed his last of the fifty major 4000m mountains. Of the eight remaining summits of Alps 4000, only the three tops on the Brouillard Ridge were unknown to us. I'm loathe to admit to peak-bagging, but since the Aiguille Verte, I had been assiduously watching the progress of our cumulative total.

The anticipated fatigue overtook me as we slogged back over the Dôme du Goûter and joined the normal route from the Goûter Hut to the summit of Mont Blanc. So far the night had been ours alone, but now we became part of a torchlit procession as dozens of parties headed slowly towards the Bosses Ridge. This is just the stage in the ascent of Mont Blanc when people really begin to feel the altitude, and yet there remains a climb of 550m from the Col du Dôme to the summit, which is exposed to the wind throughout.

The Vallot Hut at 4362m offers a temporary respite before this last climb, but the decision to enter should not be taken lightly. The hut was built to shelter up to fifteen people in comfort, but it is likely that as many as three times that number will be found piled inside in the hour before dawn. Simon and I badly needed a hot drink and half-an-hour of rest. We had no choice but to enter the fray. Angus and Martin had just arrived after following our route across the Corridor, and stove, pan and snow for melting were somehow balanced in a tiny square of free floor-space.

I felt a silent gratitude to Simon as he took on the job of holding the stove. I passed him my mug and then slumped down on what I presumed to be a pile of rucksacks. My head was swimming with fatigue and the moment I lay down all conscious thought drifted into hazy hallucination.

'Mon Dieu! Bougez, bougez, monsieur.'

I was thrust out of my dreams by a great shifting in the pile of gear beneath me. Two indignant faces emerged, their shouts indicating that I had been lying across their bodies. I shoved their legs to one side and squeezed into a tiny gap where I was undisturbed until the brew arrived.

The hot sweet coffee shot to my bloodstream as if it had been injected direct. Although my powers of concentration were restored, it was a matter of concern as to just how long the stimulative effects of the caffeine and sugar would last.

Dawn was close when we emerged from the hut and joined the human crocodile on the Bosses Ridge. This final snow arête is pleasingly sculpted and sufficiently narrow to give a sense of exposure, particularly on the Italian flank, where great ice slopes sweep down the Miage Face. Our memories of guiding this ridge were of toiling slowly with clients who had reached their limits of acclimatisation and in the process were suffering torment from the icy wind. This morning we romped up in little over an hour and stayed warm throughout.

Our only hindrance was in passing parties on narrow sections, but we did not resent the crowds. After so many days of isolation we were glad of some company, especially among folk who were nearing their own pinnacle of personal achievement. The final ridge rises in a long convexity which taxes the last reserves of many and only broadens at the very top. Some fifty people were already gathered there and well over a hundred more were following on the ridge. Some of the summiteers were waving a flag, a group of Germans was singing with great gusto and a few were lying motionless on their sacks, their energies totally spent.

The view was one of unbroken splendour. A single cumulonimbus cloud towered 6000m into the sky somewhere beyond Monte Rosa. This apart, the only clouds were close-knit canopies formed from the overnight condensation of sinking air in the valleys of the Pennine Alps. Although many of the nearby peaks appear dwarfed when viewed from Mont Blanc, each was outlined like cut crystal in the sharp morning air. The sprawling tourist developments of Chamonix, 3800m below, were no more than the tiniest blot in the overall scale of this scene. The top of Mont Blanc is a good place for anyone who needs reassurance that the world is still a big place.

We might have prolonged our stay had the Brouillard Ridge not clouded our thoughts. To leave the warm conviviality of the summit and descend the mountain's South Face in the full heat of the day seemed wholly irrational now that we were presented with the task. Of the three great classic climbs on the south side of Mont Blanc, the Brouillard Ridge was the only route that neither of us had done. Moreover, it had a reputation as a long and tiresome route of AD+ grade, with more than its fair share of loose rock. The famous climbs on the Innominata and Frêney Faces finish along its upper crest, but we knew nobody except Will McLewin who had done the ridge in its entirety from the Col Emile Rey.

Three 4000m tops lie on the Brouillard Ridge. Our first objective was the obscure Pic Luigi Amedeo (4460m), which Karl Blodig had imagined was his final '4000er' when he joined Young, Jones and Knubel on the first complete ascent of the ridge in 1911. Beyond the Pic Luigi the ridge drops steeply to the Col Emile Rey at 4030m. This remote col offers the only possible passage between the Brouillard and Miage basins, but it is rarely visited except by the most determined collectors of '4000ers'. The last two tops, Mont Brouillard (4069m) and the Punta Baretti (4013m), lie a short distance south of the col.

Our departure from Mont Blanc at 6.50am on 7 August was one of the lonelier moments of the expedition. Angus and Martin were returning to collect the tent at the Col Maudit and would then descend to Chamonix. They wished us luck and photographed us striding down the narrowing crest towards Mont Blanc de Courmayeur before they, too, left the summit. Once more we were thrown back on our own wit and resource.

I feel bitterly cold and uncomfortable on the top of Mont Blanc, so I am glad to get going. The initial descent takes us in a long rightward curve on to an exposed snow arête interspersed with loose rock steps. On the south side of the arête the face seems to drop straight down to Courmayeur 3¹/₂km below. However, we are now old hands at this style of ridge and I am able to relax and take a workmanlike approach to the task. We cover the ground steadily.

At the beginning of every serious passage on the expedition we had automatically suppressed our fears and channelled our emotions, thus gaining a heightened state of alertness and awareness. Despite its significance as the last great unknown of Alps 4000, we did not dare approach the Brouillard Ridge in any other way. Simon's feeling of 'relaxation' was simply the achievement of that singular state of mind where nothing in the world matters except the stability of the next step of snow.

The snow quality varied greatly from a firm pack on the north side of the ridge to a crust of sugary granules on the south. With 6m of rope between us and no other protection, we tried to weave a route that would keep us on opposite sides or, failing that, would follow the safer north flank. But the north side was regularly too steep to be traversed comfortably and on several occasions we were both forced on to the rotten slush on the Brouillard flank which was melting quickly in the sun. Despite our growing commitment, we still seemed no more than a stone's throw away from the dome of Mont Blanc, for we could see every party on the Bosses Ridge in clear profile.

Occasionally, the shaded depths of the Miage flank began to draw my eye away from the immediate ground at my feet and in my fatigue felt slightly giddy. The slope below seemed so smooth and simple that it began to look inviting. An unspeakable thought crossed my mind:

'How easy it would be to let go and slide down there.' The survivor in me immediately responded.

'Keep a grip, Martin. For Joy and your children you've got to come through this one. It's only a few hours more.'

This fleeting temptation returned several times. I blotted it out on each occasion, but I knew I was getting desperately tired.

> Close to the Pic Luigi we are stopped by a smooth rock step and decide to abseil. As we pull the rope to retrieve it, the free end jams completely in a crack at the top of the step. It is infuriating. The rest of the rope has run through the crack smoothly and only the plastic tape wrapped round the end has jammed it. Martin offers to go back up, but he finds it harder than he thinks. The step is overhanging. He comes back down, removes his crampons and finds an easier way to climb back up round to the left. He repeats the abseil and this time we flick the rope clear of the crack. We've got our rope back, but we've lost half-an-hour.

We stood on the Pic Luigi Amedeo at 11am. Having climbed it, we were now doubtful whether it has a height separation of more than 35m. At that moment the thought was irrelevant and we decided that the top would stay on our list anyway. The Pic Luigi was quite definitely the most inaccessible top we had climbed, surpassing even the Pointe Marguerite on the Grandes Jorasses, which is its closest rival.

The exposures of the ridge now eased and we were thrown into a long diagonal movement across the south flank towards the Col Emile Rey. Not all of Mont Blanc is composed of solid granite. At the edges of the igneous mass which forms the core of the range, there are bands of shale and other rotten conglomerates. These were metamorphosed by extreme heat and compression and are weathered rapidly under the action of frost and sun. The lower Brouillard Ridge is a striking example of such disintegration. Its rocks of biotite gneiss were fairly described by Geoffrey Winthrop Young as 'a hot jumble of cyclopean fragments'.

Virtually everything we touched beyond the Pic Luigi moved. Several pieces detached altogether and we noticed that any debris we sent down was channelled towards the crucial couloir which gives access to the Col Emile Rey. I remembered all too well the words of our guidebook that, in ascending the ridge, it is essential to be well above the col by dawn.

With the sun now approaching its zenith, the wisdom of descending further towards the couloir needed little debate.

'We can't go down there,' I said.

'I agree,' said Simon, 'but if we can't go down there, then where the hell can we go?'

'Maybe we could wait until tonight.'

'But what about the storm? We can't just sit here waiting for it.'

'I'm running out of steam. How about a cuppa?'

Finding a crow's nest of solid rock, we set up the stove and chopped some ice blocks from a shaded crevice. With the brew underway, I radioed to the Val Veni, secretly hoping for an improved weather forecast that would enable us to sleep for the remainder of the day.

'There's no real change,' said Joy. 'Storms tonight and tomorrow.'

David Litherland then gave us a verbatim recital of the morning's forecast from Chamonix.

'You'll have to keep going. You can do it,' he said.

'Yes, come on,' came a shout from Joy, behind. 'You're doing great. Just keep going and you'll make it.'

These encouragements were given in total ignorance of our exact position and predicament, but they had the desired effect. With a team down there rooting for us, we no longer felt completely marooned. Even if the couloir was unjustifiable, surely there was some other way.

'We might be able to keep to the side of the couloir on the rocks,' suggested Simon.

'We'll head for that gendarme where the couloir narrows and see what's what.'

An hour's rest and a hot drink helped revive us and on continuing the descent we immediately found some reserves of energy. We dropped down another 150m, keeping off the long snowfields which were exposed to rocks falling from above. At the mouth of the gully we stopped. A waterfall sprang from the base of the snows and cascaded into the narrows. Tiny fragments of stone bounced down in the flow. We could no longer keep out of the line of fire on the side wall. Neither of us were tempted to chance the gully, even though we stood at its brink. The memory of the Géant was still too vivid. Simon began to scout for alternatives.

> I take a look over the edge of the cliff to our right. The wall is vertical for 150m, but if we can find anchors we might be able to reach the col with safety. A good spike at the top encourages us to try. I fix the rope and Martin takes all the old slings and wired nuts which we've picked up on other routes over the past weeks. They have been stored in our sacks in expectation of a situation like this. Then he swings out over the edge and ventures down the cliff. At his shout I follow. I reach his stance and pull down the rope. We are committed to the second rappel, and are past the point of no return.
>
> The cliff is steep but well cracked. After each abseil Martin gets a good belay. There is no evidence of anyone else having climbed or descended this face, but after five 30m rappels, we reach broken rocks level with the Col Emile Rey.

Emile Rey was the most eminent of the Courmayeur guides of the nineteenth century and he was described as a man cool in his doings but passionate in his feelings. At a particularly difficult passage on the Aiguille Blanche de Peuterey, he was heard to yell in a fit of anger: 'I have never turned back in my life; I shall not do so today.' Rey's self-belief was unshakable, but he died descending easy ground beneath the Dent du Géant in 1895. Jumping down on to a sloping ledge, he slipped on loose pebbles and could not save himself.

The col is a wild spot, but was infinitely more friendly than the ridge we had descended. At 3.15pm, we left our sacks and tackled the last two tops. Mont Brouillard took only ten minutes, but the Punta Baretti lies ½km further along the ridge. The linking crest was mainly easy but very loose. I now felt as though I was climbing by remote control. We were locked into a slow but steady pace and, without halting, we took 2¼ hours to make the return journey.

We now knew that we could not possibly continue to the Aiguille Blanche de Peuterey that evening. It lay across two steep and difficult glaciers and would have taken us well into the night. We could see the tiny Eccles Bivouac Hut, perched on the Innominata Ridge between the Brouillard and Frêney Glaciers. There was no issue. We needed sleep and the Aiguille Blanche would have to be left to the whims of tomorrow's weather.

As we left the Col Emile Rey there were already long streaks of cirrus cloud in the west and a milky sheen in the evening sky that suggested an approaching weather front, although it might be 6, 12 or 18 hours before the storm broke. At that moment, we were too tired to care about anything save a safe descent to the hut.

Simon led us down the couloir towards the upper plateau of the Brouillard Glacier with a show of determined step-kicking in rotten snow. I was climbing last and therefore held the most vulnerable position. But we had bought one hammer axe along for just such a situation and I enjoyed the extra security of a second axe, whereas Simon managed with just one. On several occasions the steps collapsed into a hidden cavity under my weight and I threatened to topple backwards. The angle was constant at 45 to 50°. I yearned for an end to the mental torment, for anything that would get us off this infernal slope.

We crossed a great avalanche runnel descending from the access couloir to the Brouillard Ridge, which we had avoided earlier. We had neither seen nor heard any major activity in the couloir all afternoon, but we were taking no chances. Simon was in and out of the runnel in seconds and we continued traversing at speed until clear of objective danger from further gullies to its right. A short descent took us down to the plateau, which is no more than a shelf sandwiched between the soaring Brouillard Pillars and an impassable icefall. We climbed off the far end of the shelf and traversed 30m to the hut door.

In fine weather the Eccles Hut can be impossibly crowded. There are, in fact, two huts, the second lying 30m higher on the slope, but in total they offer only twelve bed-spaces. When the Central Pillar of Frêney is in condition, a dozen climbers can come here for that one route alone, never mind other great routes like the Innominata Ridge. We were relieved to find that only a French guide from the Oisans district and his client from Marseilles were in residence. After 33 hours on the move and just 6 hours after being stranded on the Pic Luigi, we had secured a bed for the night.

Our new companions had just climbed the Red Pillar of Brouillard and had seen us descending from the Pic Luigi Amedeo. Such unconventional behaviour aroused their interest.

'Why do you descend the ridge?' asked the guide.

'To get to Mont Brouillard and the Punta Baretti,' Simon replied by way of feeble explanation.

'I don't understand. Please, tell me where you started from.' His countenance evinced an increasing puzzlement.

'The Col du Géant,' announced Simon with a flush of pride.

Our guide now looked incredulous.

'You have very little food? Please, take these biscuits. Now, which route do you do?'

'Well, we started up the Diable Ridge . . .'

More disbelieving glances were exchanged and half a loaf of bread passed our way.

'And then where?' he asked.

'We went out to the Aiguille de Bionnassay.'

This revelation brought a low whistle and two cartons of pot-noodles. I thought it was time we explained about the 4000m peaks before they declared us utterly insane, but the disclosure was lost on the pair. What was an entirely rational choice of route to us, in the circumstances seemed to them an extended form of suicide. After that, we were embarrassed to tell them that we were qualified guides and, like our French colleague, were fully paid-up members of the UIAGM (Union Internationale des Associations des Guides de Montagnes). Nevertheless, the conversation had served to replenish our meagre remaining food stocks.

Whether out of pity for us or fear of what we might do to them later in the night, the pair departed at 8.30pm to descend 1300m to the Monzino Hut. We were grateful to be left an empty hut and the need to sleep hit us like a pole-axe. I stretched out on a hammock bunk, supped a last cup of tea and remembered no more.

*

It is 3am and the alarm is trying its best to wake us. I look over towards Martin and see that he has not stirred. My body feels stiff from head to toe, the result of 33 hours' exertion and only 5 hours of sleep. I must first look out and check the weather. Expecting snow to blow in, I slowly ease the door open, but am pleasantly surprised. No snow has fallen and the cloud is broken.

This chance to climb the Aiguille Blanche must be taken. I know the route from the bivouac hut well, having used it to approach both the Innominata Ridge and Frêney Pillar and descended it after guiding David Litherland over the Blanche in 1991.

Nevertheless, the Aiguille Blanche de Peuterey remains the most remote of the major 4000m mountains and still deserves our respect. I shake Martin from his slumber and start the stove for a brew.

I feigned sleep until the tea was ready.

'Bed-tea! This is an unexpected surprise,' I said, as Simon handed me my mug. He was definitely showing an improvement in his morning performance. His favourable weather report enabled me to savour every second of my lie-in. I felt comparatively refreshed and wonderfully relaxed. Having coped with the rigours of the Brouillard Ridge, today's route held no fear. With luck, we might be back in the valley within ten hours.

We left at 5am, traversed back to the Brouillard Glacier and climbed up to the base of the couloir leading up to the Col Eccles. The snow was crisp and there was only one section of ice just above the *bergschrund*. Thanks to this abnormally snowy summer, the remainder of the couloir yielded to simple step-kicking. Simon recalled having to climb rocks on the right edge due to an impossible rimaye and bare ice in the couloir on his last visit in 1992.

The Col Eccles provides the only route between the upper Brouillard and Frêney Glaciers. It was first traversed in 1877 by James Eccles with the guides Michel-Clément and Alphonse Payot. From a bivouac close to the site of the present hut they had crossed the col and descended its far side, thus becoming the first humans to stand on the upper plateau of the Frêney Glacier. The commitment of that descent undoubtedly impressed Eccles who recalled:

It might have been an illusion, but at that time I thought it the most formidable piece of work I had ever done. Possibly the light – the couloir then being in deep shadow – had something to do with the impression.

From the upper Frêney basin, the party continued to climb the upper section of the Peuterey Ridge to the summit of Mont Blanc. Although they did not climb the Aiguille Blanche, they had unlocked the key to its ascent, which was made by a party led by Rey eight years later.

The descent to the Frêney plateau caused us little trouble. The snow was firm and there was barely a hint of a *bergschrund* at the bottom. In these conditions, our route to the Aiguille Blanche, although circuitous, is much the easiest way to climb the mountain, rating no higher than AD in technical standard. It should certainly be considered by parties who are deterred from climbing the classic route to the Aiguille Blanche via the Peuterey Ridge, which is rather more serious and difficult.

As we gained the plateau, the famous pillars of Frêney glowed briefly in the dawn and then retired into the gloom as dark blue flagships of the gathering storm enveloped Mont Blanc. It was eerily silent and I could not help but think of Walter Bonatti and the Frêney Pillar tragedy of 1961. Directly above rose the slim *chandelle* of the Central Pillar where Bonatti, Pierre Mazeaud and their five companions had endured three nights of continuous storm while attempting to make its first ascent.

Just below us, the plateau ended in a great plug of sheer ice. Bonatti's party had abseiled down the Rochers Grüber on the left side of this huge serac during their desperate retreat from the pillar. One by one the party succumbed to hypothermia on the Frêney Glacier and only Bonatti, Mazeaud and Roberto Gallieni reached the Monzino Hut alive. I wondered how they might have fared had they tried to get over the Col Eccles and descend the much easier Brouillard Glacier.

The memory speeded our steps. This was no place to be caught in a storm. We hurried over to the Col de Peuterey and by 6.40am were engaged on the final rocky buttress of the Aiguille Blanche. Two pitches of mixed climbing took us to the summit crest. We went first to the central and highest top, the Pointe Güssfeldt (4112m). This was ignored by early ascensionists of the mountain, who treated the 4107m south-east top, which is known as the Pointe Seymour King, as the true summit.

A curving knife-edge of snow led over to the south-east summit. We felt it proper to climb it, especially since its height separation is close to 35m. The top is an easy angled dome of snow. We reached it at 8am and immediately radioed our success to Carole and Joy in the Val Veni.

On the mountain's first ascent by Rey's party in 1885, the summit cele-
brations were unrestrained. Henry Seymour King wrote afterwards:

> The guides had with great trouble dragged up an alpenstock and
> fastened to it an Italian flag, leaving the traditional bottle of champagne
> to our noble selves.

Even had we carried up the champagne, Simon and I are not the types
to make such an effusive display. We sat quietly on the snow and
allowed a couple of minutes for the moment to sink in. Alps 4000 had
just become a reality. The official finish might be on the Barre des
Ecrins in six or seven days' time, but this was our private moment of
success. Nothing could now stop us, save being knocked off our
bicycles on the main road to Aosta. We allowed ourselves a brief glow
of pride and relief and then commenced the descent.

We were back at the hut by 10.40am and stopped no longer than it
took to fold our blankets and collect our rubbish. In good snow conditions the descent from the Eccles to the Monzino Hut down the left side
of the Brouillard Glacier is one of the fastest imaginable. We took off
our crampons after the first slope below the hut and then plunged
downhill in a series of leaps and glissades, forsaking all normal precau-
tionary measures for glacier travel, save for a very slack rope. What
matter a few crevasses now that we were free? The sense of euphoria
grew as we lost height. All I could think of was the prospect of seeing
Joy, Alex and Hazel in the valley. We passed the Monzino Hut at
12.20pm, scrambled down the buttresses beneath the hut and strode
through the young pine woods which cover the former snout of the
Miage Glacier.

Carole was waiting at the roadhead at La Visaille with our bikes. Our
campsite was 3km down the valley. I dropped my sack in the Land-
Rover, changed out of my boots and pedalled off. The warm valley
wind streamed through my hair as I swooped down a series of hairpins
and into the camp ground. The kids ran out to greet me. Hazel jumped
straight into my arms, while Alex tugged at my trousers.

'Mummy, Dad's back.'

Joy emerged from the van looking pleased and relieved. We
embraced with more feeling than for several weeks.

'Well, that's it,' I said. 'We've done it now.'

Simon arrived a few minutes later. Carole handed him a mug of his
favourite weak tea and he stretched out in the back of the Land Rover.

Surrounded by Carole and friends I feel light-hearted. As my mind skims back over the past ten days, I find it hard to grasp the scale of effort we have applied to gain this result.

Just an hour later the storm broke.

11

UPHILL ALL THE WAY

Val Veni to Val Savarenche – Gran Paradiso – Col du Galibier – Barre des Ecrins

One of the greatest pleasures of the expedition lay in journeying continuously towards new horizons. This sense had been most keenly felt when we combined the climbing with walking and biking to move across and between the massifs. Now that the mental stress of completing the Mont Blanc summits was over and with our eventual success no longer in doubt, the last phase of the trip promised the best opportunity to indulge in the delights of mountain travel as opposed to serious climbing.

It is fortunate that Italy can at least lay absolute claim to one '4000er', the 4061m Gran Paradiso. All of its other 4000m mountains are shared with Switzerland or France. Lying 40km south-east of the main watershed of the Alps, the Paradiso massif enjoys warmer and sunnier weather than is found in the Mont Blanc and Pennine ranges. From the Val Veni we faced a half-day cycle of 67km to reach Pont at the head of the Val Savarenche, which for all and sundry is the starting point for the ascent of the Paradiso.

Sporadic thunderstorms rumbled through the night, but cleared to leave a warm, bright morning on Monday 9 August. After an undisturbed seven-hour sleep I felt refreshed. However, yesterday's euphoria had worn a little, and we were coming to terms with the fact that the best part of a week of hard work still lay between us and the Barre des Ecrins. If all went well, we would be there in five days, finishing on the auspicious date of Friday the 13th. That would give a total time of fifty-two days, just four days behind our original base schedule. Considering that we had endured much the worst summer weather since 1987, that would be a respectable performance. We

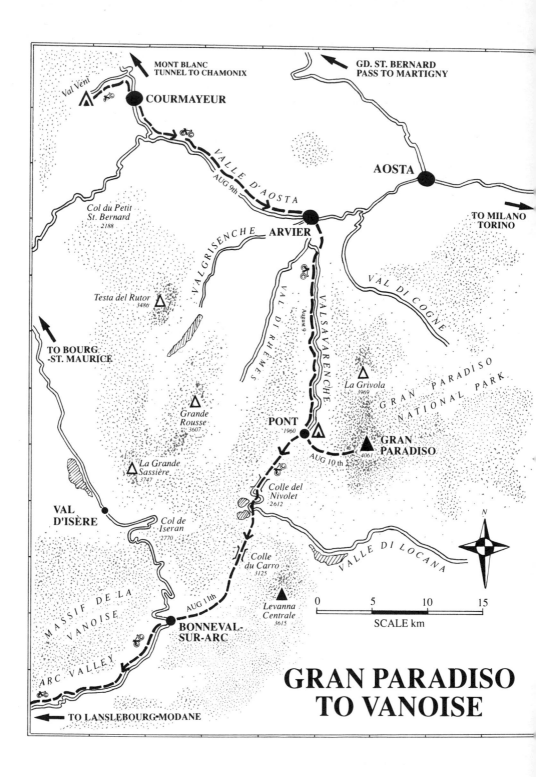

MONT BLANC
TUNNEL TO CHAMONIX

GD. ST. BERNARD
PASS TO MARTIGNY

Val Veni

COURMAYEUR

AOSTA

Col du Petit
St. Bernard
·2188

V A L L E   D' A O S T A

AUG 9th

TO MILANO
TORINO

VALGRISENCHE

ARVIER

VAL DI COGNE

Testa del Rutor
·3486

VAL DI RHÊMES

Anghin 9

VALSAVARENCHE

G R A N   P A R A D I S O

TO BOURG
-ST. MAURICE

La Grivola
3969

N A T I O N A L   P A R K

Grande
Rousse
3607

PONT
·1960

GRAN
PARADISO
·4061

AUG 10.th

La Grande
Sassière
3747

Colle del
Nivolet
·2612

VAL
D'ISÈRE

Col de
Iseran
·2770

V A L L E   D I   L O C A N A

N

Colle
du Carro
·3125

MASSIF   DE   LA
VANOISE

AUG 11th

Levanna
Centrale
3615

0   5   10   15

BONNEVAL-
SUR-ARC

SCALE km

ARC VALLEY

TO LANSLEBOURG-MODANE

GRAN PARADISO
TO VANOISE

informed Bill Shannon and Jackie Ross. Bill began to gear all media coverage to that target date and Jackie declared that he would fly out to meet us at the finish.

With these arrangements sealed, we were ready at 11am. Today, Simon and I decided to have a change from each other's company and I stayed back a few minutes before setting off. The gentle spin of the pedals and the rush of a cool breeze sent a wave of happiness through my body as I coasted down the Val Veni. I kept glancing up to my left, past the towering buttresses of the Aiguille Noire de Peuterey and up the crumpled icefalls of the Brenva Glacier to the shining dome of Mont Blanc, 3500m above. Its summit was wreathed by the last tentacles of morning mist. I found it hard to believe that we'd been up there for the last three days. Even when conquered, Mont Blanc remains supreme and unmoved and it left me with the same sense of awe as when I'd first seen the mountain as an alpine novice fourteen years previously.

The Val Veni road runs alongside the gravel-covered snout of the Brenva Glacier, then twists down to join the Aosta trunk road 2km from its emergence from the Mont Blanc Tunnel. I turned right and pedalled steadily past the clustered roofs of Courmayeur town centre. Although disturbed by the continuous noise of lorry traffic on the road up to the tunnel, Courmayeur has retained much of its traditional character, in marked contrast to its bigger and busier French rival, Chamonix, yet very few people other than Italian mountaineers make it their base for a climbing holiday in the Mont Blanc range.

From the town the road follows the Dora Baltea river down into the Val d'Aosta, which brings a corridor of warmth and fertility into the heart of the high Alps. We had expected heavy traffic. Juggernaut convoys usually ruin any appreciation of the churches, villages and fortresses which are perched high above the valley gorge. Happily, this must have been the time when the truck-drivers were taking their lunch-break and I enjoyed an untroubled ride, during which I dropped 550m in height down to the village of Arvier.

Simon was waiting here for Carole to arrive in order to have a snack and a drink, but I preferred to push on up the 28km ride to Pont on an empty stomach. I had not forgotten my torment on the Grand St Bernard a fortnight previously and wanted to tackle the 1270m ascent of the Val Savarenche while there was still some shadow across the valley.

The high valleys of the Italian Alps are wilder and more wooded than their Swiss counterparts and less disfigured by ski-ing development than those in France. Once the main routes are left, you can feel transported back a century to an era when the pace of life was wholly tuned to the demands of the land. The folk of the Val d'Aosta retain French as their native language, keeping faith to the time when the region was part of the dukedom of Savoy, and few of them have acquired the hard-nosed commercial mentality that has blighted many other areas of the Alps.

The hamlets above Arvier were just commencing their siesta as I pedalled through. My muscles had to work hard on the initial twisting climb, but once I had gained the floor of the Val Savarenche and the gradient had eased to a more gradual incline, I found a growing strength and stayed in my middle set of gears all the way to the final steepening below Pont.

'It's incredible,' I said to myself. 'I'm feeling as strong as an ox.'

Our powers of recovery had grown so much through the summer that they were now astounding even ourselves. By all normal expectations, I should have been flat on my back in a shaded room after the three days we had just experienced on Mont Blanc. The journey was showing us how much can be achieved where there is a will and an aim.

After the rustic tranquillity of the Val Savarenche, my arrival at Pont was something of a shock. Two large hotels, a packed car park and a campsite large enough to accommodate five hundred people filled the valley floor. A continuous stream of trekkers could be seen ambling up the track towards the Paradiso. Nevertheless, the camp was clearly defined and well managed, and did not ruin the essential beauty of the surrounding scenery. A few rock-climbers were attempting bolt-protected routes on the granite crags which flanked the camp. The snowy cap of the Ciaforon (3640m) could be seen up on the left, but the Paradiso itself was wholly hidden behind the bulk of the immediate valley-side.

The main hut base for the Gran Paradiso is dedicated to Vittorio Emmanuele II, the King of Sardinia and Piedmont who saved the ibex from being hunted to extinction in the nineteenth century. The area is the native home of the ibex, but the animal has since been released in many parts of the Alps and has prospered. Appropriately, the Paradiso region is now a national park and some 4,000 ibex are known to live in the 56,000 hectare reserve.

The mountain's ascent is extremely popular on account of its technical simplicity and proximity to the urban conurbations on the northern Italian plains. Places at the Emmanuele Hut must be reserved by telephone in the high season, but more space may be found at the nearby Chabod Hut, which is only slightly more distant from the normal route up the Paradiso's western flank. We decided to avoid any complications with accommodation by doing the whole 2100m ascent from valley to summit in the morning and were therefore able to spend the afternoon relaxing with our families.

We left Pont at 4.15am. I guessed that Simon was on good form by the speed with which he led us up to the hut. Despite the darkness, we were there by 5.45am, half-an-hour inside the normal guidebook time. Our prompt arrival surprised Angus Andrew and David Litherland who had been staying at the hut and were only just preparing to leave. They had hoped to get some film of us on the summit.

We were in no mood for delays.

'You'll just have to catch us when we are descending,' we said and pressed on across the moraines to the snout of the Gran Paradiso Glacier where several other parties had stopped to put on rope and crampons.

Simon continued to push a hard pace up the gentle convex swell of the glacier on its right-hand side. We were at the final rocks by 8.30am.

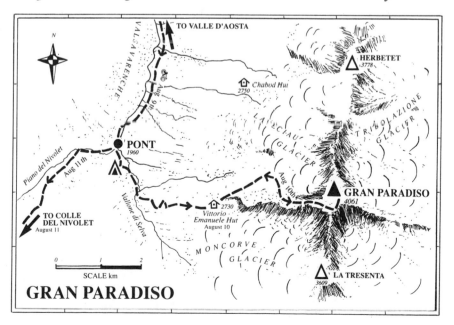

The Paradiso has two summits 100m apart. One has a statue of the Madonna and seems the obvious choice, but on my last visit I'd been convinced that the other top to its north was higher by a metre or two.

Simon thought otherwise.

'I've been to both and I can tell you the Madonna summit is the higher.' He sounded adamant, but I pressed the point.

'Well, I'm sure that Goedeke's guide says that the Madonna is lower.'

'Who's to say that he is always right?'

There was now an edge in Simon's voice. We were close to open argument for the first time in the trip, over what was an entirely trivial point. There had been occasions of resentful silence between us which had not lasted more than a couple of minutes, but never a row. We had always been able to keep a lid on our emotions when they did rise close to boiling point, and that had been essential to our progress. It was a sure sign that the journey was nearly over that we were now prepared to risk an argument.

The issue was quickly defused by our visiting both summits and I was almost glad to admit to Simon that the Madonna looked just as high when viewed from the northern top. The view from the Gran Paradiso is one of the finest in the Alps. The mountain lies at the hub of an arc of great peaks stretching from Monte Viso in the south to Monte Rosa in the north-east, but this morning a swathe of grey storm clouds hid the majority of the high ranges. We felt glad that we were not still engaged on Mont Blanc.

In the lee of the storm the clouds sheared off into magnificent lenticulars which streamed out over the black cone of Monte Viso and the plains of Piedmont. A bitter wind was rising on the summit slopes. Many people climbing the Paradiso are merely mountain walkers who are attracted far above their normal altitudes by the prospect of a *facile* '4000er'. Several were inadequately clad to withstand the piercing gale. I felt chilled even with a full set of Gore-tex clothing and offered my spare fleece jacket to a bearded chap who was ambling slowly towards the top with no more than a stringy woollen jumper to protect him from the cold. He looked pleased that I'd asked, but steadfastly refused.

Angus and David met us at 3800m. The clouded view and the wind rather spoilt Angus' film session. In fine weather the Paradiso would have been the ideal place to get a wide-angle panoramic shot of the '4000er' ranges, all of which are visible from the top except for the

Bernese Oberland and the Piz Bernina. Fighting camera shake and wind interference on his microphone, Angus recorded an interview with us. Once he had finished, we were pleased to get moving again and descended to Pont in two hours.

With so much of our route completed and only the Barre des Ecrins ahead, our mood was becoming more reflective. We were glad to have these last few days during which we could consider our pending success while still enjoying the journey. That afternoon at Pont, I began to wonder how I'd react at the finish.

My body was still strong, but I'd been through too much mental stress over the last fifty days to wish for any more. When close to completing the winter ascent of all Scotland's Munros in 1985, I had thought how nice it would be to go on climbing new hills for ever and had fallen into a slight depression after the finish. However, the Munros had presented neither the technical trials nor the sustained dangers of this expedition.

Furthermore, Joy had been my partner on half of the Scottish summits. The Munros traverse had brought us as close to marital bliss as a pair of hill-lovers could ever wish. It was little wonder that we would have happily extended that trip.

By contrast, the intensity of Alps 4000 had surprised and occasionally shocked me. Many times I had repeated the utterance that had first come to my lips half-way to the Adlerpass. The expedition was, and probably always would be, the toughest thing I'd done in my life, not only in terms of physical effort, but also in the immense task of organisation. Standing so close to its fulfilment, I did not think that I'd regret the finish this time.

I also knew how much Joy wanted to get home. Even the children were becoming unsettled by the constant moving about and now deserved some prolonged attention from their father. I had been troubled and sometimes perplexed that this challenge which was born from my natural passion for the mountains should have inflicted unhappiness on the person closest to me. I realised that, however laudable its aims and deeds, mountaineering can never be blindly pursued without regard for the feelings of others. Having almost won what was essentially a personal battle, I wanted more than anything else to repay the debt I owed my family. Only with the finish could I begin to do that.

We left Pont at the crack of dawn on 11 August. The quickest route back into France and towards the Ecrins Massif was overland on foot across the Colle del Nivolet and the Colle du Carro. These two passes would take us to the head of the Arc Valley on the southern edge of the Vanoise National Park. Knowing no more of the route than was suggested by our 1:50000 map, we took our boots, axes and crampons in case we encountered glacial terrain.

The morning was chill and clear with a dew-frost clothing the hillsides. A zigzagging path took us up through bluffs and *roches moutonnées* into the Piano del Nivolet, a wide ablation valley which provided excellent grazing for docile herds of cows and ibex. Dozens of curious marmots poked their heads out of their burrows at the approach of our steps and then scuttled down to safety as we walked past. At the head of the valley, we picked up a metalled road which led past two lakes and a pretty *pension*, then climbed to the 2612m Colle del Nivolet.

In the morning sunlight the surrounding hills looked exquisitely beautiful.

'I can't think that many Brits ever get here,' said Simon.

'It makes a nice change; they'll all be sitting in Chamonix moaning about the weather,' I laughed.

Ten minutes later we were stopped in our tracks by the sound of English voices. Our fellow guide, Martin Doyle, and his wife Sue were sitting at the summit of the pass.

'I've got a week off work, so we thought we'd get away from Chamonix and do some trekking,' said Martin.

The fact that they were as surprised to see us as we them was proof that the Paradiso National Park is still a good place to escape one's countryfolk. A ten-day east–west trekking route, the Grand Traverse of the Gran Paradiso, passes through the Colle del Nivolet. With a bountiful supply of huts, the area offers tremendous trekking potential, with plenty of additional scope beyond the official tours.

The crest of the col offered a breath-taking panorama across the Lacs Agnel and Serru. The hairpins of the road disappearing down into the Valle Locana lent scale and dimension to the scene. We scanned the opposite skyline in search of our second pass, the 3125m Colle du Carro. Due to the artistic licence of Italian cartography, it took some time to match the topography to the map.

Our map also proved less than frank on the matter of footpaths. We walked down past the lakes and then turned right on what the map showed as a track leading round into the side valley from which we would commence the 1200m climb to the col. Our way soon became completely overgrown and a little bushwhacking was needed to reach the valley floor. We stopped here by huge boulders to have a snack and bathe our feet.

The day was already so hot that for the duration of our rest I sat in a cool, clear brook which coursed down an old drainage aqueduct. The valley had once been habited by summer pastoralists. Like the footpaths, their way of life has been virtually erased from the landscape, except for a few sad ruins and these aqueducts, which were still functioning efficiently decades after their abandonment. An ugly bulldozed road on the opposite side of the valley indicated the modern means of exploiting its grazing potential. My image of the Paradiso was left a little tarnished by this sight.

We climbed up through encroaching scrub vegetation and out on to long scree slopes at the valley head. No obvious paths were visible leading to the col. We chose a fairly direct route and ended up having to surmount a rock step on which my fell-running shoes coped well with a couple of grade IV moves. Above the step we gained the crest of an enormous moraine which must at one time have shored up a vibrant glacier. Only benign slopes of névé and a few shrinking tongues of ice now remain of the Carro Glacier. There is every sign that it might disappear altogether in the next century.

We were now 250m below the pass which was $^1/_2$km wide and devoid of cairns or prominent landmarks. Happily, the sight of two other climbers high on the snow-slopes above confirmed the correct line of the route. We changed into boots and followed them up to meet the French border at the crest. Standing at the very head of the Arc Valley, the pass offered an extensive vista across the Dauphine Alps. The Ecrins Massif was central in the scene and though fully 60km away, the glacier face of the Barre des Ecrins was clearly discernible. Within forty-eight hours we should be there.

The French flank of the pass was busy with trekkers. We dropped down past the Carro Hut to well maintained valley pastures. Judging by the number of electric fences and admonitory notices, these alps were held in far greater value than the neglected Italian slopes. We picked up a good jeep track on the valley floor and this took us down to the roadhead and car park by the picturesque village of L'Ecot.

We were right on time for our arranged meeting at 1.30pm, but there was no sign of either Carole or Joy here. We had suggested that a three-

or four-hour drive would be sufficient for them to drive round from the Val Savarenche. They had to retrace their route almost as far as Courmayeur, climb over the 2100m Col du Petit St Bernard, then drive up the Val d'Isère and cross the 2770m Col de l'Iseran to reach us. We continued walking 4km down to Bonneval-sur-Arc and waited for half-an-hour. Eventually Simon found Carole waiting up a side road.

The drive had been the toughest of the summer and had been slowed by the swell of summer tourist traffic. Having just enjoyed one of the finest day's trekking imaginable, it was not the time for us to complain of the delay, and indeed Carole was in somewhat abrasive mood.

'That three hours you told me was a load of old baloney; it's taken at least five,' she said.

Tomorrow Carole faced the prospect of another marathon drive to Grenoble airport in order to collect Jackie Ross. Like Joy, she was becoming a little battle-weary.

As for Joy herself, she was presumed to be still somewhere on the drive. Simon and I decided to get on our bikes and commence the 60km cycle down the Arc Valley. At the first good campsite we would stop. Joy knew that this was our plan should the initial rendezvous fail. We cycled 18km down the valley against a stiff breeze and stopped at Lanslebourg. The town was bustling with its weekly street market in full swing. David and Angus had met us at Bonneval and Martin Welch returned from Chamonix where he had been processing films and despatching them to Bill Shannon. The whole support team was thus assembled ready for the last two days and Joy arrived an hour later.

> The hot dusty road had been jammed with traffic. The children had wanted to stop for a snack when we were close to Courmayeur, so we drew into a lay-by. As I fed them, passing lorries shook our van every twenty seconds and there was no chance to let them play outside. Then we had to face a grinding climb over the two passes. The van's exhaust silencer had been holed and the engine noise was deafening. I was definitely tired. Was it really going to end so soon? The pressure of my routine has not only come from coping with the kids. I also seem to have followed Martin's every step on the mountains in my mind, so there'll be relief when he finishes safely.
>
> I'd have preferred a quieter summer, but who am I to quell such an ambition? As soon as Martin had committed himself to this expedition there was no turning back, and in my deepest heart I hadn't wanted to let him down. And would he have been easy to live with if he hadn't attempted it? I doubt it! Nevertheless, if I'm ever asked to support another similar expedition, I may well request an early retirement.

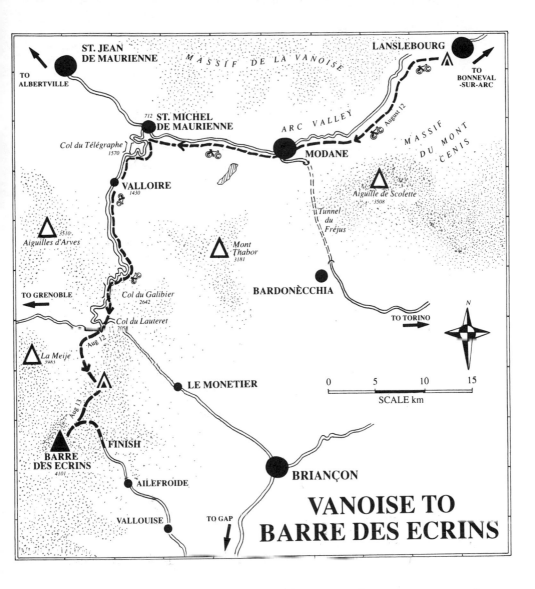

The 2642m Col du Galibier can justifiably be regarded as an *Eigerwand* of cycle touring. The 2000m climb to the col from St Michel-de-Maurienne in the lower Arc Valley was frightening us far more than the ascent of the Barre des Ecrins that was to follow. Our personal pride and competitive spirit were now such that we were determined to put in a performance on the col worthy of the whole expedition. No one was forcing us to push ourselves to our limit on the pass, but once we started a climb there would be no stopping. Happily, the 2000m ascent is split into two sections with a short downhill run to the village of Valloire in between. We could fairly allow ourselves a break at Valloire for drinks and snacks before tackling the 1200m upper section of the pass.

The morning of 12 August promised another hot day. We left at 9.10am and cycled a further 40km down the Arc Valley to St Michel. Half-way down we passed the industrial town of Modane where the busy route from Italy through the Frejus Tunnel is joined. From here both the traffic and the heat built up and the run no longer seemed an appropriate warm-up. I drank steadily from my bottle all the way to St Michel in order to be at my maximum state of hydration when the climb began.

There was relief when we turned off the main route and commenced the first stage of the ascent through thickly wooded hillsides to the 1570m Col du Télégraphe. Reality is never worse than nervous anticipation. The road was quiet and shaded and we soon slotted into a relaxed pace, each taking turns in the lead. Carole and Joy passed us at the summit and then we free-wheeled down into Valloire. In this busy but attractive little resort we called a twenty-minute break. For me, a custard tart and two raisin patisseries seemed the right sort of food for rapid digestion along with two cups of tea. I prayed that my stomach would cope with the coming effort. Any cramps or a stitch would be agonising.

Angus and David had already gone ahead to Ailefroide in order to try to make reservations for themselves and Martin Welch at the Ecrins Hut. Martin was staying with us to film the ascent of the col and would then go round to Ailefroide and walk up to the hut in the evening. All three would then climb up the Glacier Blanc at dawn to meet us on the final slopes of the Barre des Ecrins. From Valloire, Carole departed for Grenoble, leaving Joy to support us on the big climb to the Galibier.

As we remount our bikes Martin declares that we have 1200m of continuous ascent to the col. I'm sure he told me it was only 1000m when we looked at the route last night. I shudder at the prospect of doing 20 per cent more climbing than I've psyched myself up for. I suspect that Martin has been playing with the numbers in order to see how I react. Perhaps I should have looked at the map a little more closely myself!

The first section is one long straight and in oppressive heat I struggle to find a rhythm. Martin is in the lead and starts to creep away from me. I know the pace I must hold to reach the col and battle on. If I can only get my chain on its centre ring, my efficiency will much increase. The road eases by a couple of degrees. I change up in gear and press on in pursuit of Martin.

Some 3km after leaving Valloire I realised that I was strong and able to sustain the effort, even though there were some 900m still to climb. My legs felt finely tuned and responsive. I could dare to push them harder and would probably survive. The feeling was mildly intoxicating. I was surprised that Simon dropped back so quickly.

The road climbed the straight and deeply enclosed Valloirette to Plan Lachet at 1940m where it turned sharply to the right and commenced a series of sinuous switchbacks towards the summit. I saw Simon slowly regaining his lost ground and I eased to allow him to catch up so that we could tackle the hairpins together.

The switchbacks are steep and unrelenting. Joy, Alex and Hazel douse us with water from pistols and buckets as we ride past lay-bys, which keeps our temperature down. The pass is sometimes used as a stage on the Tour de France and the names of famous cyclists are daubed on the tarmac in huge white-washed letters, presumably to encourage their efforts.

Followers of the Tour must be totally fanatical. Every 100m we passed a string of painted slogans: '*Allez Fignon; Bugno, le Roi; Allez Indurain* . . .' All the great names of the past decade of cycle touring were there and we began to feel a pride to be following in their tracks. Then we passed one which said '*Allez Simon*'. I sensed that my partner had been strengthening, but now he surged forward, the veins on his neck bulging with the extra effort. Happily, his spurt was not prolonged as the next rise revealed a further series of hairpins twisting up to a little notch on the rocky skyline which marked the summit.

On the last 500m I feel a painful pressure on my knees and slightly ease my pace, unwilling to cause any muscular damage before our final day. It is just after 2pm when we pull up the final rise. It is a great moment. We've held our mettle and the reward is a brilliant view of the Barre, only 16km away.

The crest of the pass was crowded with cars and other cyclists, but it couldn't spoil our delight. After fifty-one days of toil and danger, the Barre des Ecrins lay right before our eyes. The folds of its noble glacier face seemed almost touchable across the intervening depths of the Romanche Valley. Behind us and some 80km to our north the great white swell of Mont Blanc rose on the northern horizon. Our time there was already a distant memory.

However, one other great mountain in the view captured our

attention, La Meije, which rose above La Grave to our south-west in a magnificent sweep of buttress and glacier. More than any other peak, La Meije deserves to be among the ranks of the '4000ers', but it falls short in altitude by just 18m. Its exclusion from our journey illustrated the futility of applying height as the sole criterion of a mountain's worth.

By keeping our sights to 4000m and above, we had climbed the majority of the great peaks of the Alps, but by no means all. Other summits that we had seen on our travels, like the Bietschhorn (3934m) in the Bernese Oberland and La Grivola (3969m) in the Graians Alps, had impressed us more than many of the '4000ers' we had climbed. There was no shortage of new challenges for our future years of guiding in the Alps.

When Martin had completed filming at the summit, we sped down to the 2057m Col du Lauteret, which runs transverse to the Col du Galibier and provides the crossing between the Romanche and the Guisane Valleys. For the last time we dismounted from our bikes. They had served us better than we could ever have hoped. We had grown to enjoy and respect cycle touring as a physically gruelling yet scenically rewarding sport. There can be few better ways to see the Alps than by bicycle. To people like me, whose knees can no longer stand intensive running, cycling offers a new outlet to dormant energies.

The remainder of the journey would be made on foot. The Barre des Ecrins lay on the far side of the watershed at the head of the Romanche Valley. We needed to cross that watershed and descend to the Glacier Blanc by dawn. The lowest crossing was from the Glacier d'Arsine and over the 3286m Col du Glacier Blanc, but this appeared to involve loose rock and possible objective danger. The most direct route lay over the 3376m Col de la Roche Faurio, but this required us to climb a 500m ice couloir.

We decided to reserve our final choice until we had walked from the Col du Lauteret to the Alpe de Villar d'Arêne Hut later in the afternoon. There we could ask the advice of the hut guardian. Meanwhile, Joy cooked us a meal and we changed back into our climbing clothes. We confirmed final arrangements with both Martin and Joy. We'd make radio calls at 6, 8 and 10 in the morning and Joy would station herself at the Ailefroide roadhead by the Cézanne Hut to meet us on our return from the mountain.

At 4.15pm we set off again and followed the GR 54 footpath on a long

traverse round into the upper Romanche Valley. We had now entered
the Ecrins National Park and the area's popularity with holidaymakers
was immediately evident. A constant stream of walkers passed us from
the opposite direction. The GR 54 offers a circular *grand randonnée*
around the edges of the massif. Like the Tour du Mont Blanc, it is a
hugely popular route, whether for serious trekkers who complete the
whole circuit using huts for accommodation or just for day strollers.

The path formed a narrow balcony weaving in and out of gullies high
above the valley floor, which rises and broadens into grazing flats
where the hut stands. Immediately behind the hut the rocky Pics de
Chamossière divide the valley, the shorter left branch leading to the
Col d'Arsine and the deeper right fork containing the Glacier de la Plate
des Agneaux. We were glad to get off the narrow single-file path and
stretch our legs across the broader upper valley to the hut.

Here the guardian told us what we had begun to suspect. The easiest
crossing of the watershed took neither of the cols which we had originally considered, but climbed rather higher, almost to the top of the
3613m Pic de Neige Cordier, before dropping through the 3491m Col
Emile Pic to the Glacier Blanc basin. With a height gain of 1500m from
where we stood just to get to the base of the Barre des Ecrins, we had
our night's work well cut out.

We wanted a quiet bivouac for the last night of the trip, so left the
hut and wandered up broad grassy meadows to the Col d'Arsine, where
clusters of boulders offered obvious sites. The evening was warm and
dark clouds on the mountains threatened a thunderstorm. We were
glad to stop and lay our tired limbs on a carpet of turf. With a good
sleep we might restore the energy expended on the Col du Galibier.

Simon produced the rations for supper, which inevitably included
instant leek soup. Knorr had failed to consider the need for variety in
our diet when offering to support the venture and had supplied 120
packets of the same flavour. Luckily, we were partial to leek soup, even
though we clasped our stomachs mockingly and groaned every time it
emerged from our sacks.

We were happy to be alone for this last night. We were still the same
close companions who had sat in the Diavolezza Hut fifty-two nights
previously and we knew how much we owed each other.

The traverse could not have been successful without our partnership on the
mountains. It is hard to quantify our relationship as so much of the support

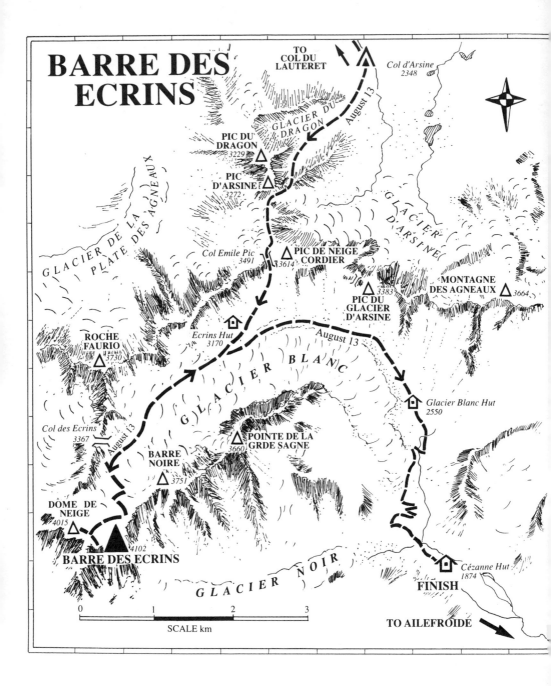

BARRE DES ECRINS

TO
COL DU
LAUTERET

Col d'Arsine
2348

GLACIER DU DRAGON

August 13

PIC DU
DRAGON
3229

PIC
D'ARSINE
3272

GLACIER DE LA PLATE DES AGNEAUX

GLACIER D'ARSINE

Col Emile Pic
3491

PIC DE NEIGE
CORDIER
3614

3383

MONTAGNE
DES AGNEAUX
3664

PIC DU
GLACIER
D'ARSINE

Ecrins Hut
3170

August 13

ROCHE
FAURIO
3730

GLACIER BLANC

Glacier Blanc Hut
2550

Col des Ecrins
3367

August 13

POINTE DE LA
GRDE SAGNE
3660

BARRE
NOIRE
3751

DÔME DE
NEIGE
4015

4102

BARRE DES ECRINS

GLACIER NOIR

Cézanne Hut
1874

FINISH

0   1   2   3

SCALE km

TO AILEFROIDE

*we have given each other is unspoken and it has been as equals that we
have faced the same problems. We have shared our weaknesses as well as
our strengths. Our styles of climbing, although different, do match up well
when put to the test. As to our relationship off the mountain, it should
survive because I believe that we have an understanding and respect for one
another which goes beyond any single disagreement.*

As the senior partner by eight years, I'd gained a lot of pleasure from
watching Simon's development since we had first met on the cliffs of
Stoney Middleton in Derbyshire eleven years previously. Then just 19
years old, he was one of the many youths who spend the best part of
their time messing around the crags and the rest of it thinking about
climbing, much to the despair of their parents and educational mentors.

Simon had given up a degree course, broken his leg in a fall and spent
a good deal of time on the dole in those days of youth, but he had never
lost his determination to climb. Starting from nought he had slowly
worked his way through every qualification in the hills from summer
mountain leader to international mountain guide, and was now the
equal of any mountaineer. His success on Alps 4000 proved that young-
sters who get bitten by the bug of climbing can, with long application
and determination, make good and confound those who think it a
pointless and dangerous activity.

The night was so warm that I felt stifled, even though we slept in no
more than our clothes and a bivouac bag. After just three hours of restless slumber, the 1.30am alarm was not altogether unwelcome. We had
a bowl of porridge and departed at 2.15am. The sky was starry and the
sliver of the waning moon lit our way into the narrow valley of the
Glacier de la Planche. A long plod up screes and then the icy glacier
slope took us to a shoulder on the Pic d'Arsine. We descended loose
rocks on the far side for 100m to the Glacier d'Arsine and traversed its
upper slope until we found the shallow couloir leading up to the 3217m
Brèche de la Plate des Agneaux.

From the brèche we climbed an easy rock ridge towards the summit
of the Pic de Neige Cordier, but turned right just before the top and
traversed a snow-slope to reach the Col Emile Pic at 5.15am. We
switched off our headtorches on the descent to the Ecrins Hut which
sits at 3170m above the edge of the Glacier Blanc. We had done 1300m
of climbing and we hadn't even started on the mountain that we
wanted to tackle. The hut was empty, its one hundred guests having

departed towards the Barre more than an hour previously.

I was possessed by a sense that we had missed the party and a feeling of lassitude as we sat on the deserted balcony. We could see a line of dots zigzagging slowly up the lower slope. Angus, David and Martin were somewhere among them. We had to get moving. A beautiful two-tone alpenglow momentarily struck the glacier slope of the Barre as the sun rose and gave us a little impetus for the 2km slog to the base of the climb.

The glacier trail now rose in long diagonal zigzags towards the 4102m summit crest, which was hidden in cloud. This was hardly the place I'd expected to hit a depression, but I couldn't help my loss of spirit. Fatigue is no respecter of occasion. Did I really have to push my legs uphill for another 750m? Thank goodness this was the last day!

We met our support team only half-way up the slope. We were dismayed by their lack of progress, but Martin had wanted to stop to do some filming, while David was suffering from a stomach bug and struggling to continue. Just at the time when we wanted to move quickly and get the last climb over, our pace was slowed. We had offered to share our rope with David on the final summit, because we owed him much of the inspiration for the '4000ers' traverse as well as a lasting debt of friendship. Now that the reality was presented, this symbolic gesture no longer seemed so appealing. We bottled up our impatience and tied David into our rope.

Angus and Martin also looked a little frustrated and our feelings boiled over on the final slope to the Brèche Lory. In a rather arrogant manner I waved Martin to go in front, saying:

'Why don't you go ahead and get some film of us with David?'

The Glaswegian temper was quick to respond.

'Look, I'm not going to take that crap from you or anyone.'

'I'm sorry,' I said. 'I just thought you might as well use the time and get some footage.'

Martin did go ahead and filmed the sequence. We approached with David and I did a little commentary on David's role in the expedition. My words of eulogy sounded a little hollow after the dispute, especially given that their intended beneficiary was for once silent due to his illness.

Surely we could do better than this on the final climb? Yet there was nothing in the surrounding scene to raise us from the doldrums. A persistent mist covered the summit ridge. The route was crowded with large guided parties and disfigured by piles of excrement which lined the track at regular intervals.

'For heaven's sake,' I thought, 'if people have to make their toilet on the glacier, why can't they be bothered to go a sociable distance away from the trail to do it?'

The situation seemed to exemplify everything that was wrong with modern alpinism – crowds, pollution and a follow-the-path mentality. This was all a far cry from the unfettered climbing we had enjoyed throughout the trip.

At the Brèche Lory we turned left and mounted a short rock step on to the final crest. The ridge now rose as a narrow PD arête, but at an easy incline. We were relieved to see that nearly all the guided parties had stopped at the brèche or else turned right to ascend the easier subsidiary summit, the 4015m Dome de Neige des Ecrins. David rallied now that the top was near. We were going to make it by 10am.

As we crossed a little forepeak, the mists which had shrouded the ridge began to roll back. A shaft of diffuse sunlight filtered through the cloud and revealed the summit crown in vague profile. In an instant the scene was magically transformed. My gloom lifted and suddenly I remembered why I was there.

We made the final steps 51 days, 13$^1/_2$ hours after leaving the Piz Bernina on that snowy evening back in June. There were only four other climbers at the summit cross and, to our surprise, we heard Scots accents. One of them turned and gasped:

'Martin, Simon, it's you. Don't tell me you're just finishing. We saw you on television before we left home last week. Congratulations.'

It was Ian McCullough, one of our past clients. This coincidence further raised our spirits. A prolonged session of handshaking and back-thumping followed. Simon looked dangerously close to letting his emotions run loose.

In a way the Ecrins feels no different from any other summit, except for an overwhelming sense of achievement. I cannot stop smiling.

Then I got the radio out and called the valley.

'We're on the Ecrins, Joy.'

'Well done. I'm really pleased for you. I can't pass you over to Carole as she hasn't arrived back from Grenoble. When are you expecting to be down?'

'About 3pm. We'll see you then.'

After half-an-hour at the top, we made ready to descend. Simon and I needed to get down quickly in order to meet Jackie and call Bill Shannon before the press deadlines for tomorrow's newspapers. Martin wanted to come with us to film our arrival back in Ailefroide. Without a murmur of discontent, Angus agreed to rope up with David, who was likely to be considerably slower than ourselves. That was typical of the willingness which Angus had shown since he had first joined the expedition in Zermatt. Meanwhile, our mentor was still feeling pretty wretched. Nevertheless, David had just notched up his 49th '4000er'. With determination such as he had shown on this climb, we could be sure that he would continue his quest and climb his remaining 26 tops over the next three or four years.

As Simon and I scrambled down the ridge to the Brèche Lory, a wicked thought came to me:

'I don't know what all the fuss was about up there, because we still haven't done all the '4000ers',' I said. 'What about the Dome de Neige?'

'It doesn't look 35m above the col, but we can't very well not do it,' replied Simon.

In fact, our 1:25000 map put the Brèche Lory at 3974m and the Dome de Neige des Ecrins 4015m, which gives a 41m height difference. This humble snow hump thus became our 75th and final 4000m peak.

After the ten-minute detour to make its ascent, we slid down the glacier slope in a near-continuous standing glissade, then hiked around the long and gracious curve of the Glacier Blanc past the Ecrins Hut. Simon charged ahead at times, his strides lengthened by the prospect of a final end to the effort.

As yet the achievement is hard to comprehend as a whole. I've always pushed myself to the boundaries of my ability and experience on the mountains and perhaps this has been the greatest challenge of all. To have gone non-stop for fifty-two days has been an extraordinary experience. Along the way I've learnt a lot about Martin's inner strength. The depth of thought he applies to problems is considerable and the resulting solutions have been impressive.

For myself, I've been left with an ⌐ncreased metabolism and am over a stone lighter in weight. I wonder if I'll put it back on as quickly? Having put aside the practicalities of life to indulge our love of climbing over the last two months, I know that it is time to step back into the flow and catch up with the real world.

As Simon drew in front on the rocky path, Martin Welch suddenly stopped and pulled me to one side.

'I don't care what we said back up there this morning,' he said. 'I think that what you boys have done is something really special. I've been glad to be part of it.'

Coming from the man who had faithfully followed our progress for the past forty days, those words meant far more than any of the empty plaudits which the media might bestow.

The path below the Glacier Blanc Hut was horribly crowded with trekkers. This was hardly an appropriate way to finish an enterprise which had been a lonely adventure for its greater part. I ceremoniously submerged myself in the glacier stream just before the Cézanne Hut to clear the sweat of the day. Joy, Carole and Jackie Ross were waiting at the car park.

Jackie had just taken a walk up towards the great South Pillar of the Barre des Ecrins. As a non-mountaineer, he was beginning to grasp the scale of what we had done. Had he known just what was involved when we had approached Blythswood nine months earlier, he might have thought twice about supporting our venture. Now that we had succeeded, he would hopefully see a rich return in funds and publicity for the charity which he had founded. One thing was sure, that with the continuing plight of so many countries of Eastern Europe, Blythswood's work would continue long after our own achievement was forgotten.

When Angus and David returned, we all went down to Ailefroide for a celebration meal. Everybody's mood had mellowed and all the irritations and frustrations which had got in the way of our enjoyment of the day were forgotten. We made the essential call to Bill Shannon who was in a state of great excitement. Within the next two hours he had contacted half-a-dozen television companies and twice the number of press agencies, many of whom phoned through to our restaurant for an interview. The string of incoming calls left the kitchen chefs and waitresses almost as bemused as our French guide at the Eccles Hut. To use Bill's own favourite words, 'things had at last come together.'

At midnight I was lying in the back of the van alongside the kids while Joy drove. I felt warm and relaxed, but was far too happy to sleep. We had hit a sudden downpour somewhere near Grenoble and as I watched the steady sweep of the van's wipers across the windscreen, the mountains already seemed far away. By 9am I would be at Calais and another life would begin. Whatever trials, frustrations or sorrows the future held in store, I drew strength from the knowledge that I would always look back on the summer of 1993 with a mixture of pride, humility and occasionally disbelief that it really happened.

Stripped of all its pretensions as a last, great challenge or first-ever traverse, our journey had granted us all the hardships and joys that we could ever wish from the mountains. Indeed, it had provided an education in all that life should be. The Alps had proved that they are by no means exhausted as a playground for adventure and exploration. The bad weather had, in fact, enhanced our appreciation of the mountains. They had grown in stature with each successive storm and the great pioneers of a century past had come to be our heroes. More than anything, the Alps had realised my childhood vision of the mountains as a world of fantasy where I could live my dreams and stand at the fragile edge of existence.

APPENDICES

GLOSSARY

Topographical and Climbing Terminology

The following foreign-language words for topographical features and technical climbing terms are used habitually by mountaineers and appear throughout the text:

ABLATION	Process of wastage of snow or ice, especially by melting
ABSEIL	Rope descent using friction device for control
AIGUILLE	Rock needle or spire (Fr)
ANCHOR	Climber's means of attachment to the cliff
BELAY	General term for the climber's anchorage, the attachment of rope to anchors and method of feeding the rope to moving climbers
BERGSCHRUND	The crevasse which forms at the break of slope between the ice of a moving glacier and the mountainside above (Ger)
BOLT/ EXPANSION	Inserted into hole drilled in the rock as a means of
BOLT	progression or protection
BRÈCHE	Narrow gap between peaks or pinnacles (Fr)
CALOTTE	The snowy summit cap of the mountain (Fr)
CHANDELLE	Candle or pillar of rock (Fr)
CIRQUE	Armchair-shaped glacial valley with steep headwall (Fr)
COL	Pass or saddle between mountains (Fr)
COOMB	Stony hollow in hillside
CRUX	Hardest section of a climb
DIÈDRE	Groove or corner of rock (Fr)
FIRN	Dense compacted snow between one and three years old in the intermediate stage of transition between snow crystals and glacier ice; forms large fields at the heads of glaciers (Ger)
GENDARME	Rock tower or pinnacle (Fr)

GRAUPEL	Hailstones or hard-frozen snow pellets (Ger)
HANGING GLACIER	Detached glacier clinging to steep mountainside or side valley
ICEPALL	Steep, heavily crevassed portion of a valley glacier
KARABINER	Metal snaplink for clipping the rope into anchors
MORAINE	Ridge or mound of debris deposited by a glacier (Fr)
NÉVÉ	French term for firn snow
NORDWAND	North face (Ger)
NUNATAK	Island of mountain bedrock projecting above the surface of an ice cap
NUT	Tapered metal wedge inserted into rock crack for protection
PITCH	Individual stage of a climb between belay points
PITON	Metal blade or wedge hammered into crack in the rock as a means of protection or progression
RAPPEL	French term for abseil
RIMAYE	French term for bergschrund
ROCHE MOUTONÉE	Rocky bluff, smooth on its upper side, resulting from glacial plucking (Fr)
RUNNING BELAY/RUNNER	Nut, sling or piton anchor attached to rope by karabiner to provide protection between climbers
SERAC	Unstable tower of ice formed in icefalls or on steep hanging glaciers (Fr)
STANCE	Ledge occupied by climber while belaying
VERGLAS	Thin film of water ice covering rocks (Fr)
VOIE NORMALE	The normal or easiest route up a mountain (Fr)

Fr: French language term
Ger: German language term

Climbing Grades

1 *Overall grading* The overall difficulty of an alpine climb, taking account of its length, altitude, objective risk and technical difficulty, is denoted by the following adjectival grading scale:

| *Facile* | F: | Simple glacier climbs and rock scrambles |
| *Peu difficile* | PD: | Steeper or longer snow ascents or sustained rock scrambles with rock pitches of grade II |

Assez difficile	AD:	Snow/ice faces of 45–50° average angle or mixed climbs of considerable length and complexity with rock pitches of grade III
Difficile	D:	Snow/ice faces of 50–55° average angle or mixed routes involving considerable length and commitment with rock pitches of IV and possibly V
Très Difficile	TD:	Face routes with sustained difficulties and possible objective risk, 55–60° average angle on snow/ice; ridges and buttresses with sustained rock-climbing of IV and V
Extrêmement Difficile	ED:	The hardest face routes in length, difficulty and commitment; snow/ice above 60° in average angle; rock pitches of IV, V and VI – this grade is now subdivided into four classes, ED1 to ED4

The grades F to TD are refined by the adding a plus or minus sign; an AD+ is thus significantly harder than an AD–.

2 *Rock-climbing grades* Rock pitches on alpine routes are classed according to the UIAA numerical system. Their equivalent British grades are as follows:

I:	Easy/moderate
II:	Difficult
III:	Very difficult
IV:	Severe
V:	Very severe – Hard very severe
VI:	Hard very severe – Extremely severe

As with the overall grading, the refinement of a plus or minus sign is used with each grade. Thus a IV– might be Mild Severe in standard and a IV+ as hard as Mild Very Severe.

When interpreting these grades, allowance must be made for the greater length and more sustained nature of alpine rock pitches, as well as the fact that at grades of V and below the climber will probably be wearing boots and carrying a rucksack.

3 *Winter climbing grades* At several places in the text an equivalent Scottish winter climbing grade has been given as the most appropriate way of classifying pitches which were covered in snow or else heavily iced. Scottish winter grades are given on a I–VIII numerical scale.

APPENDIX II

THE 4000m PEAKS OF THE ALPS

The 75 Peaks Climbed: 23 June –13 August 1993

(All heights in metres)

Major Mountains

#	Peak	Height	#	Peak	Height
1	Mont Blanc	4807	27	Dreithorn	4164
2	Dufourspitze	4633.9	28	Jungfrau	4158.2
3	Nordend	4609	29	Bishorn	4153
4	Signalkuppe	4554	30	Aiguille Verte	4122.2
5	Dom	4545.4	31	Aiguille Blanche de Peuterey	4112
6	Liskamm	4527.2	32	Barre des Ecrins	4101.8
7	Weisshorn	4505.5	33	Mönch	4099
8	Täschhorn	4490. 7	34	Pollux	4092
9	Matterhorn	4477.5	35	Schreckhorn	4078
10	Mont Maudit	4465	36	Ober Gabelhorn	4062.9
11	Dent Blanche	4356.6	37	Gran Paradiso	4061
12	Nadelhorn	4327	38	Aiguille de Bionnassay	4052
13	Grand Combin	4314	39	Piz Bernina	4049.1
14	Lenzspitze	4294	40	Gross Fiescherhorn	4048.8
15	Finsteraarhorn	4273.9	41	Gross Grünhorn	4043.5
16	Mont Blanc du Tacul	4248	42	Lauteraarhorn	4042
17	Castor	4228	43	Dürrenhorn	4034.9
18	Zinalrothorn	4221.2	44	Allalinhorn	4027.4
19	Hohberghorn	4219	45	Weissmies	4023
20	Piramide Vincent	4215	46	Dôme de Rochefort	4015
21	Grandes Jorasses	4208	47	Dent du Géant	4013
22	Alphubel	4206	48	Lagginhorn	4010
23	Rimpfischhorn	4198.9	49	Aiguille de Rochefort	4001
24	Aletschhorn	4195	50	Les Droites	4000
25	Strahlhorn	4190.1			
26	Dent d'Hérens	4171.4			

Subsidiary Tops defined as those summits having a height separation of 35m or over from higher adjoining summits.

51	Zumsteinspitze	4563
52	Liskamm West Summit	4479
53	Pic Luigi Amedeo	4460
54	Parrotspitze	4432
55	Ludwigshöhe	4341
56	Weisshorn North Ridge Gendarme	4331
57	Corno Nero	4321
58	Dôme du Goûter	4304
59	Il Naso, Liskamm	4272
60	Grand Combin de Valsorey	4184.4
61	Pointe Whymper, Grandes Jorasses	4184
62	Breithorn Central Summit	4159
63	Grand Combin de Tsessette	4141
64	Breithorn West Twin	4139
65	L'Isolée, Mont Blanc du Tacul	4114
66	Pointe Carmen, Mont Blanc du Tacul	4109
67	Breithorn East Twin	4106
68	Grande Rocheuse	4102
69	Pointe Chaubert, Mont Blanc du Tacul	4074
70	Mont Brouillard	4069
71	Pointe Marguerite, Grandes Jorasses	4065
72	Aiguille du Jardin	4035
73	Hinter Fiescherhorn	4025
74	Dôme de Neige des Ecrins	4015
75	Punta Baretti	4013

Other Tops Climbed with height separations of less than 35m; estimated height differences shown

Point 4011, Lauteraarhorn	4011	25
Point 4015, Lauteraarhorn	4015	30
Wengener Jungfrau	4089	25
Stecknadelhorn	4241	25
Pointe Hélène, Grandes Jorasses	4045	25
Point Médiane, Mont Blanc du Tacul	4097	25
Aiguille Blanche de Peuterey, South-East Top	4107	30

* We suspected that the Pic Luigi Amedeo may not have a 35m separation. This and a few other tops do need to be accurately surveyed.

Note 1: North Ridge Gendarme, Rimpfischhorn (4108) was the only top in this category not climbed due to bad weather; its height separation is around 30m.
Note 2: Additionally, the following tops are included in the UIAA list of the '4000ers' on account either of their topographic importance, or their historic or sentimental appeal. All of them have a height differential of 20m or less:

Roccia Nera, Breithorn	4075
Punta Giordani	4046
Corne du Diable, Mont Blanc du Tacul	4064
Pointe Croz, Grandes Jorasses	4110
Mont Blanc de Courmayeur	4748
Grand Pilier d'Angle, Mont Blanc	4243

The inclusion of these enables dozens of other minor summits to claim the status of '4000ers'. Therefore they were not considered as part of the Alps 4000 expedition, although some were climbed inadvertently. In the event, the only tops on the UIAA list of 82 which we did not climb were the Grand Pilier d'Angle, Corne du Diable and Punta Giordani. Nearly all of the minor tops are listed in Richard Goedeke's climbing guide to the 4000m peaks.

ALPS 4000 ROUTE SCHEDULE

Distance, height gain and climbing time are shown for each day; statistics for cycling sections are given in italics.

	DATE	ROUTE	DISTANCE	HEIGHT GAIN	CLIMBING TIME
PIZ BERNINA	22 June	Climb to Diavolezza Hut from Val Bernina	5km	870m	2hr
	23 June	Ascent of Piz Bernina (4049m) via Fortezza, Bellavista Terraces and South Ridge (PD); descent to Marco e Rosa Hut	10km	1430m	11hr
	24 June	Descent to Morteratsch via Fortezza and Morteratsch Glacier	12km	160m	8hr
ENGADIN TO OBERLAND	25 June	*Cycle St Moritz–Julierpass (2284m) – Tiefencastel – Bonaduz Ilanz – Trun*	*125km*	*1150m*	*7hr*
	26 June	*Cycle Disentis – Oberalppass (2044m) – Andermatt – Furkapass (2431m) – Grimsel Hospice*	*86km*	*2600m*	*7¹/₂hr*

	Date	Description	Distance	Ascent	Time
BERNESE OBERLAND	27 June	Walk in to Aar Bivouac Hut via Grimselsee and Unteraar Glacier	19km	800m	6hr
	28 June	Ascent of Finsteraarhorn (4274m) by Finsteraar Glacier, Agassizjoch and North-West Ridge (AD), 7½hr; descent via Finsteraarjoch to Obers Ischmeer basin and Schreckhorn Hut	13km	1775m	13hr
	29 June	Ascent of Schreckhorn (4078m) by Schrecksattel and East-South-East Ridge (AD+), 5hr; traverse of Lauteraargrat to Lauteraarhorn (4042m) (D+), 5½hr; descent by South-West Ridge to Schreckhorn Hut (AD+)	10km	1900m	16hr
	30 June	Ascent from Obers Ischmeer to Finsteraarjoch (AD), Fiescherfirn and Hinter and Gross Fiescherhorn (4025m and 4049m) (PD); ski descent to Ewigschneefeld and Mönchsjoch Hut	13km	1520m	12hr
	1 July	Ascent of Jungfrau (4158m) by Rottalsattel and South-East Ridge (PD), 4½hr; detour to Wengener top; return to Mönchsjoch	11km	1220m	7½hr
	2 July	Ascent of Mönch (4099m) by South-East Ridge (PD); ski descent of Ewigschneefeld to Konkordia Hut	11km	580m	7hr
	3 July	Ascent of Gross Grünhorn (4043m) via Grünegghorn and South-West Ridge (PD+), 5 hr; return to Konkordia Hut	10km	1370m	7½hr
	4 July	Ascent of Aletschhorn (4195m) by Hasler Rib and North-East Ridge (AD+), 6hr; ski descent of Mittelaletsch Glacier to Märjela and Fiesch	24km	1550m	13hr
		BERNESE OBERLAND TOTALS:	**111km**	**10,715m**	**82hr**
SAASTAL	5 July	*Cycle Fiesch – Brig – Visp –Saas Grund*	*50km*	*900m*	*3hr*
	6 July	Walk up to Weissmies Hut	6km	1170m	2hr
	7 July	Ascent of Weissmies (4023m) by South-West Ridge (PD–), 3½hr; traverse under Lagginjoch and ascent to Lagginhorn (4010m) across West Face (AD–); descent of West Ridge (PD); return to Saas Grund	19km	2100m	10hr
	8 July	Walk up to Mischabel Hut	7km	1800m	4½hr

9 July	Traverse of Nadelgrat (AD), Dürrenhorn (4035m) – Hohberghorn (4219m) – Nadelhorn (4327m) – Lenzspitze (4294m); descent to bivouac on Lenzjoch	8km	1600m	9¹/₂hr
10 July	Ascent of Dom (4545m) by North Flank; descent via Festijoch to Dom Hut	6km	550m	7hr
11 July	Descent to campsite at Täsch	6km	–	2hr
12 July	Cycle to Täschalp; walk up to Mischabeljoch Bivouac Hut via Weingarten Glacier	*9km* *6¹/₂km*	*790m* *1640m*	*1hr* *5hr*
13 July	Ascent of Täschhorn (4491m) by South-East Ridge (AD), 5hr; return to Mischabeljoch, traverse of Alphubel (4206m) by North and South-East Ridges (PD); Alphubeljoch – Mellich Glacier – Allalinpass	8¹/₂km	1160m	13¹/₂hr
14 July	Ascent of Allalinhorn (4027m) by South-West Ridge (PD); return to camp on Allalinpass	2¹/₂km	470m	3hr
15 July	Ascent of Rimpfischhorn (4199m) by North-West Face (AD+), 4 hr; descent by West-South-West Ridge (PD+), then back across Allalinpass and up Allalin Glacier to Adlerpass; ascent of Strahlhorn (4190m) by North-West Ridge (PD-); descent to Stockhornpass via Adler and Findel Glaciers	16km	1740m	12hr
16 July	Traverse to camp on Monte Rosa Glacier at Pt 3303m	5¹/₂km	270m	3hr
17 July	Traverse of Nordend (4609m) by Monte Rosa Glacier and South-West Ridge (PD), 4¹/₂hr– Dufourspitze (4634m) by Silbersattel and North Ridge (AD) – Zumsteinspitze (4563m) – Signalkuppe (4554m) – Parrotspitze (4432m) – Ludwigshöhe (4341m) – Corno Nero (4321m) – bivouac hut at Balmenhorn	8¹/₂km	1890m	11¹/₂hr

EASTERN ZERMATT SKYLINE

Date	Description	km	m	hr
18 July	Traverse of Piramide Vincent (4215m) – Il Naso (4272m) – Liskamm (4527m) by Cresta Sella (PD+) – Liskamm West Summit (4479m) by main ridge traverse (AD) – Castor (4428m) (PD–) – Pollux (4092m) (PD) – Roccia Nera; descent of Verra Glacier to Val d'Ayas Hut	14km	1580m	11½hr
19 July	Linkage of the summits of the Breithorn: East Twin (4106m) West Twin (4139m) – Central Summit (4159m) – West Summit (4164m) (AD); descent to Schwarzsee by Breithorn-plateau and Trockenersteg	17km	1270m	9½hr
EASTERN ZERMATT SKYLINE TOTALS:		98½km 9km	12,170m 790m	87½hr 1hr
20 July	Ascent of Matterhorn (4477m) by Hornli Ridge (AD), 6hr; return to Schwarzsee; walk via Stafelalp to camp at Schönbiel Hut	18km	2440m	15hr
21 July	West-North-West Face of Dent d'Hérens (4171m) (AD); return to Schönbiel camp	12km	1760m	7½hr
22 July	Dent Blanche (4357m) by Wandflue and South Ridge (AD), 6hr; return to Schönbiel camp	10km	1660m	11½hr
23 July	Ascent of Ober Gabelhorn (4063m) by Mont Durand, Arbengrat and North-West Face (AD), 6½hr; descent of North-East Ridge (AD) over Wellenkuppe to Rothorn Hut	9½km	1590m	10½hr
24 July	Ascent of Zinalrothorn (4221m) via Gabel Notch (AD–), 4½hr up and down; traverse of Unter Äshjoch and Hohlicht Glacier to Schalihorn (3974m) (PD); descent of Schalihorn's North Ridge to Schalijoch Bivouac Hut (AD+)	10km	1660m	12hr
25 July	Stormbound at Schalijoch Bivouac Hut			
26 July	Ascent of Weisshorn (4505m) by Schali Glacier and East Face (AD), 4½hr; descent of North Ridge (AD+) over Grand Gendarme (4331m) to Bishorn (4153m) and down to Zinal	13½km	1000m	12hr
WESTERN ZERMATT SKYLINE TOTALS:		73km	10,110m	68½hr

	Date		km	Elevation	Time
GRAND COMBIN	27 July	Cycle Zinal – Sierre – Martigny – Bourg-St Pierre; walk up to Valsorey Hut	8km *103km*	1230m *1160m*	2½hr *5hr*
	28 July	Ascent of Grand Combin de Valsorey (4184m), de la Tsessette (4141m) and de Grafeneire (4314m); approach and descent via Plateau du Couloir and South Face (PD+); return to Bourg-St Pierre and cycle up Val Ferret to La Fouly	14km *28km*	1490m *790m*	8½hr *2hr*
MONT BLANC MASSIF	29 July	Walk up to l'A Neuve Hut	5km	1100m	2hr
	30 July	Cross Col d'Argentière (3552m) and Col des Cristaux (3601m) (PD+); descent to Couvercle	10½km Hut	1650m	9hr
	31 July to 1 August	Ascent of Les Droites (4000m) by South Ridge (AD), 4 hr; return to upper Talèfre Glacier, ascent of South Couloir of Col Armand Charlet (AD+) and traverse of Aiguille du Jardin (4035m) Grande Rocheuse (4102m) – Aiguille Verte (4122m); descent of Whymper Couloir (AD+) to Couvercle Hut	10km	2300m	14hr
	2 August	Pierre à Bérenger– Leschaux Glacier – Col des Grandes Jorasses, (AD) 4½hr; ascent of West Ridge of Grandes Jorasses over Pointe Marguerite (4065m) – Pointe Whymper (4184m) – Pointe Walker (4208m), (D) 7hr; return to Canzio Bivouac Hut on Col des Grandes Jorasses	9½km	2070m	17hr
	3 August	Traverse of Rochefort Arête over Dôme de Rochefort (4015m) and Aiguille de Rochefort (4001m), (D–); ascent of Dent du Géant (4013m) by South-West Face (AD); descent to camp on Col du Géant	5km	780m	10hr
	4–5 August	One rest day and one day stormbound on Col du Géant			
	6 August	Ascent of Diable Ridge of Mont Blanc du Tacul (4248m), (D+), over Pointe Chaubert (4074m) – Pointe Carmen (4109m) – L'Isolée (4114m); descent to support tent on Col Maudit	5½km	1080m	9hr

	Date		km	m	hr
MONT BLANC MASSIF	6–7 August	Traverse of Mont Maudit (4465m) – Grand Plateau – Dôme du Goûter (4304m) – Aiguille de Bionnassay (4052m) – Vallot Hut – Mont Blanc (4807m) – Brouillard Ridge (AD+) – Pic Luigi Amedeo (4460m) – Mont Brouillard (4069m) – Punta Baretti (4013m) – Eccles Bivouac Hut	14km	1990m	22hr
	8 August	Ascent of Aiguille Blanche de Peuterey (4112m) by Col Eccles and Frêney plateau (AD), 3hr; return to Eccles Hut; descent to la Visaille in Val Veni	8km	780m	8hr
		MONT BLANC MASSIF TOTALS:	**67½km**	**11,750m**	**91hr**
GRAN PARADISO – BARRE DES ECRINS	9 August	*Cycle Val Veni – Courmayeur – Arvier – Val Savarenche – Pont*	*67km*	*1270m*	*3hr*
	10 August	Ascent of Gran Paradiso (4061m) by West Flank, (F+), and return to camp at Pont	16km	2100m	7hr
	11 August	Traverse of Colle del Nivolet (2612m) and Colle du Carro (3125m) to Bonneval-sur-Arc; *cycle to Lanslebourg*	28km / *20km*	1860m / *100m*	9hr / *1hr*
	12 August	*Cycle Modane – St Michel-de-Maurienne – Col du Télégraphe – Valloire – Col du Galibier (2642m) – Col du Lauteret;* walk to Alpe de Villar d'Arène Hut and bivouac on Col d'Arsine	*81km* / 9km	*2000m* / 350m	*5½hr* / 2½hr
	13 August	Traverse of Col Emile Pic to Ecrins Hut; ascent of Barre des Ecrins (4102m) by North Face and West Ridge (PD+); descent of Glacier Blanc to roadhead at Cézanne Hut	20km	2240m	12hr
		GRAND TOTALS:	**504km** / *569km*	**61,545m** / *10,760m*	**408hr** / *35hr*
		TOTAL TIME: Piz Bernina to Barre des Ecrins: 51 days 13½hr			

EQUIPMENT AND FOOD

Personal Clothing and Equipment

Boots We both commenced the expedition with Scarpa Vega plastic boots which were compatible to our ski bindings. The Vega is a comfortable and versatile climbing boot. From the Saastal onwards I changed to Scarpa Fitzroy leather boots. These were slightly lighter in weight and performed better on rock pitches than the plastic models, but did not give such good support for ice climbing.

Gaiters Berghaus Yeti gaiters were essential to keep our feet warm and dry throughout the summer. We stuck them to our boot rands and insteps with Superglue and repaired any minor tears in the rubber with the same. The use of the adhesive ensured the durability of the gaiters.

Outer shell clothing Berghaus Trango Extrem jackets and Super GTX Overtrousers, both in Gore-tex, provided the highest level of warmth, weather-proofing and durability throughout the trip

Windshirts Berghaus polyester windshirts received our joint commendation as the most useful single garment of the summer, despite their weighing only a few grams. On sunny but breezy days on the tops and on fast night approaches to climbs, they kept off any icy winds without our overheating. They were also our best protection against sunburn, when worn on top of our vests with the hood up.

Fleece clothing We both wore Berghaus Ascent fleece jackets which provided our warmth layer.

Trousers Troll Rock Bottoms have been our choice for alpine mountaineering for many years. Their stretch material and double pannelling offers comfort and warmth and they dry remarkably quickly. They are also considerably cheaper than breeches or salopettes.

Undergarments We both used Berghaus ACL vests and zip-neck shirts which were comfortable and warm.

Headwear For the whole journey we had fleece caps and used Phoenix light-weight helmets for protection during our traverse of the Mont Blanc massif. The absence of stonefall danger earlier in the trip meant that we could dispense with helmets in order to save weight.

Gloves/mittens We both used thick woollen mittens in the Dachstein style plus Gore-tex overmitts for really cold or windy conditions. For technical climbing we used plastic-coated work gloves, available in many hardware shops for between £1 and £2 a pair. For grip and durability these are worth ten times their price.

Harnesses We both used Troll two-piece sit harnesses of some vintage.

Ice axes The Grivel Super Courmayeur axe system has served us well over many years of alpine climbing. We used axes with 55cm shafts and banana-shaped picks. For steep couloirs or ice faces, at least one of us carried a second hammer-axe if possible.

Crampons I used Salewa Messner scissor crampons which have chisel-ended front points and vertically inclined second points. They are thus ideal for the mixed climbing encountered on alpine ridges. Simon used an old Camp model with strap bindings, which proved perfectly adequate for the grades of ice and mixed climbing which we encountered.

Rucksacks We set out determined not use any rucksack larger than the 45-litre Berghaus Ice Star sacks with which we were provided. They helped us to keep to our lightweight strategy. However, the Ice Stars could carry all supplies and gear for a three-day trip and were both comfortable and hard-wearing. We carried loads of between 10 and 18kg during the journey. Our support teams were provided with Berghaus 80-litre FGA rucksacks which carried loads well in excess of 30kg.

Ropes In the interests of saving weight, we used only a 40m length of 8.2mm diameter rope for the first two-thirds of the journey. This was only just long enough for some of the pitches and abseils encountered. For the Mont Blanc massif we used a 60m length of Beal 8.2mm diameter rope, which is an ideal length for the classic 'grandes courses' of the range. We could also climb, if desired, with this rope doubled for greater abrasion resistance.

Climbing hardware Five wired nuts, two Friends, half-a-dozen slings and two ice screws sufficed for most of the routes; harder rock pitches usually had *in situ* pitons.

Cameras We both used Olympus compact cameras and Fuji 100 slide film throughout the journey. All my pictures were taken on a simple 35mm AF10 model which is reliable and has a good quality lens. Simon variously used a 35–70mm zoom model and an XA2. Our roving film team, Angus and Martin, used Canon and Olympus SLR cameras with zoom lenses.

Altimeter Simon's Thommen 8000 altimeter was a crucial navigational aid and predicted weather changes far better than the Swiss forecasting service.

Sleeping- and bivouac bags We both had light Rab sleeping-bags with 500gm of down-filling plus Phoenix Phreeloader Gore-tex bivouac bags for outer protection and possible emergency use. The sleeping-bags were only carried when we were camping or bivouacking in the open.

Skis Our skis were 130cm Kastle Firn Extrem models with Silvretta 404 bindings, adhesive brushed-nylon skins for climbing, and *harcheisen* (ski crampons) for icy ground. It would be hard to find a lighter and more portable alpine ski capable of performing on variable mountain terrain. The skis were specially imported via Kastle's agents, Europa Sport of Kendal.

Ski poles Apart from their use when ski-ing, telescopic Grivel ski poles proved an essential aid to progress in deep snow, as well as saving our knees a brutal battering on the many long descents. We always carried one each.

Bicycles Our cycles were Dawes 'Street Sharp' hybrid models with straight handlebars, treaded tyres and 21 gears. They gave us no maintenance problems whatsoever and handled the steepest passes with aplomb. Although we never used them off the road, they are adaptable to gentle off-road terrain. We carried a full set of maintenance accessories and cycle clothing, including helmets.

General Support Equipment

Radio transceivers Radios were essential to co-ordinate the complex support operations, especially when we were away for many days. Without them we would have suffered a complete breakdown in the lines of supply on several occasions. The use of this one piece of advanced technology enabled us to travel fast and light without sacrificing our margin of security.

The expedition had four Yaesu FT 26 paging transceivers throughout the expedition which were bought from Electronic System in the Rue de Lyon in Geneva. Their rechargeable battery packs gave a fortnight's use at an average of 10 minutes air-time per day. We kept the use of radios to a minimum. The use of unlicensed radios for rescue purposes by guides is tacitly accepted in the alpine countries, but unlicensed equipment should not be used for regular communication.

Video film equipment All filming was done on Sony PR805 cameras with Sigma 0.6 wide angle and Tokina 2.5mag telephoto lenses. A back-up camera was always carried or else readily available in case of breakdown. 90-minute Sony HMEX film tapes in Hi-8 format were used. A DSM Battery Belt with a 7-hour charge capacity was carried and was essential to sustain filming over several days in subzero temperatures. A video camera light, mini tripod and external microphone, plus other minor accessories, were also carried.

Support tents We had two Phoenix Phreedome four-person tents of dome-shaped geodesic design, which were roomy and comfortable for both ourselves and our support teams. For lightweight operations, such as the Col Maudit camp, we relied on a single-skin Phoenix Phreerunner bivouac tent. All tents had snow valances for use on glaciers.

Support vehicle Our motor home was a Swift Kon-Tiki 6-berth model, 4 years old with 45,000 miles service. We purchased it from Perthshire Caravans of Errol, Perth, who bought it back from us at the end of the journey. We added 5,000 miles to its clock and lost £3,000 in depreciation on the resale. Although expensive to run, we were impressed with its comfort, reliability and suitability for alpine road touring. Simon and Carole, and Martin Welch were provided with Land Rovers by Blythswood.

Food

With such an effective support operation and regular visits to staffed huts we were not severely constrained by the need to save weight in our food supplies. Indeed, we regarded a plentiful and varied food supply as essential to sustain our effort. We must have been consuming close to 5000 calories a day throughout the expedition. Fresh fruit and vegetables were always added to the support team rucksacks, despite the protests of the carriers.

Carole and Joy divided the job of preparing food supplies, with Carole doing the shopping and packing loads and Joy cooking flans, loaves, cakes and biscuits in the oven in our motor home.

Simon and I needed solid, filling foods with plenty of complex carbohydrates like cereals, rice and pasta, and generous helpings of fat. We ate nothing like the quantities of sweets and chocolate that might be imagined. Basic staples like flapjacks and oatcakes were far more palatable and sustaining on the hill. We passed through several food cravings during the journey, my most regularly occurring desire being for eggs, while Simon never seemed to tire of dried bananas. At the end of the trip our only craving remaining to be fulfilled was for fish and chips. That pleasure had to await our arrival back in Britain.

As I don't eat animal meat, Simon was quite happy to have a largely vegetarian diet. Our menus were little different from those we have shared over many years of climbing and mountain guiding. All cooking on the mountains during the expedition was done on Epigas Backpacker stoves with resealable propane/ butane gas fuel cartridges.

I took multi-vitamin pills and Evening Primrose Oil tablets throughout the expedition to ward off infections and stress injuries. Simon took none and remained every bit as healthy as me. Clearly, our basic food diet was giving us all the nutrients we required. Our metabolisms worked differently during the expedition. Simon finished the journey over a stone lighter. I lost no more than 3 or 4 kilos in bodyweight, and quickly put this back on after a few days' indulgence at home.

A typical menu plan when Simon and I carried our own food in the mountains was:

Breakfast	Muesli, semolina (boil and serve), or porridge, bread, margarine, jam or honey
Lunch	Oatcakes, chocolate bar, flapjacks, cheese, fruit cake, caramel wafer biscuits, dried bananas, pre-prepared trail mix of nuts and dried fruit, ice tea or powdered fruit drink
Dinner	Soup (usually instant leek!) with bread or oatcakes, tuna and fresh vegetable stew with pasta and cheese, custard (boil and serve) or instant mousse

This would be supplemented by any of the following during support operations:

Quiche Lorraine, tuna and mushroom flan, lentil bakes, soya loaves, nut burgers, chicken steaks (for Simon), vegetarian sausfry, eggs, pre-cooked baby potatoes and carrots, mixed salads, patisseries, fresh bread, tinned and fresh fruit, canned beer.

Food and Equipment Sponsors

Although we were unable to secure any form of financial sponsorship for the expedition, many companies generously donated equipment and food, or else arranged preferential discounts for us.

In particular we would like to thank Berghaus Ltd for the supply of clothing, rucksacks and boots, Phoenix Mountaineering for providing tents and helmets, and Dryburgh Cycles of Dingwall for procuring our bicycles and providing all cycle clothing and accessories.

Our appreciation is also due to the following manufacturers, agents and retailers:

Quiggs of Glasgow (Fuji films), Europa Sport (import of skis), Knorr (soups), McCowans (Highland toffee), Highland Wholefoods (trail mix), Nairns (oatcakes), Tunnocks (caramel wafers), Rowntrees (chocolate bars), Mrs Margery Jenkins (Simon's mum) (memorable fruit cakes), Dave Millar of Perthshire Caravans (sale and repurchase of motor home), Ken Vickers of Cordee (maps), Uvistat (sun cream).

REFERENCES

Blythswood Care

Our appeal to fund Blythswood Care's work in Eastern Europe had raised a total of £20,000 by the autumn of 1994. Blythswood's work to alleviate the material and spiritual suffering of those countries goes on and our appeal remains open. Donations or enquiries for further information can be sent to:

Rev Jackie Ross
'Blythswood – ALPS 4000'
Main Street
Lochcarron,
Ross-Shire IV54 8YD
Scotland

Alps 4000 Video

A video film of the expedition has been made and is available on order from the production company:

Chrisfilm & Video Ltd
The Mill Glasshouses
Pateley Bridge,
North Yorkshire HG3 5QH
Tel: 01423 711310

General References

Three recent texts are indispensable to all those with an interest in the high mountains of the Alps. Those who set their sights on the 4000m peaks need look no further for information and inspiration:

The Alpine 4000m Peaks by the Classic Routes by Richard Goedeke, (Diadem Books, 1991)

A concise practical guidebook to climbing the normal routes on all the '4000ers'.

The High Mountains of the Alps Volume 1: The Four-Thousand-Metre Peaks by Helmut Dumler and Willi P. Burkhardt, (Diadem/Baton Wicks Publishing, 1993)

A vastly enlarged and magnificently illustrated revision of Karl Blodig's original guidebook to the '4000ers' with superb historical detail on their conquest and inspiring narrative; one of the finest coffee-table books on mountaineering ever produced.

In Monte Viso's Horizon: Climbing the 4000 metre Peaks by Will McLewin (Ernest Press, 1992)
Lively anecdotal account of one man's life-long love affair with the '4000ers'; winner of the Boardman-Tasker prize for mountaineering writing in 1992.

Historical References

Several extracts from the classic literature of alpine mountaineering have been used in this text. Those who wish to delve further into this genre should refer to the early editions of *The Alpine Journal* (and its forerunning bulletin *Peaks, Passes and Glaciers*). These are housed in full in the Alpine Club library:

The Alpine Club,
55 Charlotte Road,
London EC2A 3QT
Tel: 0171 613 0755

Of the many books of this era two stand out:

Scrambles Amongst the Alps by Edward Whymper (Webb & Bower/ Michael Joseph, 1986)
This latest edition of Whymper's classic book retains the format and all engravings of the original, but is accompanied by colour photographs by John Cleare.

On High Hills – Memories of the Alps by Geoffrey Winthrop Young (Methuen, 1927)
No longer in print, but worth seeking for its accounts of Young's great days in the Alps; the narratives are dense and florid, but they are probably the finest examples of the romantic mountain writing which flourished in the nineteenth century and remain an inspiration.

ACKNOWLEDGEMENTS

Simon and I would like to thank the many people who made the Alps 4000 expedition possible, and who gave so much of their time and energy to help us.

Of our many supporting climbers, we would like to offer our special appreciation to Martin Welch who joined us in many high and difficult places to make his film and supported us throughout the trip without any guarantee of success or reward at its end; and also to David Litherland who has sustained our interest in climbing the '4000ers' over the last eight years and is as responsible as anyone for our attempting the challenge.

We acknowledge the other support teams in no particular order. They all did a magnificent job. Thank you:

Angus Andrew; Roger Coppock and Bruce Taylor; Ian, Sandra and Craig Dring; Graham Forshaw; Julie Hodges; Bob Neish; Martin Stone and Mike Walford; Graham Walton.

Bill Shannon, the expedition press officer, Rev Jackie Ross, President of Blythswood, and Donald McLeod, Blythswood Appeals Officer, gave us constant support and encouragement throughout a risky and often difficult enterprise. We'd also like to thank the other staff at Blythswood for their help in mounting our appeal.

Finally, and most importantly, Simon and I would like to pay tribute to the loyalty, love and support of our wives, Carole and Joy, who endured a tough and often thankless summer, yet kept us going from start to finish.

In the writing of this book I am indebted to my editor, Jo Weeks of David & Charles, for her interest, help and advice throughout the project, and to David Litherland for his meticulous review of the manuscript. If any florid, mawkish or overly sentimental passages remain in the finished text, they most certainly cannot be blamed on him.

The maps were drawn with painstaking care, skill and enthusiasm by Richard Singerton.

Trevor Braham and Paul Mackrill also contributed information for the text, and I thank Mr Jocelin Winthrop Young for permission to quote from his father's book *On High Hills*.

Lastly, I'd like to thank Simon for his contributions and comments on the text, which have ensured that this book is by no means a one-sided story of what went on in the expedition.

INDEX